Leo Eitinger and David Schwarz
(Editors)

Strangers in the world

Hans Huber Publishers
Bern Stuttgart Vienna

CIP-Kurztitelaufnahme der Deutschen Bibliothek

Strangers in the world / Leo Eitinger and David
Schwarz (Ed.). — Bern; Stuttgart; Vienna:
Huber, 1981.
    ISBN 3-456-80972-7
NE: Eitinger, Leo [Hrsg.]

© 1981 Hans Huber Publishers
Type-setting by Paul Stegmann Bern
Printed by Lang Druck Ltd. Liebefeld-Bern
Printed in Switzerland

Contents

Part III: Transcultural approaches

List of the authors

ALI ABDOLELL, M. A. Doctoral candidate in applied linguistics at the Ontario Institute for Studies in Education, Toronto, Canada

RACHELLE BANCHEVSKA, Mental Health Education Officer, Mental Health Authority of Victoria, Melbourne, Australia

JACQUES BAROU, Ph. D. Sociological Counsellor in the Société Nationale de Construction pour les Travailleurs Immigrés and in the Ministère du Travail, Paris, France

W. BÖKER, M. D. Professor of Psychiatry, Direktor der Psychiatrischen Universitätsklinik Bern, Schweiz

MARIANNE CEDERBLAD, M. D. Ass. Professor, Director, University Clinic for Child and Adolescent Psychiatry, Regionssjukhuset, Linköping, Sweden

JIM CUMMINS, Ph. D. Visiting Professor of Third Language and Multicultural Studies at the Ontario Institute for Studies in Education, Toronto, Canada

LEO EITINGER, M. D. Professor of Psychiatry, Head, University Psychiatric Dept., University of Oslo, Vinderen, N – Oslo 3, Norway

DAN G. HERTZ, M. D. Professor of Psychiatry, Director, Psychiatric Clinic, Hadassah University Hospital, Chairman, Psychiatric Faculty, Hebrew University – Hadassah Medical School, Jerusalem, Israel

FREDERIC H. HOCKING, M. D. Honorary Consulting Psychiatrist, Alfred Hospital, Melbourne, Australia

DIANA HULL, Ph. D. Associate Professor of Psychology, Dept. of Psychiatry, Baylor College of Medicine, Houston, Texas, U.S.A.

ERWIN K. KORANYI, M. D. Professor of Psychiatry, Director of Education, Royal Ottawa Hospital, Ottawa, Ontario, Canada

MIRJANA MOROKVASIČ, Ph. D. Research fellow, Centre Nationale de Recherches Scientifiques, Paris, France

KIVUTO NDETI, Ph. D. Professor, Director, Center for African Familiy Studies, Nairobi, Kenya

HARALD OFSTAD, Cand. jur., Mag. art., Professor of Philosophy, University of Stockholm, Stockholm, Sweden

PHILIP H. RACK, MA, MB, FRCPsych. Consultant Psychiatrist, Transcultural Psychiatry Unit, Lynfield Mount Hospital, Bradford, England

VIVIAN RAKOFF, M.D. Professor of Psychiatry, Director, Dep. of Psychiatry, Clarke Institute of Psychiatry, University of Toronto, Toronto, Canada

DAVID SCHWARZ, Fil. lic. Chief Editor of the bi-monthly «Scandinavian Migration and Ethnic Minority Review» (Invandrare och Minoriteter), Box 4063, S – 10261 Stockholm, Sweden

ALAN STOLLER, M. D. Chairman, Victorian State Council for Special Education, Australia. *Formerly,* Chairman, Mental Health Authority, Victoria, Australia

Preface

It can be stated without fear of exaggeration, that dislocation — the moving from one place to another — is the basis of human civilization. Moving to new pastures, new surroundings, urged human beings to new forms of adaptation and new inventions to master the new demands. This form of evolution is still operative since human dislocation is perhaps more prevalent than ever, and the demands of present-day migrants no less exacting than those of former times. Today, however, problems of mental adaptation have become the object of numerous and different scientific studies.

The first question to ask would be — *why* do people move? The motives are manifold, just as motives for all human actions usually are. It would be meaningless to try and enumerate all of them. On one side of the broad spectrum lies the genuine interest in knowing and learning what is «beyond the horizon» or «behind the high mountains». However, this interest in broadening one's knowledge and experience is hardly the most important reason for mass-migration. The Bible describes two quite different aspects of mass dislocation, both of «political» importance. The liberation and exodus of the Hebrews from bondage in Egypt, and the forced exile of the same people to Babylon. The conquest of neighbouring countries and the dislocation of their populations has continued throughout history, varied by different forms of colonization or the finding of new markets. Among the forced mass migration of «conquered individuals», the infamous slave trade from Africa must not be forgotten. Political upheavals and persecution of political adversaries were further motives for migration. In our time we have witnessed a nearly explosive growth of these tendencies, with more and more masses moving, or rather, being driven from one country to another, often with tragic results.

In the history of migration, religion has played a not unimportant role. It was often a pretext for conquering other countries, in order to bring to them the «only true faith». Not less frequently, religious intolerance led minorities to flee their own countries in order to find refuge elsewhere. Politically, religiously, culturally and socially persecuted or underpriviliged groups were often the largest proportions of migrating people. Individuals who actively wanted to change the state of affairs in their homeland, or who were discontented with their individual fates, were important parts of the migrating masses. Their less active family members often followed them, their motivation being less political or religious than personal and emotional. Differences in the life-style and in wealth between the industrialized and the developing worlds on one hand, and open or semi-open borders between many countries on the other, have fostered a relatively new form of dislocated population: the so-called «guest-workers» with their own specific problems.

A quite different kind of dislocation took place after the First World War, when the world witnessed the expulsion or the re-emigration of large ethnic groups and their re-settlement in the original homelands of their fathers (e.g. Greeks, Turks). After the Second World War we saw the recurrence of the same phenomenon on an even larger scale, especially after the liberation of the colonies in Africa.

Less dramatic though not less important forms of dislocation can be found inside the boundaries of practically all the countries of the world. The steady movement from the country-side to the cities, the so-called urbanization as the expression of a social evolution, is a trend we find everywhere in the world. And everywhere this form of dislocation, the others we have mentioned as well as many more, generate mental problems of tremendous dimensions. Migration has a profound effect on everyone involved in it. Most influenced, of course, are the persons migrating, but the families and societies whom they are leaving cannot remain completely unchanged. Not less important is the effect on the receiving countries and on their populations, *their* attitudes and *their* level of understanding.

Among the migrants themselves, the degree of successful adaptation will often be dependent on their motivation and degree of tolerance to all kinds of difficulties. Both will vary with the original reason of dislocation. People migrating because of an (unconscious) dissatisfaction with themselves, will continue being dissatisfied in the new country. But all migrants — whether they are the so-called «guest-workers» wanting to better their social situation, or refugees barely escaping death — have basic physical needs. They must eat, have a place to stay, a place to work. And after the basic needs have been satisfied, more complex, mainly psychological needs will become apparent. If these remain unsatisfied many tragic situations may arise, especially psychological maladaptation and mental health problems. The difficulties confronting the children are obviously not less complicated. In this connection, the attitude of the receiving society is of paramount importance.

Acknowledging this important field of research, the World Psychiatric Organization decided to investigate the problem of dislocation and mental health more thoroughly. It was made the subject of a plenary session at the last World Congress of the association in Honolulu in 1977, and chaired by one of the editors of this book (L.E.). This volume is partly built on the papers delivered at this session. In order to cover a broader field of the problems in question, it has been enlarged by many contributions from both psychiatric and non-psychiatric workers in the field of migration and human dislocation. It should be of interest not only to psychiatrists, but also to psychologists, social workers and members of all other professions coming in daily contact with migrants, refugees, «guest-workers» and other dislocated persons. It is our hope that the different contributions will give an all-encompassing picture of the many-faceted problems encountered by both the migrants and these professionals and lay-personnel dealing with the dislocated population groups.

We would like to express our thanks to all those who assisted us in preparing this publication. Special thanks must be extended to the fellow contributors in this volume, not only for the excellence of their studies, but also for their co-operation in the production of this book. Thanks also to Ester Sonja Bergene for her invaluable secretarial help, and to Jan Skarsgård whose critical review of the entire manuscript was most helpful and stimulating.

LEO EITINGER   DAVID SCHWARZ

Part I

General problems

Chapter 1

Foreigners in our time: Historical survey on psychiatry's approach to migration and refugee status

Leo Eitinger

It is natural that the problems of migration and mental health should first have been taken up in the United States of America — the «original» immigrant country. At that time the attitude of Europe, the «old country», was to rid itself of all undesirable elements by shipping them to the colonies. This led to protests by the colonists who wished to control immigration in order to ensure that anyone likely to become a public charge (paupers, criminals, the infirm, etc.) would not be allowed entry. Included in this group were mentally disturbed persons, unable to work or adjust (for detailed references see ØDEGAARD [11]).

As time passed, the immigrants, now considering themselves «oldtimers» began to doubt the abilities of «newcomers» to live up to their own excellent standards. This was a fluctuating attitude — prominent during times of economic decline and unemployment but receding in importance during periods of economic affluence (neither is this attitude entirely unknown today). As a simplification one can say that two groups exist: one group advocating immigration and seeing it as an advantage from both the economical and cultural angles — and one rejecting immigration, seeing its influence only as negative, their individual spheres of influence depending on the economic climate of the moment.

As an argument against immigration it was said that new immigrants meant more mental patients who would eventually penetrate the receiving society. This unfounded argument can even be heard today. A problem involving disease should not be dependent on beliefs and opinions only. Psychiatrists did not always live up to the ideal required of them and were often active members of misguiding discussions. Often their publications were not based on scientific findings and were both used and misused by opposing factions. The Norwegian psychiatrist ØDEGAARD [11] has given a review of the literature on insanity and immigration from the earliest researches until the appearance of his trailbreaking study of mental diseases amongst the Norwegian-born population of Minnesota. He writes that the older psychiatric literature «illustrates very interestingly how an essentially scientific problem is frequently obscured and distorted when social and political factors are allowed to figure too prominently». In actual fact, many of the papers published on the topic of psychiatric diseases amongst migrants were more in the nature of pleas and one-sided presentations than scientific works. Since many of the authors had preconceived meanings or rigid political convictions, it was more important for them to prove the correctness of their prejudices than to find the facts. Most of them were merely interested in proving or disproving that there were more psychotics amongst migrants than amongst the local population. The methods used were often crude, mostly consisting of counting the patients in a mental hospital and controlling how many were foreign-born and how many native-born. It usually turned out that the percentage of foreign-born was much higher among the patient population than among the population in the catchment area of the mental hospital in question. The most obvious sources of error were statistical, not taking into account the different age distribution of the foreign-born and the native-born population groups [11]. Since severe mental diseases are extremely rare amongst children and since there were very few children among the immigrants, the statistical results were necessarily in disfavour of the migrant population. Another very frequent source of error is that different mental diseases require different lengths of hospitalization, and the patients who «remain» in the hospital are by no means representative of all the patients admitted.

17

Based on such erroneous statistics, it was easy to jump to false conclusions e.g. that certain races have a higher frequency of mental disease than others [12]. Statements like these soon became «evidence» for senseless prejudices both in psychiatry and in the general discussion on migration.

In his pioneering work, ØDEGAARD [11, 12] controlled the admission rates of Norwegian-born immigrants to Minnesota mental hospitals and compared them (controlled for diagnoses, age and sex), on the one hand, with admission rates of native-born patients, and on the other hand with admission rates of Norwegian-born in Norwegian mental hospitals. The Norwegian immigrants in Minnesota had, in both comparisons, higher admission rates than the two controls. ØDEGAARD could thus prove that the higher admission rate of Norwegian immigrants in Minnesota could *not* be related to the «Norwegian race», but must be in some way connected with the problem of migration. He could, furthermore, demonstrate that emigrants who returned to Norway also had a higher admission rate in Norwegian mental hospitals than Norwegians who had never emigrated, thus confirming his assumption that the fact of migration and not «the race» was of decisive importance.

There can be two different causal factors influencing the frequency of mental diseases among migrants. It can either be the selection of the individuals who are migrating, or it can be the complex stress of migration itself, hardships of the newcomers, the difficulties of adaptation to new environments, the disappointments when the expectations have been too high etc., etc. From his own patient groups, ØDEGAARD could demonstrate that it was mainly the «self-selection» of emigrants which was the decisive factor, while the stress of migration was considered of subordinate importance. The instability of the personality, his difficulty in social adjustment to the local milieu, his former psychotic or pre-psychotic episodes – in short – being a mentally «poor risk» – is, according to ØDEGAARD, the driving force that brings a person to leaving his own country to become a migrant, and eventually, a patient in a foreign country.

Though ØDEGAARD's work is very convincing, it does not settle, once and for all, the question of «either selection or stress» as the main cause for a higher psychiatric morbidity amongst migrants. In the United States MALZBERG with his co-workers [6, 7, 8, 9] were trying to solve the problem. They could also demonstrate, in large scale investigations, that migrants have higher admission rates than the native-born, and they even found that immigrants from different European countries have consistently different frequencies of mental diseases. These differences can, however, not be ascribed to any sort of «race». Some of the mental diseases diagnosed to a higher degree in certain nationalities, were clearly dependent on cultural patterns, such as the abuse of alcohol — and mental diseases resulting from it (see chapt. 10).

Further investigations with more sophisticated methods have taken into account the fact acknowledged in psychiatry for many years — that there is not *one* cause of a mental disease. There are always several more or less important causal factors working together, influencing each other and the personality in question. These factors are the individual's make-up, moulded by influence of parents, siblings, the harmony of the family and the home, the experiences in school and further life, the exposition to stress, to intoxicating agents, etc. All these factors and many more also have an active role in the forming of a migrating population. Who wants to become an emigrant and whom is society slightly pushing towards becoming an emigrant? In some countries it will be the most active, interested, the person of above average intelligence who wants to achieve more than the too limited possibilities will allow him in his native environment. «He must get out and grow.» In other countries or other cases, it will be the failure who cannot adapt to the requirements of the normal society, and who will be pushed away. In some countries the economic situation makes it impossible for large parts of the population to feed themselves and they want to find better living conditions (without any sort of local selection). The reason, motives and possibilities are nearly infinite, as is the case with the emigrating individual's and population's personality make-up. But this is only one side of the problem.

The other side, and from the point of view of mental health or breakdown, just as important, if not more so, is the situation in the receiving country. We know from general psychiatry that it makes a great difference if a person is bound to live without close personal ties, or if he/she lives in contact with others who can be of personal support in daily life or in difficult situations. We also know that the kind of society one lives in is just as important, and that an accepting, well-organized and integrated society will have less psychiatric patients than a disintegrating society with large groups of unemployed who are specially hostile towards newcomers. All these factors will be of the greatest importance for the mental health or breakdowns of migrants when they start settling in a new country.

In addition to the selecting processes and problems in the country of origin and the inter-human relationships in the receiving country, there is a third set of problems confronting most of the migrants: the shift and change in their professional roles and living circumstances. One migrant may come from a relatively isolated rural country and be forced into living in a city and working with many strange people in a large restaurant kitchen or even in a factory. Another, who has been a skilled industrial worker, is suddenly forced to work in an isolated and rather subordinate position. Again we know from general psychiatry that sudden and substantial changes in life enhance the disposition towards becoming a patient, not at least a mental patient. It is obvious that it cannot be an easy task to take into account all these very different factors afflicting the mental health of migrants and causing a higher frequency of mental breakdowns.

To be fair it must also be mentioned that not all accounts on migration end up with a negative conclusion as far as the migrants or their mental health are concerned.

ØDEGAARD [11] quotes a nonmedical author who writes that the northern emigrants are on the average «mentally and morally superior to those who remain at home . . . The earnestness and depth of their character coupled with a strong imagination and poetical nature infits many of the immigrants for enduring the intense pressure of American life . . . The emigrants leave the old country with a wounded heart, with fear of the old rather than hope of the new in their minds.»

Another aspect of the whole problem is raised by PARK [10] in his paper *Human Migration and the Marginal Man.* PARK shows that a migrating personality lives in two different cultures and is able to look at both with a critical view, without prejudice. There is a certain «moral dichotomy», but this is compensated by the broader cultural outlook, and by the possibility to live under the controlled influence of quite different backgrounds.

Summarizing the psychiatric view on migration from an historic point of view, one must admit that the older investigations have not been able to discern all the concurrent and/or conflicting factors influencing the outbreak and development of mental diseases among migrants. The different published works have, however, demonstrated that «migration» is not a unitary concept, that there can hardly be a conclusive answer to the question whether migrants have more (or less) mental breakdowns than the native-born. On the other hand, one must be aware of many complications immanent in a problem before a proper solution can be found.

Refugees

Most of the investigations mentioned [6, 7, 8, 9, 11, 12] have been carried out on so-called voluntary migrants, those who had left their homeland because they had wished to do so. The motivation may differ, as may the degree of voluntariness. The social difficulties, unemployment, even hunger may have been driving forces, but still

21

the act of emigration had been a voluntary one, based on the decision of the individual. In contrast to this we have migration on a forced basis, not planned by individuals for their own prefered reasons. Political, religious or national differences are usually the driving forces in these cases. The individual who does not emigrate has to reckon with extreme hardships, or even with loss of life. Even though this form of involuntary migration — both individual and in groups — has been known throughout history, it is only during the last three or four decades that these migrant-refugees have been objects for more detailed scientific psychiatric investigations. It has been a complicated task as many of the refugees went through extreme stress-situations before leaving their homelands. Examples are: Survivors of Nazi concentration camps emigrating after World War II to USA, Canada, Australia, etc., persecuted and tortured political ex-prisoners from South American fascist countries, or people who had been inmates in forced labour camps in Siberia. And who would ever be able to investigate today's so-called «boat-people» from South-East Asia, and to decide how much their personality make-up and how much the hardships of their escape and rescue are the main factors in a possible breakdown? It is a tragedy of our time and a proof of the unsatisfactory status of the world's humanism and culture, that the problem of refugees is threatening and growing practically every day. It has been estimated that since World War II there have been more than 50 million refugees needing international help [1].

The differences between voluntary migrants and refugees have been discussed, among others by BERNARD [1]. He writes that the popular assumption has been that a migrant should be expected to be more «normal» than a refugee. This theory does not hold water under detailed scrutiny. As mentioned earlier, researchers have often found more or less specific personal traits in persons making the decision to emigrate. These traits would, owing to the circumstances conducive to voluntary emigration, not necessarily be present in refugees. On the contrary, newer investigations have shown that refugees often are people with an above the average interest in public affairs and therefore more exposed to persecution in their homeland. From a psychological point of view, these refugees would show a greater power of resistance and thus, a lesser tendency towards breakdowns. Another point which is not elaborated upon by BERNARD, is the question of motivation. A person who has just escaped a really dangerous, life-threatening situation in his country of origin will more easily and often gladly cope with all the problems of adjustment in his new surroundings, considering them unimportant trivialities. «What does it matter if I don't have the same food or the same kind of work when I can breathe freely?» «What does it matter if some people are not friendly, I am allowed to say what I mean and nobody would arrest me for that» are reactions one often hears from refugees. «Not everything is as good as at home, neither as wonderful as I had expected in my dreams, but of what importance is that as long as I am alive and able to work and change my circumstances without risking my freedom and/or my life» is another reaction often heard. This attitude will prevail, in any case, during the first year(s) of political migration. The threshold of tolerance that persons with such an attitude can rely upon is quite different to that of a voluntary migrant coming to his new country with the intention of getting rich as quickly as possible and who is extremely disappointed when he learns that one has to work hard, even in this new country, in order to make a living. While the quoted attitudes expressed by the refugees will increase the power of resistance towards unpleasant life experiences and make him less inclined to become a psychiatric patient, the opposite will be the case with a voluntary migrant having unrealistic expectations.

On the negative side comes the often long-lasting persecution, insecurity, defamation and other difficulties the various minorities, dissidents and refugees are exposed to long before they manage to escape. They cope as long as they have the slightest hope of getting rid of the oppressors or of coming to a new country. The group of refugees perhaps investigated in the greatest detail are the survivors of the infamous Nazi concentration camps. They are dealt with separately in this volume (chapter 11). Another group under close investigation are the tortured ex-prisoners from South America. However, these results are not yet available.

The author of this chapter investigated all the refugees who came to Norway during the first 15 years after the outbreak of World War II, who had had mental breakdowns and been admitted to psychiatric institutions. This study was done at the end of the fifties and may by now be considered «historic». We found that the frequency of severe mental disturbances in the refugee population was much higher (up to five times as high) than in the matched Norwegian population, varying for the different forms of mental diseases. It was not posible to demonstrate *one* single and absolute causal factor for the substantially higher frequency of breakdowns. All the patients had gone through extreme hardships, persecutions, forced labour camps and some even concentration camps before arriving in Norway. But proportionately more refugees had occupations of a lower standard or belonged to a lower social order than the Norwegian controls which could, according to existing psychiatric theories, be a reason for the higher psychiatric morbidity amongst the refugees. Furthermore, the refugees lived under far more unharmonious circumstances than their Norwegian counterparts. More than half were unmarried and every third married couple was separated. The number of divorced, widowed and those married several times was nearly three times that of the Norwegian controls.

The experiences of the refugees were not determined by the then – officially – very positive attitude of the population as displayed in friendly articles in the newspapers and official reports. On the contrary, one had the impression that these patients had been isolated and rejected. They felt insecure and referred to experiences in their occupational and private lives characterised by difficulties with which they were unable to cope. They felt economically dependent and exploited, not appreciated in their work, subjected to unfair competition. All these negative feelings resulted in a paranoic attitude which reduced the mental resources and led to psychotic breakdowns.

Also in their personal, erotic lives the refugees felt insecure, unaccepted, especially by the families of the Norwegian partners to whom they were engaged to be married. This was proven by the fact that there were ten times as many jealousy reactions among refugees than among the controls. Even in a relatively homogenous group such as the post-war refugees could be considered, there are many different factors that can be causally connected with the higher frequency of mental breakdowns. Further and more detailed observations and investigations should therefore be carried out.

In spite of the present necessity of such investigations, it is our hope and our plea, as it is surely that of all scientists engaged in the problems of the refugee: May all politicians and decision-makers of all countries of our world be endowed with so much understanding of and consideration for human beings and their sufferings that, in the very near future, there will be no refugees but only voluntary migrants left to study.

Bibliography

1 BERNARD, W.S.: Immigrants and refugees: Their similarities, differences, and needs. Internat. Migration *14*, 267 – 281, 1976.
2 EITINGER, L.: The incidence of mental disease among refugees in Norway. J. Ment. Sci. *105*, 326 – 338, 1959.
3 EITINGER, L.: The Symptomatology of mental disease among refugees in Norway. J. Ment. Sci. *106*, 947 – 966, 1960.
4 EITINGER, L.: A clinical and social psychiatric investigation of a «Hard-Core» refugee transport in Norway. Int. J. soc. Psychiat. *5*, 261 – 275, 1960.
5 EITINGER, L.: Psychiatric investigations among refugee patients in Norway. Ment. Hyg. *44*, 91 – 96, 1960.
6 MALZBERG, B.: Race and mental disease in New York State. Psychiat. Quart. *9*, 538 – 569, 1935.
7 MALZBERG, B.: Mental disease of foreign-born whites, with special re-

ference to natives of Russia and Polan. Amer. J. Psychiat. *92,* 627 – 640.

8 MALZBERG, B.: Mental disease among native and foreign-born whites in New York State. Amer. J. Psychiat.*93,* 127 – 137, 1936.

9 MALZBERG, B. & LEEDS, E.S.: Migration and mental disease. Social Science Research Council, New York, 1956.

10 PARK, R.E.: Human Migration and the marginal man. Amer. J. Sociol. *33,* 881 – 893, 1928.

11 ØDEGAARD, Ø.: Emigration and insanity. Acta psychiat. Suppl. 4, København, 1932.

12 ØDEGAARD, Ø.: Emigration and Mental Health. Ment. Hyg. *20,* 546 – 553, 1936.

Chapter 2

Foreigners in our time:
The present situation

ALAN STOLLER

The phenomenon of human dislocation

Human dislocation has been the lot of mankind since
earliest times and must be seen as inherent in the evolution
of the human race. However, with the development of
technology, growing world population, and the freeing of
communications, the process has become of increasing
significance to humanity. RICHMOND [20], in discussing
the Canadian scene, has postulated a pre-industrial era,
when assimilation had distinct utility; the current industrial era, with growing urbanization and pluralistic integration of the subcultures of different ethnic groups, and
with society requiring to adapt to both population increase
and diversification; and an era which we are now entering,
the post-industrial era, where transport is easy and widespread, and where migrants are cosmopolitan and mobile,
do not need to integrate or assimilate, and act as resonating
agents of change within an increasingly mobile population. Whilst this may be the case for advanced industrial
societies, the world as a whole has been facing a wide diversity of human dislocations, many of which have created
problems.

A vast literature has grown up since World War II in regard to forced (involuntary) international migration (refugees, concentration camp survivors, exiles, forced labour,
etc.) as well as in regard to free (voluntary) international
migration (migrants, guest workers, temporary and long-
stay), students, professionals (for job enhancement), adventure groups, repatriates, etc. There is also the phe-

nomenon of rural-urban intra-national migration, urban-suburban migration in the more affluent societies, and displacement arising from the re-drawing of old colonial boundaries. Finally, there is also the human displacement of national and international commissions and other personnel.

It must be obvious that a good deal of the so-called voluntary migration is dictated by economic and discriminatory pressures, and that much of a host society's acceptance of migrants is dictated by economic or political considerations.

In all these dislocations, there is an adjustment required of the individual in terms of himself, his family and his traditional community — in other words, his personal and social identity — in relation to the requirements of the new community he is entering. Outcome will be affected by the attitudes and organization of the host community. It is therefore necessary to consider the process of uprooting and resettlement in these terms.

Uprooting and resettlement

As already stated, dislocation invariably involves uprooting from one's traditional milieu, with all its personal and social ramifictions, and adaptation to a new way of life. The phenomena of uprooting and resettlement are complex and require the insights of numerous professional disciplines for their elucidation, as applied to both the immigrating and the receiving populations. It is just as important to concentrate on the psychodynamics of the individual as on the socio-cultural changes in the larger group to which he belongs. It is also necessary to appreciate that whilst anxiety is a natural consequence of uprooting, this may provide for many the basis for a constructive personality growth.

There are many factors which may affect the capacity of the individual to adapt. At one extreme, refugees may have suffered severe concentration camp experiences, the trauma of flight, the hopelessness and frustration of a prolonged camp experience and then a lack of recognition of qualifications by a discriminatory receiving society; at the other extreme, one sees the professional who emigrates with his family intact to a well-paid job in a country with a similar language and culture to further his career. The majority lie in between.

When a person adapts from one community to another, traditional values and beliefs are gradually replaced by those of the host society, a process which is called *acculturation.*

Movement towards the total values and behaviour of the host society is termed *assimilation* and this may occur to varying degree over time. The basic personality of the immigrant has developed through identification and learning (*core personality*) with added elements from his social experience (*social personality*). His previous traditional way of life has given him a status, a sense of communal belonging, a set of supporting beliefs and a sense of continuity. Thrust into a new environment, he has to develop coping mechanisms to deal with the interaction between the old and the new, and this produces *culture conflict* which, if prolonged, merges into *culture tension.* The process of acculturation moves through *behavioural assimilation* to *structural assimilation,* when sufficient mobility has occured for the individual to enter the political, social and cultural institutions of the host society.

Interaction can be traumatic, depending on such factors as the suddenness of the dislocation (rate of change), the impersonality of the environment (urbanization), a relative devaluation of the immigrant's perception of his place in society *(loss of status),* the lack of traditional supports *(alienation)* and, in all, the need to change to new ways of language, dress, food, recreation, etc. Acculturation does not necessarely equate with assimilation. Its degree can be assessed through *a shared frame of reference,* involving the values, attitudes and behaviours common to both the immigrant and the host societies [24].

Acculturation is inevitably a two-way interaction process and it is now being more and more accepted that the monistic *melting-pot* type of assimilation, where the immigrant is expected to give up his own ways rapidly and conform to the mores and behaviour of the receiving society, is neither practicable nor desirable.

In Australia, and in other countries taking in immigrants in a systematic way, a pattern of interactionistic *cultural pluralism* is currently developing. This implies in practise an acceptance of the core values of the receiving society with tolerance for the retention of less important, even of enriching, values of the old country. In this circumstance, the individual can integrate and compete in his own right at the same time as he preserves his own identity in its individual and communal aspects. Erikson's formulation of the concepts of *identity formation* and *identity change* are applicable here. It is important to note that cultural pluralism cannot exist without institutional duplication in the host society *(social pluralism)*.

In some situations, the type of societal adjustment which occurs is termed *multi-culturalism* where ethnic groups retain their traditional cultural and social identities as part of a larger State. As is evident from such recent experiences as those in Lebanon, Cyprus and Northern Ireland, this situation can become explosive.

The final theoretical stage of interaction is *amalgamation,* where host and receiving societies become one and indistinguishable, a process which must take many generations and require that different cultural beliefs with strong emotional content (e.g. religion) are institutionalized in acceptable form to the whole society. How far this occurs in its finality is questionable, as one studies those countries with indigenous minority cultures going back many centuries which are now beginning to reassert themselves in the light of changing socio-political circumstances.

Problems of adjustment

Turning more expressly towards the individual and his problems in establishing a new identity, these are not infrequently associated with low socio-economic status and a change from rural to urban living, resulting in feelings of being devalued, manipulated and separated from the fruits of his labour [19]. Those who cannot adapt satisfactorily and derive ego-strength from overcoming obstacles may become anxious, frustrated, angry and possibly paranoid, or sink into an apathetic, existential vacuum. In the initial phase of the translocation, the immigrant tends towards a sense of euphoria; but later, faced with the difficulties of adjustment, an idealization of the homeland may occur which inhibits satisfactory integration with the host society; or alternatively, if overvaluation of the culture of the country of settlement takes place, a conspiciuousness may result which makes the individual not only abrasive to the host country but also renders him marginal to his own ethnic group.

Family and societal problems may result from differential assimilation of individuals such as, for instance, the maintenance of homeland authoritarian patterns in the face of adolescent freedoms within the new location. Crises, such as illness or accidents, may lead to personality decompensation, with regression and associated psychopathological symptoms. Those coming from developing countries and rural backgrounds tend towards more primitive types of reaction – either confusional psychotic-type behaviour of short duration – or alternatively, denial of mental illness with symptoms of bodily diseases of the emotional conflicts. Expressions of illness tend to be coloured by the culture of the particular immigrant group and both recognition of illness and help-seeking behaviour are also determined thereby.

Evidence has accumulated that certain groups of migrants have greater problems of adaptation because of negative self-selection – in other words, individuals who are more vulnerable to mental illness emigrate to a greater degree. This has been well documented by such as MEZEY [13, 14, 15] with respect to Hungarian refugees from 1956 and SCHAECHTER [21] in regard to Southern European females in Australia. COCHRANE [3] in considering the reason for differential rates of mental hospital admissions among groups of immigrants in England and Wales, hypothesised that where migration is relatively easy (as with the Irish), less stable members of the population self-select; whereas, where migration is relatively difficult (as with Pakistanis), only the most stable individuals can achieve migration. Where a total population migrates, as with some Asian immigrant groups to Israel, patterns of mental illness tend to conform to the overall homeland patterns.

Concepts such as culture shock, culture change, alienation and status discrepancy have been formulated to explain rates of breakdown. These, however, have limited roles to play in explaining the overall picture of mental maladjustments in migration groups [10]. In a recent review of migrant mental health, MURPHY [17] has highlighted the need to consider each migrant group in terms of ‹factors operating in the society of origin, factors relating to the migration itself, and factors operating in the society of resettlement›. He stated further that ‹all three sets need to be considered if one seeks to reduce or merely understand the level of mental disorder in any immigrant group›. HULL [5] makes the pertinent point that migration, as a social phenomenon, provides special situations in which to develop and test hypotheses having to do with the relative and/or collective influence of heredity and environment, the potency of the change factor itself, and the differing impact of the environment depending on the time of life the change has taken place. Not only must one be concerned with the actual patterns of mental illness but consider intervening variables relative to psychological, socioeconomic and anthropological inputs.

Among the various groups of individuals who have been described at risk for the development of psychopathology in a series of studies in Victoria, Australia, were those of low socio-economic status and especially poor language attainment: women who were relatively isolated within an otherwise assimilating family; young people caught between two cultures and experiencing culture tension within the family; old people in whom all traditional supports were wiped out; those who faced a lack of recognition of professional qualifications and suffered a loss of status; and, finally, those traumatized individuals who had suffered severe experiences such as concentration camp survivors or other political refugees [22]. There is no migrant psychopathology as such but there are various groups of vulnerable individuals who develop maladaptation in relation to migration — presenting with more unhappiness, social behaviour problems, psychosomatic disorders, neuroses or frank psychotic disorders.

The amount of mental illness manifested will depend on the type of dislocation, previous background, the degree of social protection afforded the group, the perception of illness, the accessibility of helping services, and the bureaucratic structure and organization of the host society. It will also be affected by the degree to which ghettoes form and protection is afforded within the organization of these, and the current economic climate within the receiving population will also play a part. Mental illnesses reflect psychopathological reactivity in its severe forms and it is to a consideration of these that we now turn.

Mental illness

Whilst the recording of admissions to mental hospitals has proved a useful index of migrant maladjustment in the past, this is becoming more problematical as the management of mental illness shifts more into the community. The treatment of the overall migrant intake into a country as a homogeneous entity has proved to be methodologically unsound, since the varying national and ethnic groups which compose the inflow demonstrate different rates of breakdown as well as different diagnostic-specific rates [22].

Issues which need to be considered are whether migrant groups suffer higher, or lesser, rates of breakdown? Whether mental hospital rates truly reflect overall rates of psychological disturbances, including the more ubiquitous psychosomatic disorders and social breakdowns? And moreover, what factors are likely to be involved in individual cases? It needs to be decided how, and to what degree, environmental stress factors play a part in individual breakdowns; how far predisposition is involved; and, to what extent, individual or social crises can be implicated in those who break down after a prolonged period in the new situation, taking into account the natural history of such disorders in the population in general.

Epidemiological studies will continue to remain controversial, and comparisons between ethnic groups inadequate, so long as insufficient attention is paid to methodology — such as the adequate definition and collection of cases of mental illnesses and the refining of crude rates in terms of factors such as age, sex, marital status, and occupational and cultural background.

Other variables need to be considered, such as country of origin, length of stay, severity of experiences, urban or rural background, the degree to which mental illness is perceived, and the availability of diagnostic and treatment facilities. Furthermore, consideration needs to be given to variations in rates of breakdowns over time, the degree to which immigrants return to their homelands, or relocate, changes in the economic or political climate, and the effect of bureaucratic process in increasing, or diminishing, group supportiveness.

Diagnostic tools relating to the study of morbidity have not, as yet, proved adequate to encompass the varying cultural differences in the expression and recording of psychiatric illnesses in different ethnic sub-cultures. From a statistical viewpoint, the findings in a particular group under study needs to be related to its proportion in the total population if any generalization is to be made, and adequate census data is therefore essential.

Studies such as that of KRUPINSKI and STOLLER [8] have

demonstrated that there can be considerable variations in rates of mental illnesses as between different groups of origin. They were able to relate rates of mental hospitalization in Victoria, Australia, to adequate census data, tapped a wide range of facilities (in-patient, out-patient and day hospital), and diagnoses were established on a fairly uniform basis and included a wide range of psychiatric disorders. They were able to establish several groups-at-risk.

Eastern Europeans, who had the severest war experiences, had the highest rates of psychiatric problems of all the groups of origin. EITINGER [4] had noted irreversible psychological changes in severely traumatized individuals and their tendency to break down soon after immigration. Analysis of sub-groups within the Australian refugee group showed that the Jewish refugees, who had suffered most severely, nevertheless had lower rates of psychosis than non-Jewish; the latter however were experiencing a considerable degree of status discrepancy and frustration. Status discrepancy (gap between expectations and achievement) has also been demonstrated in another context; an inflow of higher educated negroes into Philadelphia had higher rates of breakdown than southern-born U.S. negroes in the same circumstances, the latter having lower expectations and therefore less in the ‹way of frustration› [18]. The Jewish group in Australia was highly positively selected, in that, not only were they survivors but they had chosen additionally an apparently more difficult assignment in travelling so far from their origins. They demonstrated nevertheless a high degree of neurotic symptoms which carried over to their children, who had higher rates of emotional and behaviour problems than non-Jewish children in this study. There can be little doubt that neurotic drives had positive value in enabling many Jewish refugees to succeed in their new situation, and it is not surprising that some developed a late ‹let-down› after apparently attaining comfortable circumstances [9].

Southern European middle-aged females constituted a further risk group. They demonstrated a bimodal pattern of breakdown in terms of length of stay. At least 60% of those who broke down soon after migration were found to have had a history of earlier breakdowns or emotional instability [21]. A larger number broke down in the period 7 – 14 years after migration, a situation which was ascribed to poor assimilation resulting in a loss of status and esteem within the family group, the other members having integrated to greater degree with the host community [23].

Elderly persons coming to help their children's families adapt in the early stages of their settlement found ready roles and were not at risk. However, when brought out after the family had established itself, they were at greater risk in that they found their traditional values challenged by the already locally-integrated family, and their reduced physical capacities added to their inability to adjust.

Adolescents were shown to be at risk for the development of behavioural disorders because of differential assimilation within the family and peer-group pressures. Inter-generational conflict occured , especially in families with authoritarian backgrounds. To detect these, it was necessary to extend studies to second-generation immigrants, born in the new location from immigrant parents. Immigrant children arriving after age 10, without language, have been found to have relatively poor prospects of entering higher studies and are also at greater risk. Furthermore, with the development of ethnic concentrations, schools in such areas have a high proportion of children with language deficiencies and lack resources to cope with communication difficulties so that, once again, movement into higher education is restricted. Despite this, adolescents of Southern European origin have low rates of behaviour disorders, presumably attributable to the cohesiveness of the family. Whilst the family is protective in this circumstance, it is not so for the Southern European middle-aged female, as already mentioned. Family is also found to be non-protective for another group-at-risk, the young male immigrant from U.K., in whom a carry-over of alcoholic problems result in the breakdown of his marriage and the family pathology as a consequence, and not a cause, of his alcoholism.

MURPHY [16] has drawn attention to the importance of the size of the immigrant group in protecting against mental illness, as well as a traditional climate of acceptance in the host society. When an optimal size is reached, it is considered that the ethnic concentration builds in sufficient supports to reduce the development of mental illness in some individuals and to contain them in others. He has collected evidence to support the thesis, in that higher rates occur in dispersed immigrants as compared with ethnic group concentrations. However, in Victoria, Italians have the same rates, whether in concentrations or dispersed, a situation which may be influenced by relative affluence and car ownership facilitating easy communication. One needs to ask also the question why mental illness rates for Greeks and Italian populations in this Australian State has remained constant over a 15-year period and only the Yugoslavian ethnic group has shown a decline with increasing size [6]?

Sufficient has been stated in this section to show the great complexity of the topic «mental illness in migrants». Certain perspectives have emerged as at this time. Migrants should not be seen as constituting a homogeneous mass, but as consisting of a number of groups-of-origin which need to be delineated and defined in terms of background origin, transit experiences and degree of host acceptance. Note also needs to be taken of changes over time.

Similarly, mental disorder is not a uniform concept. There is a need to assess the ways particular migrant groups express their emotional conflicts and determine a system of case-finding so that more meaningful comparisons can be made as between rates of specific illness in different migrant groups, as well as between the patterns of illness in both homeland and host societies. Socio-cultural factors are especially significant in this regard, so that multi-cultural as well as multi-professional inputs are necessary. Psychiatric disorders need to be teased out from social phenomena such as criminality, delinquency, suicidal behaviour and accident-proneness, as well as from psychosomatic disorders presenting to general medical facilities. It is, moreover, important to note that anxiety and unhappiness may constitute spurs to achievement and act positively towards adaption; thus, degree of impairment needs to be included in any diagnostic assessment.

Whilst epidemiology should aim at groups which are totally representative of their proportions in the population as a whole, limited studies on special groups of migrants in specific situations can provide useful data for the establishment of hypotheses for testing factors involved in adaptation and maladaptation of immigrants. KRUPINSKI & COCHRANE [7] have been able to compare mental hospital admissions in Victoria, Australia, and U. K. and have found interesting correlations in terms of countries of origin, even though social circumstances have been different.

Previous attemps to relate the occurrence of mental illnesses in migrant groups to either self-selection or environmental stress have failed to take into account the complexity of factors involved or the degree to which they are integrated. Certainly, both individual vulnerability and environmental factors need to be teased out and has been shown to have some value in distinguishing between some immigrant groups. This holds for status discrepancy, which cuts across socio-economic status. In fact, social factors are difficult to relate in any aetiological way to the occurrence of mental illness in immigrants. The earlier emphasis on low socio-economic status is now largely seen as the result, rather than the cause, of mental breakdown. However, low socio-economic status tends to produce more institutionalization, longer stay and less tendency to discharge, thereby affecting prevalence rates.

Length of stay in the country of settlement has already been attended to, in that evidence of previous illness or instability has been found to high degree in those who break down early; whilst later breakdowns tend to occur in those who remain relatively isolated and unassimilated within a family group, or suffer a let-down after a long period of struggle. As might be expected, evidence has accumulated that the longer an ethnic group stays in a new country, the more its patterns of mental illness will move towards the host picture. BURVILL [2] in relation to suicidal behaviour of U.K. immigrants in Western Australia, has even postulated an index of assimilation based on the degree to which the suicide method changes from U.K. to a local Australian pattern after a number of years. Statistics relating to length of stay need to be assessed in terms of the natural history of mental disorders as they occur in an aging population.

Rural-urban migration is of special significance in developing countries in that community disintegration is a potent factor in the production of social pathology and associated mental health problems [11]. The truncated families which are left behind create an overall demographic imbalance which has distinct mental health consequences in the homeland situation [12]. We have not yet begun to evaluate the situation in regard to urban influxes, such as the «shanty towns» in South America or Asia, where nutritional deficiencies and infectious diseases must play a highly significant part in the overall picture of mental health functioning.

Finally, the role of host acceptance requires to be assessed for each immigrant group. MURPHY [17] drew attention to the importance of this factor, in addition to the size of the ethnic community, as being protective for the immigrant. However, there is considerable variation in the way in which different immigrant groups are accepted in the one host society, taking into regard such factors as race, colour, sociocultural background [1], and even historical traditions.

Final remarks

In studying human dislocation, it is clear that methodology still needs to be refined to take in all forms of maladjustment, take note of all areas of functioning (psychological, social and cultural), carry out prospective studies of defined cohorts with suitable control populations, and operate with multi-disciplinary teams from both host and immigrant societies.Insights, leading to action, must essentially be in the social area and, in this task social psychiatry has a vital role to play. Over-arching social theory is not possible in our present state of knowledge. One needs to still systematically collect data, set up hypotheses and test these in the light of experience. There is need for a systematic attempt to be made to develop some global immigrant assessement techniques which will make comparisons possible as between different ethnic groups, taking into account social and cultural variability.

Bibliography

1 BAGLEY, C.: A comparative study of mental illness among immigrant groups in Britain. Revue Ethnics *1,* 23, 1972.
2 BURVILL, P.W., McCALL, M.G., REID, T.A., STENHOUSE, N.S.: Methods of suicide of English and Welsh immigrants in Australia. Brit. J. Psychait. *123,* 285, 1972.
3 COCHRANE, R.: Mental illness in immigrants to England and Wales: an analysis of mental hospital admissions. Soc. Psychiat. *12,* 25, 1977.
4 EITINGER, L.: Pathology of the Concentration Camp Syndrome. Arch. gen. Psychiat. *5,* 371, 1961.
5 HULL, D.: Migration, adaptation and illness: a review. Soc. Sci. & Med. *13A,* 25, 1979.
6 KRUPINSKI, J.: Sociological aspects of mental ill-health in migrants. Soc. Sci. & Med. *1,* 267, 1967.
7 KRUPINSKI, J., COCHRANE, R.: Migration and mental health: a comparative study. Ethnic Studies *3,* 2, 1979.
8 KRUPINSKI, J., STOLLER, A.: Incidence of mental disorders in Victoria, Australia, according to country of birth. Med. J. Aust. *2,* 265, 1965.
9 KRUPINSKI, J., STOLLER, A., WALLACE, L.: Psychiatric disorders in East European refugees now in Australia. Soc. Sci. & Med. *7,* 31, 1973.
10 KUO, W.: Theories of migration and mental health: an empirical testing on Chinese-Americans. Soc. Sci. & Med. *10,* 297, 1976.
11 LEIGHTON, A.H., LAMBO, A.T., HUGHES, C.C., LEIGHTON, D.C., MURPHY, J.M., MACKLIN, D.M.: Psychiatric Disorders among the Yoruba. Cornell Univ. Press, New York, 1963.
12 LYKETSOS, G.: Emigration: psychopathological reactions in the families left behind. Ment. Hlth. Soc. *4,* 263, 1977.
13 MEZEY, A.G.: Psychiatric illness in Hungarian refugees. J. Ment. Sci. *106,* 628, 1960.

14 MEZEY, A.G.: Psychiatric aspects of human migrations. Int. J. Soc. Psychiat. *5,* 245, 1960.

15 MEZEY, A.G.: Personal background, emigration and mental disorder in Hungarian refugees. J. Ment. Sci. *106,* 618, 1960.

16 MURPHY, H.B.M.: Migration and the major mental disorders: a reappraisal. In: Kantor, M.B. (Ed.): Mobility and Mental Health. Chas C. Thomas, Springfield, Illinois 1965; Chap. I., pp. 5 – 29.

17 MURPHY, H.B.M.: Migration, culture and mental health. Psychol. Med. *7,* 677, 1977.

18 PARKER, S., KLEINER, R.J., NEEDLEMAN, B.: Migration and mental illness: some considerations and suggestions for further analysis. Soc. Sci. & Med. *3,* 1, 1969.

19 PFISTER-AMMENDE, M.: The symptomatology, treatment and prognosis in mentally ill refugees and repatriates in Switzerland. In: H.B.M. Murphy (Ed.): Flight and Resettlement. Unesco, Paris 1955; pp. 147 – 173.

20 RICHMOND, A.H.: Immigration and pluralism in Canada. Int. Migr. Rev. *4,* 5, 1969.

21 SCHAECHTER, F.: Previous history of mental illness in female migrants admitted to the psychiatric hospital. Royal Park. Med. J. Aus. *2,* 277, 1965.

22 STOLLER, A.: Migration and mental Health in Australia. Brit. J. Soc. Psychiat. *1,* 61, 1966.

23 STOLLER, A., KRUPINSKI, J.: Immigration to Australia: Mental Health Aspects. In: Zwingmann, C., Pfister-Ammende, M. (Eds.): Uprooting and After. Springer, Berlin/Heidelberg/New York 1970; pp. 252 – 268.

24 TAFT, R.: The shared frame of reference concept applied to assimilation of migrants. Hum. Relat. *6,* 45, 1963.

Chapter 3

Identity and Minority:
Value conflicts and conflicts of identity

HARALD OFSTAD

External Identification

If we were to order a spare part for a tractor, we must be able to identify it in some way, e.g. with the help of a number. Stating this requisite number identifies the desired part and avoids confusion.

With regard to people, their names usually suffice as identification instrument. For example, «There was a phone call for you when you were out.» «Who was it?» «It was David Schwarz.» If we were still uncertain, the questioning would continue something like this, «Which David Schwarz?» «You know, the one who is the co-editor of the book *Strangers in the World.*»

In similar ways we identify groups or nations we are talking about. «Where have you been this summer?» «In England» – a specific land is identified. «How did you like them?» «Who?» «The English.» The name identifies a particular population. It is about them that the person's opinion is desired.

But identification does not have to occur by the use of names, and, quite often it cannot be obtained in that way, since the object under consideration does not have a name or because the name is inadequate for identification purposes. In such instances, one may use some type of description. We say, «You know the sensation the taste of lemon leaves in your mouth.»

Identification with the help of proper names is usually relatively neutral – from an evaluative point of view. But quite often an identification implies a positive or negative evaluation, as, in the case of America's troops during the Vietnam war calling their enemy a «Slope» or a «Gook», etc. Americans knew who was being talked about partly just because the names were derogatory. A strong negative evaluation is likewise implied in the statement: «A nigger was here asking for you,» or, in «Out with the pigs» — as was said during the German occupation of Norway in World War II. The situation clarified who was being referred to — despite the fact that the identification was nothing but an insult, serving to strengthen the group feelings among Norwegians and identify the enemy as an outgroup.

When the function of identification is to delimit a particular person, group or object(s), I shall talk about *external identification.*

Internal Identification

I distinguish between *internal* and *external* identification. By internal identification, I mean the kind of identification that groups or individuals undertake when they attempt to answer such questions as, «Who am I?» or «Who are we?».

In certain cases proper names may function as answers even to questions concerning internal identification. «Who am I?» «But of course, you are Peer Gynt.» «Oh, that's right. I almost forgot!» Suddenly one remembers that one is the individual referred to by that name — which, in this instance, was all one had to know. But usually it is not a proper name we are after when we are seeking for our identity.

Feeling of identity and criteria of identity

The experience that this is me, this is we — the feeling of identity — presupposes the fulfilment of certain conditions or criteria. Hence, we should distinguish between *feeling of identity* and *criteria of identity.*

In the case of an individual person, his feeling of identity may presuppose that his body looks approximately as it has looked before or that he at any rate can explain the change, and further, that is mental life contains continuity and coherence. These things, then, are examples of what I call criteria of identity, that is, conditions which must be present in order for a person or a group to have, or aquire, a feeling of identity. The conditions are not necessarily the same from individual to individual nor from group to group, and they can even vary over time.

A person (or a group) searching for its identity consequently can be looking for at least two different things. He may never have had a genuine feeling of identity and is striving to obtain this feeling. But it is also possible that the person or group in question has the feeling of identity but is uncertain concerning the criteria or conditions which it is, or should be, based upon. The last possibility must also be considered for one's feeling of identity may be well anchored in certain criteria – e.g. certain personality traits which, however, one rejects from an evaluative point of view, feeling that one ought to change. «I am the heathen Augustinus, but must try to become the Christian Augustinus.»

According to my view, the experience of identity, consequently, is a feeling of identity connected to certain criteria of identity. In the following, I shall not further characterize the feeling of identity, but first of all discuss the criteria of identity and their relationships with this feeling.

Factual and ideal criteria of identity

We must distinguish between *factual* and *ideal* criteria of identity. By factual criteria I mean the conditions which actually elicit feelings of identity or, in other words, the conditions on which these feelings really are based. By ideal criteria I mean the conditions which the individual – from a normative or evaluative point of view – wishes that his feelings of identity were based upon. The individual in question may have a feeling of identity, but he would like his feeling to be based upon something other than what it actually is based upon. We can compare him with a person who is sort of happy, but whose feelings of happiness result from narcotics while, at the same time, he is wishing that they resulted from a better relationship with his wife.

It is a matter of empirical research to find out which factual or ideal criteria of identity any given person or group makes use of. As they can vary substantially, I shall limit my discussion to some of the more common factual criteria.

Different factual criteria

A group's feeling of identity can be based, first of all, on what we might call *geographic* criteria of identity. «We» are the people who exist within this or that area at a certain time-interval. In school we used criteria of this kind to identify a particular country as being bordered on the north by . . . and on the south by . . . etc.

This type of criteria may be important at the group level, at least in combination with some of the other criteria I shall discuss.

Feelings of identity can also be based on the history of the group or person, that is, on those actions and occurences which constitute its past. Let us refer to these as *historical* criteria of identity. However, a certain series of actions and occurences can be described in many different ways. According to one description, the history of the group consists of B_1, B_2 and B_3. According to another, it consists of B_4, B_5 and B_6. Both descriptions may be correct and since no description is all inclusive, the historical criteria of identity can vary.

A third possibility would be to emphasize what is typical and stable, in spite of all changes. I shall call this *criteria of continuity*. We cannot exclude the possibility that this type of criteria is inapplicable to certain people and groups, simply because nothing in their life has been stable and typical.

Historical criteria and criteria of continuity refer to how life actually has been, and , consequently, to numerous factors over which idividuals and groups have little or no control. A fourth possibility, then, is that the feelings of identity may be based upon one's conception of what one might have been, if only the circumstances had been different from what they were. Then, and only then, one's true character would have manifested itself. Let us refer to criteria of this kind as *criteria of essentiality.* An example: a person may identify himself as a psychologist because he always wanted to become one and might have been one if he could have afforded the education.

In similar ways, a social class or minority group may have its feelings of identity based on its conception of what it could have been − and in reality is − but never were allowed to become.

It is not difficult, from a theoretical point of view, to distinguish between these different criteria of identity, but in most cases they are probably united or combined within one and the same identification. «We are a group which . . . », and then follows a series of characteristics relating to historical traditions considered stable and continuous and expressing the group's essential attributes.

How does the foregoing relate to what I have called ideal criteria of identity? First, they may happen to coincide with some of the factual criteria. For example, that which is continuous and stable in one's evolution is at the same time that which one ideally would like to be. Or, one might want to base one's ideal identification on what one could have been if this or that had been different. This is what one will be, and this is what one can be, if only certain things were changed. But of course, there may also be conflicts between one's ideal and factual criteria.

As already mentioned, the feelings of identity need not be based on the same criteria all the time. The picture of one's history at a certain point of time does not necessarily coincide with the picture at a later point of time. And, similarly, the picture of one's ideal self can vary over time.

What fluctuates in these cases is not the feeling that we are ourselves, but the criteria on which this feeling is based.

Society's influence on criteria of identity

What I called «external identification» is, of course, to a large degree determined by the needs of society. This is a consequence of the fact that it functions as an instrument within social communication. But even internal identification is influenced, not only by individuals and groups, but by the larger society as well.

Quite often the internal identification is merely a repetition of the external one. «You are the baker's son» becomes «I am the baker's son». «You are the daughter of the King» becomes «I am the daughter of the King». «You are a thief» becomes «I am a thief».

The same holds for a group or a nation. They have certain pictures of themselves which are transferred to and internalized by future generations. If the community is markedly homogeneous, this process can function very effectively. But usually a society consists of competing groups, and one may be identified in different ways by different groups. One is identified as the baker's son by some, as a promising author by others and by a different group as a fighter for radical beliefs. Since it is important to influence the identification process, various groups compete to have their criteria of identity accepted.

Control of the identification process is without doubt one of society's strongest means of influence. Mastery over our identity goes deeper and has more important and extensive consequences than the manipulation which springs from rules and regulations telling us what to do in this or that situation. If society succeeds in getting us to identify ourselves as the individuals which society wants us to be, our substance is saturated — the roots of our attitudes and actions. An example: Nazi-Germany succeeded in producing a generation identifying themselves as soldiers whose function was to sacrifice their lives for what they believed was Germany's glory. Given that, the later impregnation process in the drill of war was easy.

A possible explanation of the success of this kind of manipulation is the difficulty of functioning in society if we lack the feeling of being something definite and stable. And, since we must function in order to live, we cannot always afford to be critical towards the identity which society has implanted in us.

One of the methods of oppressors has always been to influence the oppressed to identify themselves as inferiors, as slaves. If such an identification process prevails, the rulers have assured themselves a guaranteed future: the oppressed will behave as slaves.

Probably home and school usually exert the strongest influence on the identification process. Children are motivated to identify themselves, their groups, their society and nation in certain ways. However, other interest groups try to have their opinions play a part. If it becomes arduous to unite the varying identities, an identity crisis will be the likely result, producing in its turn what is called «ineffective citizens». For this and other reasons governments, including the non-totalitarian kind, attempt to gain control over the identification process.

One's own criteria of identity

As mentioned above, society and various interest groups and organizations, try to get individuals and groups to accept those criteria of identity which they consider useful. But the influence is not entirely one-sided. Society is confronted with persons having the possibility and capacity — stronger or weaker — to criticize society's influence, maintaining their own point of view.

It is important to keep this point in mind since social psychologists often seem to forget the individual's ability to resist. There are, however, two reservations. First, to a large degree we are subjected to society's influence so early in life that we are powerless to oppose it. We are being shaped without knowing that we are. Second, the methods we can use in order to unmask and criticize society's influence are themselves products of society. We use words, concepts and distinctions inherited from society.

If an individual or a group is to break free of its forced-upon identity, it is important that it possesses a conceptual system — preferably also a language — different from that of the larger community. If one masters only the concepts and language of the oppressors, one is to a large degree already taking part in their game. To rebel we need a language of our own, a language within which we can develop our independence and through which we can channel our defiance in a constructive way. Only in this way can we get that distance between ourselves and the influence process which is required in order to become aware of the possibility that our identity could have been, and can be, different from what it actually is. To become aware of this may be the first step toward altering our criteria of identity. This alteration in its turn increases our distance to the influence process and our awareness of who society wants us to be, and this awareness is a necessary condition of the development of an independent identity.

Minority groups

The problem of identity is of special significance for individuals and groups which in some important aspect differ from the larger society, since their identification often is a means with which they attempt to safeguard their distinctive qualities. I shall limit my forthcoming discussion to problems of identity pertaining to minority groups.

I shall delimit my concept of a minority group to a group which perceives itself as deviating in some important aspect from the larger community to which it belongs, and which lacks the means of forcing its own interests and views on the rest of society. Hence, according to my usage, the majority of a society can constitute a minority group. The black population of South Africa is a case in point.

There it is the Whites who numerically constitute the minority but, due to their power, they are unaffected by usual types of minority problems. On the other hand, a group is not a minority simply by virtue of not having the power to implement its interests and views on the rest of society. This would indeed be a strange concept of a minority group. As I see it, the crucial factor is that the group is, and perceives itself, as different from an ethnic, cultural or national point of view, while at the same time having a lesser amount of power than the dominating groups of society.

The criteria of identity accepted by minority groups

I have distinguished between what I have called *factual* and *ideal* criteria of identity, and between different examples of such criteria. A minority group can seek its identity in a specific geographical setting, in its history, in a certain interpretation of the stable and continuous factors in its life, or in its conception of what the group could have been – and consequently, «really is» – if certain conditions had been different, for instance, if the group had not been oppressed.

These criteria, and others I have not taken up, can be conceived of in varying versions. To illustrate, a group can find its historical identity first of all in its moral and/or religious traditions, or in its language, its culture, its struggles and wars, its solidarity during times of occupation and oppression, etc. It is a plausible hypothesis that a minority group's customs, norms, values, and language are among its most important and fundamental criteria of identity. And since I cannot discuss many different alternatives, I shall restrict my discussion to cases where the group's feeling of identity is grounded upon its norms and values.

Norms and values as criteria of identity

Let us assume that a group sees its norm- and value system and the praxis corresponding with it as its most distinctive quality. This implies that a given group member probably identifies himself as a member of the group by means of characteristics referring to this system or praxis. This is what makes him what he is, and the group what *it* is.

Identity based on a group's norms and values can be an example of what I have called a historical identification for the norms and values are usually a central element in a group's history. It can also be an example of identity based on criteria of continuity, since the group's norms and values may be part of the core of the stability of the group. Moreover, norms and values can also function as the basis of an essential identification, since the feeling of identity may be based upon norms and values which the group wants to practice, though it has been unable to do so, e.g., due to oppression. Obviously, norms and values can also be part of an ideal identification.

In the following, I shall concentrate my discussion to those cases where the various criteria coincide. This occurs when group's feeling of identity is grounded on norms and values belonging to its historical and stable traditions, at the same time as these norms and values are those which the group really wants to have.

My reason for concentrating on this form of identity is first of all that it probably plays an important role in the life of a minority group. What a minority group attempts to defend from the influences of the larger society is usually its integrated norms and values. Secondly, this type of identity is probably more important than other types, because it goes deeper and is based on fundamental factors which have significant consequences for the total life of the minority group.

What is meant by norms and values?

By «norms» I mean statements concerning what one ought to do, what is right or duty. The aim of norms, as a rule, is to guide or in some other way influence our actions, decisions, views and feelings. By «value» I refer to what has value in itself, for example happiness, knowledge, beauty, love, etc. By «value statements» I mean statements maintaining that something is good or bad. The aim of value statements, as a rule, is to point out what is, and what is not, worth striving for. They do not necessarily say anything about how we should act.

However, in the present context our thinking will become too limited if we consider norms and values solely as I have presented them. We must also imply that they are accepted in the sense that the group tries to live up to them and that they are part of the group's social system of expectations to which the group adjusts its behaviour. It is norms and values in this more comprehensive sense which I take as the basis of the identity of the minority group.

The norms and values in question do not have to be distinctive for the minority group. Other groups can have similar norms and values.

Practised norms and values versus norm- and value myths

We often talk about a group's norms and values as if they constitute a definite class. Actually, however, the norms and values tend to vary within the group. If we were to make a detailed list of the norms currently in use and the values which people strive for, paying special attention to the norms or values given priority in situations of conflict, we would be confronted with distinct variations. This variation is usually not consistent with the picture the group wants to have of itself and transfer to its members. Consequently, within a group one often finds not only concrete and practised norms and evaluations, but also a set of more abstract norms and values which do not correspond to people's behaviour. These norms and values belong to the myths of the group. The practised norms and evaluations cannot easily come into conflicts with these myths, since they are abstract and their requirements rather indefinite. The myths belong to the traditions of the group. They are carried over to future generations and retained as verbal habits and preferences, and as symbols to which one is expected to show respect.

A group normally guards its norm- and value myths more zealously than the norms and values it actually lives by. It is therefore relatively easy to accept changes in practice, given that they do not too obviously conflict with the myths.

Norm and value conflicts can become conflicts of identity

Given my presuppositions, the minority's feeling of identity is based upon its norms and values, and more strongly on its norm- and value myths than on the practised ones. But the minority group is at the same time part of a larger society with *its* norms and values which, in turn, can come into conflict with the norms and values of the minority group. (This, of course, is not always the case but, in this connection, it is just these cases which are of interest.)

The bare existence of the norms and values of the larger society can be experienced as a threat to the norms and values of the minority group. This is a natural consequence of the minority group's perception of the power which the larger community commands, and, therefore, of its ability to exercise influence. And it holds even if the larger society does not consciously try to influence the minority. But usually pressure radiates from the larger society. It can vary from extreme demands of assimilation — «be like us» — to weaker demands of polishing one's norm- and value traditions so that they do not irritate the larger community.

I shall not in this paper go into the different strategies which the larger society can use against the minority. What I wish to emphasize is that any pressure, strong or weak, will be experienced not only as a call for modifying one's traditionally accepted norms and values. It will also be experienced as a threat against the identity of the group. Conflicts between the norms and values of the larger society and of the minority group will develop into conflicts of identity. The minority group will experience the pressure as efforts to change their criteria of identity: «From now on you shall be yourself, not when you live according to the norms and values which *you* accept, but when you live according to the norms and values which *we* accept.» Especially, the pressure will be experienced in this way if it is the result of open and deliberate politics which not only conflicts with the norms and values which the minority group lives by, but also with its norm- and value myths, the pictures the group have of itself and which it cherishes as cultural symbols.

If the larger society declares that the minority's acceptance of *their* norms and values is the way to full equality, the conflict will be extremely severe, especially for the young employment seeking members of the minority group. They will feel guilty if they overthrow the norms and values of their own group. On the other hand, if they do not, they will be frustrated by overthrowing the way towards social salvation. The situation can become quite similar to the one St. Augustine describes in his endeavors to find salvation. His inner conflicts depended not only on his change from Greek-humanistic to Christian norms and values, but first of all on the fact that his identity was shattered in the process of change. Changing his view of life implied changing his personality. As long as the Christian view of life was not fully integrated, he was unsure of whether he was mostly himself when he felt Greek torments in trying to accept Christianity, or wether he was mostly himself when he felt Christian torments by clinging so hard to Greek-humanism.

The above discussion implies that a minority group fighting to keep its criteria of identity may have to fight both at the outer and the inner front: towards the pressure of the larger society, but also towards those members of its own group who depreciate the traditions of their group, wanting to become like «anyone else» believing that this is the way to better jobs.

Social scientists have collected material concerning the interactions between minority groups and the larger societies to which they belong. I do not regard it as my objective to elaborate on their efforts. Instead I shall present some ideas from a normative (and empirical) point of view with regard to the type of conflict situation I have considered.

Basic norms and values

As a point of departure, let us distinguish between those norms and values which on the whole must be followed by everyone, even the minority groups, in order that society can exist, and, on the other hand, norms and values which say something as to how life should be lived and which values striven for, given that elementary needs are met. The former type of norms and values I shall call *basic,* the latter type *cultural.*

If we assume that the norm- and value traditions of some minority groups are so constituted that certain points must be changed in order to avoid conflict with the basic norms and values, then change is necessary, just as it would be if the minority group had its own peculiar traffic laws. This must be so even if the minority group experiences the basic norms of the larger society as a threat to their identity. To illustrate: let us assume that a minority group accepts a relative's right of vendetta. On a point of this kind integration is required. We must all recognize that disagreements and conflicts are to be solved legally and with a minimum of violence. Admitting this, it is essential to underline the necessity of interpreting «basic» as narrowly as possible. For it is important that the concept of *basic* norms and values is not used as a guise for enacting norms whose function first and foremost is to prevent changes and see that society goes on serving the same interests as before.

I do not think that conflicts of the above kind, however, represent a genuine problem in relation to a minority group's feeling of identity. First of all, there hardly are any minority groups whose feeling of identity is based solely and/or mainly upon norms and values which are in conflict with the *basic norms* and values of the larger society. Secondly, even if such groups exist, their norm- and value traditions will also include norms and values which do not conflict with the basic ones, and which, consequently, can continue to function as criteria of identity.

Let us turn to what I called the cultural norms and values, presupposing that they are the ground of the group's identity.

Pluralism and conflict

We must distinguish between two different situations which can occur when a minority group's cultural norms and values confront those of the larger society. First, the cultural norms and values of the minority group may be of such a kind that even if they are followed without exception, this does not reduce the chances of the larger society to realize its own cultural norms and values. In this type of situation, we can talk about *cultural compatibility.*

Cultural compatibility is not the same as cultural agreement. While the norms of the minority group order that in situation S, one should do A_1, the larger society says that one should do A_2. For example, whereas the norms of the minority group order its members to cut their hair, the norms of the society order those who do not belong to the minority group to let it grow. The norms are different, the society is pluralistic, but the norms are compatible.

Cultural compatibility can exist even if the deviant norms of the minority group shall serve a common goal. An example: suppose that a given society must have a specific amount of chopped wood, and that a minority group follows the rule that wood should be choped with the right hand, whereas the rest of society follows the rule that one should use one's left hand. The difference in rules and practice does not prevent the realization of the common goal.

Second, the cultural norms and values of the minority group may be clearly incompatible with those of the society at large. We are confronted with a situation of *cultural conflict*. An example: suppose the larger society has the ambition of building up a strong defense system by use of military equipment, whereas the minority group consists of pacifists, distrusting military defense. Let us further suppose that the minority group has so many members that if they follow their view, it would become almost impossible for the larger society to fulfill its objective.

This is a real conflict, but as mentioned earlier it is my hypothesis that a minority group's feeling of identity seldom is based solely and/or mainly on norms leading to cultural conflicts of the type indicated. Nevertheless, I shall suggest some ideas concerning the solutions of such conflicts.

First, the large society must not use its superior power to force the minority to act against their own norms. Second, as soon as possible, and in good time before the situation becomes critical, one must start a *value analysis* on dialogical basis: What are the ends in view of the military system, as perceived by the decision-makers of the large society? How does the *people* perceive its ends? How does the minority group perceive it? How does the minority group perceive the end in view of its own policy, and how does the larger society perceive it? Does the minority group conceive of its pacifism as an end in itself, or is their idea that non-violence is a better means of defense than violence? And a means of defense for what? The best possible chance for everyone to live a good life? If so, does the minority group have the same conception as the larger society as to what constitutes a good life? And are they equally aware of the price that must be paid?

Through a value analysis of this kind the dialogue may develop into a rational dialogue permitting mutual influence without that indoctrination and pressure which the minority group will experience as an encroachment on its identity.

Let us go back to situations of cultural compatibility. Even in a situation of this kind, one can often notice that a minority, by doing something in an unusual way, can set off substantial irritations in spite of the fact that what they are doing is entirely legitimate and in no way preventing the larger society from realizing its own values. Since the larger society is superior from the point of view of power, its irritation may express itself in ways which the minority group very easily will experience as infringing its rights.

It is a plausible hypothesis that such *norm irritation* plays an important role in majority-minority relations. It is even plausible to assume that norm and value variations eliciting norm irritation will be perceived as cases of cultural conflict although the norms and values actually are compatible. As is well known, we like to rationalize our irritations in one way or another.

We must not underestimate the dejection and aggression which the larger society's norm irritation may produce within the minority group. Since the norms in question are compatible, the irritation will be perceived as completely unjustified.

The most efficient method to combat norm irritation is by showing – clearly and unequivocally – that there exists no conflict in the sense described above. By making this evident, the irrational nature of the irritation will become obvious. Further, everything which makes people emotionally more secure lessens the tendency for irrational norm irritation. Probably the tendency would also be reduced if the groups could experience, in their own lives, that it is possible to do things *our* way without inhibiting another's possibility to do the same things in *their* way. Our eating with knife and fork does not inhibit another's eating with chopsticks.

Finally, I shall say something about norm- and value differences within the field of morality. The difference between the views of the minority group and the larger society can refer to something which has value as a means to something else or to something which has value in itself, and it can refer to derived or more ultimate moral norms.

Usually, perhaps even in most cases, the disparities will not produce irritation between the two groups, but rather give rise to anxiety, insecurity and fear, since these norms and values are concerned with matters that are important also from a personal point of view. Consider the following example: a certain group has taught its members the importance of introspective contemplation. According to the group, salvation comes as the result of solitary refinement of the soul. But this group is, we assume, also part of a larger society holding that salvation is obtained through outwardly active social contribution.

The larger society has superior power. God or nature has pointed it out as the sovereign. Is it then possible that the norms and values of the minority group can be correct? Can they be correct as long as there are informed individuals who consider them incorrect?

If the minority group starts asking itself such questions, its insecurity may give way to aggression. And the aggression will be magnified since the group's feeling of identity probably is connected with its moral norms and values.

Insecurity and anguish can occur also in the larger society. And since this group has power, it is tempting to use it in more or less subtle forms in order to reduce the impression of the minority group's deviation. If this is obtained, the members of the larger society do not need to admit the conspicuous fact that there are people within their own society who believe that some of the greater community's most important norms and values are in fact erroneous.

More serious displays of power will come into conflict with the norm of tolerance, according to which everyone shall have the right to put forward and defend his norms and ideals. But even in a community where this norm of tolerance is more than empty rhetoric, it easily will function as a courtesy «von oben». The larger society can afford to be tolerant since it has the power, and perhaps also the conviction that nothing can disturb its philosophy of life. One day the minority group will wake up and see the light. Let us overlook their heresy.

Tolerance of this kind is based on arrogant and unacceptable premisses. The point is that we only in extreme cases know that these or those moral principles are more correct than these or those others. Given this, it is of value for society as a whole that minority groups argue for and practise deviant norms and values. It makes people aware of the fact that the moral questions may have other answers than the conventionally accepted ones.

The instrumental value of pluralism

If by «pluralism» we mean that within a society there are different norms and values competing with each other — one cannot possible accept all of them — the above reasoning may be summarized by saying: pluralism with regard to philosophies of life is a social value, not just something we have to tolerate.

Pluralism has value as a means, not in itself. Its value is rooted in the fact that individuals through confrontation with norm and value variations may break free from their habitual ways of thinking according to which the only acceptable possibility is that which they themselves happen to believe in. Pluralism stimulates critical comparison and reflection which may lead to modifications.

Maintaining that pluralism has value only as a means thus implies that its value is conditioned by the fact that it leads to something positive. However, a meeting between any set of norms and values does not automatically lead to anything positive. The larger society may experience the norms and values of a certain minority group as so curious that they do not take them seriously. Another possibility is that the norms express standpoints which are so extreme — e.g. fascistic ones — that they do not contain anything beneficial for the rest of society. But one has to be cautious on this point. Even a democratic society has its weak points, and may perhaps see them more clearly by being confronted with a group which openly is proud of what the larger society is ashamed of and tries to hide behind its ideological facade.

Changing norms and values

Let us suppose that the larger society is irritated at the norms and values of a minority group and perhaps even tries to change them. If this is the case, the minority group will experience the pressure as a threat against its identity. And it may experience pressure as a threat even if the larger society is pluralistic, since it may feel the norms and values of the larger society as overwhelming and demanding, especially if they are perceived as the road towards social success.

Moreover, the norms and values of the minority group are continually exposed to influence from mass media, developments and changes in the world as a whole, technical, artistic and scientific inventions and discoveries, new experiences, new thoughts and views of all possible types. Influence of these kinds carry with them the constant possibility that norms and values will be modified. Furthermore, groups within the minority group may work for specific changes.

Hence, we must reckon with the possibility that the norms and values of a minority group continuously are exposed to pressure towards changes. And changes will occur. The important question is in what way the changes will take place, and what the consequences will be for the group's feeling of identity.

Let us assume that a minority group has its feeling of identity tied to its norms and values first and foremost because they are the intermediaries of stable and continuous tradition. Under such conditions all change may be viewed as a threat to the group's identity, regardless of whether the momentum originates in the larger society, groups within the minority group or in changes in the outer world.

However, not all changes can be stopped, especially not those which are brought about through changes in society.

In a situation of this kind, different reactions are conceivable. Perhaps the most common one is that the change is accepted in practice, but not at the verbal and institutional levels. The norm and value myths remain intact. Another possibility is for the group members to take on two identities, *one* based on the group's traditionally given norms and values, and a *second* founded on the actual practice which is in conflict with the traditions. For example, we can be *one* person when functioning as the group's representative and another when functioning on one's own within the larger society. A third possibility is for a kind of double dealing to develop. When acting within the minority group, one tries to hide the fact that a new identity has been taken on when acting within the larger society, and when acting within the latter, one tries to conceal that one's roots are still in the minority group. A fourth possibility is that one becomes rather indifferent towards the norms and values of one's group, developing a superficial and uncontroversial sort of identity which one hopes will work in any situation. All four of these reactions cannot but injure the life of the minority group and, consequently, the larger society as well. Of course, a minority group's resistance to change may be stronger than what has been assumed in the above discussion. The group may perceive its norms and values, not only as bearers of its traditions, but as the final answers to life's normative questions. There is nothing more to add. But the group cannot isolate itself completely from the larger society nor from the world as a whole. Changes in the outer world will exert pressure on the group. Given that the group is of the above unflexible kind, the pressure may split the group. The young who accept changes become opposed to the dogmatic forces of tradition. The older members, on the other hand, will perceive the young ones as a threat to the identity of the group. The result may be conflict and disintegration.

Identification based on free and independent inquiry

Identification based on norms and values can be open to changes. Nothing prevents that. And I do not mean in the way previously mentioned: that changes are accepted in practice, but denied at the verbal and institutional level, but so that the changes are explicitly accepted. The crucial factor, from the point of view of the identity of the group, is whether the change is urged upon the group, or allowed to grow in accordance with the group's feeling of identity. If the changes are urged with force or through indoctrination of a more or less subtle kind, they will be experienced as alien and as an attack on the identity of the group. On the other hand, if the changes come as the result of discussion within the minority group, and are put forth in a way which the minority group accepts, e.g. through its decision-making body and after careful scrutiny by its members, the modification will be experienced as resulting from the activity of the group itself. Hence, they are not a threat to its identity, and can be accepted. It is important that the changes occur in such a way that the group's freedom is safeguarded, that the group can choose, say yes or no, and that it has it in its power to decide for or against the changes. As long as freedom is preserved, identity is not threatened.

The above reasoning has an important implication. Whether changes in the norms and values of a group shall be experienced as a threat to its identity depends upon the nature of those norms and values which constitute the criteria of identity. If the feeling of identity is based upon the entire range of norms and values which the group at a given point of time accepts, then any change may be experienced as a threat. On the other hand, if the feeling of identity is based upon a norm of a higher order, a *meta-norm,* according to which one always freely and independently should seek one's way forward to those norms and values that each new situation demands, then a change will not be experienced as a threat. If the feeling of identity is based on a particular class of norms and values, then we have to change identity each time we change opinion. But if the feeling of identity is based on a metanorm of the kind mentioned, then changes in principle will not be a problem. They are accepted if they are the result of free and independent inquiry. Assaults upon the norms and values which the group accepts at a certain time may still be unpleasant, but does not hit the group's feeling of identity.

The current situation

Norm and value myths may be found within most groups. Very likely, they also play a role in the larger society by virtue of its need to present itself as a democratic and tolerant society.

An example of how such a myth can function within an entire social group is seen in a 1953 investigation of randomly selected Oslo residents. The interviewed were asked to take a position, among other things, on the following statement: «We must be willing to give up Norway's independence if it one day becomes possible to establish a democratic world government.» Of 406, 39% accepted the statement. But when these same people later were asked to take a position on the following statement: «In a world state the coloured peoples, who have the majority in the world, must have more power than the white peoples», only 12% responded positively. And only 10% disagreed with the statement: «It would be a catastrophe, both for the whites and the coloured, if the white race should lose its position of leadership.»

A democratic world government? Of course. That is something fine. We must be in favour of that. That there will be less power for the whites and more for the coloured peoples is pushed aside. That was not what one accepted. One was in favour of the expression «democratic world government» and the associations connected with it. But when the concept is made more concrete it becomes obvious that the idea of a democratic world government is a myth, the function of which is to support the feeling of the interviewees of being persons standing for what is «true and just». The statement is experienced as so abstract that it elicits no feeling of obligation to accept its real implications, in any case not if they come into conflict with one's egoistic interests.

The larger society can arrange its relations to minority groups in somewhat similar ways. On special occasions glamorous words about tolerance and respect for minority culture and individuality are heard, but back in everyday life there is less generosity than the myths make one believe.

Lack of prejudice of this kind is not the same as respect for the identity of a group. People can be relatively free of ethnocentric prejudices but still conduct policy of assimilation. And the opposite attitude is also possible, viz., that people with ethnocentric prejudices are strongly against assimilation. The Nazis — to take an extreme example — certainly did not want the Jews to become «good Germans». But I think it is a plausible hypothesis that a policy of assimilation tends to include an ethnocentric element: «You shall be like us. But really you can never be, for basically you are, and will always remain, different.»

The policy of assimilation is a mistake not only from the point of view of respect for the cultural identity of the minority group, but even from the narrow outlook of the larger society as well. There is evidence that children's feelings of identity become more stable, and that they are better able to develop their natural abilities if they are allowed to grow up in such a way that they share language and culture with their parents. It gives them a stronger feeling of inner worth, and they avoid those feelings of self-contempt which is the price for operating with conflicting identities or playing a double game, of the type discussed above.

If a minority child learns the language of the majority, but not the mother tongue, while the parents only handle the new language poorly, the result will be emotional impoverishment of the child. That is so because only the language which has its roots in the emotional experiences of the parents can communicate to the child all the important nuances of contact, without which the world of the child becomes a world of emotional silence.

Obviously, also one's intellectual development may be impaired in a process of the above kind, but such harms may more easily be repaired. Let us also remember what linguists have stressed: it is the children who have learned to master their native language who are most able to learn the language of the larger community.

However, the language question has a deeper dimension which is part of the personal identity problem. We experience, to a large degree, our ego through the words and concepts we make use of. Descartes' thesis: «I think, therefore I am» can, from this point of view, be interpreted as expressing insight concerning the conneciton between our thinking — our use of words and concepts, and, on the other hand, our experience of our own identity. According to this interpretation, our feeling of identity presupposes that our thinking and language are experienced as *our* thinking and *our* language. But this presupposition is usually not fulfilled with regard to foreigners. The Greek is not himself in the same way when he speaks Swedish as when he speaks Greek. And even a Norwegian, whose language is so close to the Swedish, can get quite a strange feeling in his mouth — and eventually also in his soul — when he tries to speak Swedish. In the end, one does not recognize oneself, and Descartes' thesis gets the implication: «It is not I who think, therefore I am not.»

Cultural pluralism is a stimulus to critical reflection and useful for the larger society. A policy of assimilation is therefore unacceptable even from a narrow point of view. But the question concerning the larger society's relation to its minority groups should not be dealt with only from this limited perspective. For the fact that the larger society shows respect for a minority group's cultural identity and right to search for which norms and values to accept is not only useful, but a value in itself, a component in the cultural values of a society.

Bibliography

BETTELHEIM, B.: Individual and Mass Behaviour in Extreme Situations. Journal of Abn. and Soc. Psychology *38,* 417 – 452, 1943.

BETTELHEIM, IANOWITZ, M.: Social Change and Prejudice. Toronto Press, 1964.

BLALOCK, H.M.: Toward a Theory of Minority – Group Relations. New York, 1967.

BROAD, C.D.: The Mind and its Place in Nature. London, 1949.

BRONOWSKI, J.: The Identity of Man. Pelican Book, London, 1967.

CARE, N., GRIMM, R.H. (Eds.): Perception and Personal Identity: Proceedings of the 1967 Oberlin Colloqvium in Philosophy. Cleveland, 1967.

ERIKSON, E.H.: The Problem of Ego Identity. Journal of the American Psychoanalytic Association, vol. IV, 1956.

FREUD, S.: The Ego and the Id. London, 1947.

GLASER, D.: Dynamics of Ethnic Identification. American Sociological Review, 1958.

HARTMANN, H.: Ego Psychology and the Problem of Adaptation. New York, 1959.

MEAD, G.H.: Mind, Self and Society. Chicago, 1934.

OFSTAD, H., BAY, C., GULLVÅG, I., TØNNESSEN, H.:Nationalism. A Study of Identification with People and Power,vol. I. Institutt for Samfunnsforskning, Oslo, 1950.

RIESMAN, D., GLAZER, N., DENNEY, R.: The Lonely Crowd. New York, 1953.

ROSE, A.M., ROSE, C.B.: Minority Problems. A Textbook of Readings in Intergroup Relations. New York, 1965.

Part II

The individual

Chapter 4

The stress of migration: Adjustment reactions of migrants and their families

DAN G. HERTZ

Israeli immigration — A general view

Israel, as a land of immigration, has often been defined as one of the most challenging and complicated human laboratories for the study of changes which have been precipitated by the process of cultural transformation following migration.

Migration to Israel has occurred in waves, with immigrants coming from different countries at different periods. Since the establishment of the State of Israel in 1948, nearly one and a half million immigrants came to settle from more than one hundred countries [9, 21].

From some areas (North America, U.S., Canada), immigration is a continuous, slow but still as on-going steady process. From some other countries, however, due to the result of changes in international politics (increased tension or détente) short but intensive waves of immigration develop which are often interrupted with the same swiftness as they have started (Soviet Union, Iran).

Three major factors can be enumerated as high priority in the acceptance (absorption) of new immigrants to Israel. The first is a *general, politico-national* issue related to the «ingathering of the exiles» which has become a «raison d'être», a life motive for the existence of the newly re-established Jewish state. The second aspect is a combination of *historical and personal* factors; the *humanitarian* issue displaying concern for individuals, by saving and maintaining life in the spirit of Jewish humanistic and religious traditions. The third factor is on the *interpersonal-existential* level, and/or the need for utilization of manpower for assuring social and economic existence [3, 20].

At the beginning of 1978, the Israeli population consisted of three and a half million inhabitants, three million of them being Jewish. The diversity of this population does not need to be stressed. The wide scope of heterogeneity resulting from the country of origin, socio-cultural background and a pre-immigration demographic pattern, causes the Jewish population to reflect a most complex and dynamic picture. The length of residence of the different immigrant groups in the country and their consequent levels of acculturation add supplementary parameters to the already existing problem. Among the non-specifically defined «ethnic groups», marked differences can be found in age structure, educational level, family customs and beliefs, and often even in the prevalence of the different illnesses by which they might be afflicted. The complexity, however, is compounded even more when the entire population, comprising Moslems, Druze and Christians is examined [30, 31].

In most previous studies, due to methodological problems, the researchers restricted themselves in the identification of the immigrant to country of origin only. However, the definition of the country of origin often depended on the frequently changing geopolitical borders, corresponding with the immigrant's place and date of birth (e. g. members of the same immigrant family born in the same area in Eastern Europe define their country of origin respectively as Rumania, Hungary and the Soviet Union).

With the emphasis on the country of origin, in some of the studies, the terms «Ashkenazi» and «Sephardi», two major subcultures among the Jews, is often avoided. The term «Ashkenazi» is used to describe the Western immigrants who started their cultural existence in a very specific way in Eastern and Central Europe after the dispersion of the Jewish population, following the destruction of Jerusalem, nearly 2000 years ago. «Sephardi» is the term used for those immigrants from certain areas of Europe,

South America and North Africa who are descendants of the Jews expelled from Spain in 1492 [20, 30, 31].

Both subcultures carry in their history memories of persecution and threat of annihilation. Therefore, with all the demographic diversity, the basic common devotion to Israel and the common purpose of the different subgroups known as «the return to Zion» stand out even more significantly.

Yet, parallelly with the expectation and hopes, disappointments are equally intensely perceived and encountered by the new immigrants.

Over fifty percent, one out of every two persons is still an immigrant in Israel, and the difference between foreign — and native — born is much more than a matter of statistics and demographic definition. How can those differences be defined between native born and immigrants? Even with the deeply ingrained historical heritage of the immigrant, the Israeli native, the «sabra», has the genuine and natural sense of having inherited his right by birth. He was reared in the country and, therefore, through the natural course of growth and development, adopted its way of life. He can move in the milieu of the country with the absolute ease of being home, without being confronted by problems of orientation and communication facing one wishing to be an Israeli. He is never confronted with the threat of rejection and will never feel the uneasiness experienced by the immigrant when he is reminded that he just «another newcomer». Often, this sense of being and having been identified as a «new immigrant» will continue during the lifetime of an entire generation [19, 20, 23].

It goes without saying that the above description is applicable to other countries which attempt to absorb their returning foreign-born citizens (colonial Algerians in France, Dutch people returning from Indonesia to Holland).

Immigration and personality function — Theoretical considerations

This chapter attempts to describe some aspects of normal personality functions, family reactions and coping methods as reflected by immigrant and migrant groups in Israel after having been exposed to pressure of socio-cultural changes.

The main theme, as depicted by the author in previous works, deals with the reactions of individuals and families suddenly thrust into an alien culture or harboring divided loyalties to different cultures.

The methodological problems of research in this field have been extensively reviewed by FABREGA, based on the pioneer contributions of MURPHY, LEIGHTON, HERSKOWITZ and WEINBERG [15, 18, 25, 27, 36].

The difficulties of helping to assimilate a proportionally small number of newcomers to an existing system of values and pattern of customs have been experienced by most modern nations. Israel, however, as a «nation in the making» in recent past, has been and still is confronted with a much more complex problem of finding and defining her own identity while concurrently attempting to integrate a large number of new immigrants. These new citizens, originating from a large variety of cultures and countries, had very little in common with each other and with the previously established community here.

It seems that this dual problem of acculturation is more specific to Israeli society than to any other modern state in contemporary history. The integration of the process of change, together with the demand for the development of national self-identity under trying existential conditions, provides an unusual stress situation for both, the immigrant and the recipient community.

The already existing literature, relating to the stress factors and psychiatric aspects of human migration in general, reflects a wide variety of topics. The existing material is not intended to be reviewed in the framework of the present chapter. The reader is, therefore, referred to the sources mentioned in the bibliography. Particular attention must be given to contributions made by MEZEY, MURPHY, DAVID, CHAMPION and SANUA, in addition to the pioneer research carried out in Israel by A. WEINBERG [6, 7, 8, 26, 29, 36].

From the variety of factors mentioned in different publications, there is a consensus to focus attention at individual factors which may affect the immigrant's fate. However, it must also be mentioned that the decision and destination of migration does not necessarily depend on the immigrant alone but also on the law which determines who is going to migrate and to where.

Among the individual factors, specific variables play specific roles, such as age, sex, ethnic origin, socio-economic status, personal family and medical background, in addition to the manifest and hidden motives affecting the decision to make the move from one country to another [12, 14, 17, 32, 34, 38].

Social scientists understood and interpreted in recent years migration as a process of desocialization. Adaptation to the new environment has been considered as a result of resocialization. Consequently, it has been advocated that the recipient community must be prepared to show its tolerance toward the new immigrant by allowing him to learn by trial and error, before expecting him to be ready to assume his new role and social identity in terms of the new environment [1, 2, 4, 16].

ERIKSON already referred to the interrelation between identity and uprootedness, more than two decades ago. He indicated that through the influence of different crisis situations, a new and often transitory identity is assumed. Even though he had recognized the importance of social determinants (e.g. motivations for the move, process of separation from earlier environment, stages of absorption and reinvolvement in the new environment), he claimed that they do not account for the inner mechanisms involved in permitting man to maintain his individual sense of identity [13].

In continuation of the above mentioned theories, it is

necessary to quote some of the basic concepts relating to human migration, especially those which refer to the problems of acculturation. In earlier studies on migration and immigration, this author suggested the following modified definition for acculturation: «Acculturation stress is the total adaptive and coping process which occurs not only in the cultural patterning and value system but also in the psychophysiological and psychological structure and functions of individuals and families as adaptations are made to changing conditions created by the impact of populations and their cultures upon each other» [19, 22, 28, 35].

Difficulties in the process of acculturation can elicit the so-called «culture shock.» Its equivalent in migrants who return home after spending a prolonged period of time away from their own culture has been defined by HERTZ as «reverse culture shock» [19, 22].

Family reactions to changing environment

There is no unified theory about the coping mechanism of families with changing socio-cultural environment. EISENSTADT describes five different types of family constellations with various results in attempting to cope with migration stress. His definitions make a basic distinction between isolated and cohesive families. Surprisingly, not all the isolated families are prone to have adjustment difficulties. Even socially isolated families can succeed to overcome adjustment problems, depending on their ability to mobilize inner resources.

Only a combination of apathy and isolation will lead to absolute social breakdown in the family's functioning. Stable and active isolated families show reasonable favourable prognosis for positive adjustment.

Cohesive forces of the ethnic group will increase chances for successful coping. Best outlook is predicted for active families belonging to a cohesive ethnic group. Families belonging to this category will enjoy not only intrafamilial support but also the cohesive influence of the ethnic group. It will reinforce the family's ability to take active steps for self-transformation in the new environment [11].

Other studies define even more clearly the correlations between the support system originating from the family structure and the ability of the family to cope with migration and acculturation stress [5, 10].

The study of traditionally oriented, patriarchal and westernized immigrant families during and after the first year of arrival, reflects striking differences between the factors to be used as indicator for predicting their successful adjustment.

The integration of the traditionally oriented, patriarchal functioning families is mainly determined by the ability to deal adequately with the changes connected with the process of migration. Both generations, fathers and sons, are confronted with sets of demands emanating partly from the new situation, partly from the expectation from each other. In this process, the father's readiness to accept changes in the family's function has to be complemented by the sons' proneness to maintain traditional continuity to some extent.

Once the two conflicting parties, the old and new generation, reach a mutually acceptable compromise, the family will succeed to maintain undisturbed intrapsychic and interpersonal functions. If the understanding between fathers and sons fails to materialize, it will result in a breakdown of functioning, expressed by individual and family psychopathology.

The father in the traditional patriarchal family system is confronted with new situations where decisions to be made are contested and shared by other members of the family. This is expressed not only in the growing influence and participation of the wife in making decisions for the family but also in general liberalization of the family atmosphere.

Changes in the status of women (working outside the family home), and a different educational system for the children, add to development of new family constellations.

The danger exists for the father to be overruled and opposed by other family members who become better educated than the parents. The former belief that the father is the absolute and infallible authority in the family is often challenged by his unsuccessful struggle against new bureaucratic rules and demands which he never experienced before. If the father can mobilize family support for the newly presented situation, the result will become «closing the ranks» and the development of increased solidarity within the family [20, 37].

The parental generation has to overcome the painful loss of authority which might be compensated by stronger and warmer family relations. Usually, the individual frustration of the «pater familias» following the loss of status, deprives him of the ability to balance it by eventual reinforcement of family ties. Family — and clan — solidarity may grow stronger, but the father will never again become the central authority figure. He will also be forced to come to terms with the separation of his sons from the family home.

Children in the traditional family need to prove their willingness in continuing to accept parental authority. The earlier accepted ways of communication, namely requesting permission and consulting father before decisions will be made, is expected to be continued. Similarly, remaining «in the family orbit,» accepting parental participation in partner selection will decrease intergenerational conflicts originating during the process of immigration and will enhance better adjustment of the immigrant family.

In comparison with the above, Western families allowing more freedom for individual family members show a rather different set of characteristics, leading to symptoms of maladaptation. These families usually strive for acceptance by the environment, search for a feeling of security in the new setting and wish to develop immediate mastery of it.

Maladjusted westernized immigrant families present the following major emotional issues: feeling of emotional isolation, suffering from the lack of social contacts and disturbed by insecurity about the future.

Loss of previous problem-solving methods to master social situations, moral dependence on the new environment and lack of regular income are additional precipitating factors for adjustment difficulties.

Difficulties originating from the encounter with an entirely new (earlier not experienced) social and economic system, add to the problems of adjustment. Families immigrating from countries which lack democratic rule and practice restrictive migration laws, often complain about the feeling of «point of no return,» namely loss of the option to make free decisions. This may add to the difficulties experienced after immigration. Nostalgic longing, homesickness perturbs those immigrants who realize that they could not return to their country of origin, even if in reality they would hardly consider it seriously. The above experiences are often found in migrants from Eastern European and other totalitarian regimes [2, 33].

The process of positive adjustment

Based on clinical studies and observation, using the basic concepts of crisis, the evaluation of adjustment reactions of migrant families leads to the following theoretical formulation of positive immigrant adjustment which remains to some extent unaffected by the cultural and social structure of the migrant family.

Positive immigrant adjustment can be divided into three consecutive stages: *pre-immigration,* coping *stage of immigration* and *settlement.* All three of these stages comprise a combination of positive and negative emotional factors. The correlation between the two, in other words the proper utilization of the positive elements and the control of the negative ones, can be used as an indicator in the prediction of immigrant adjustment and mental health.

Pre-immigration

The family needs motivation for change, using rationalization and justification for making the move. Positive expectation from the outcome of the migration creates the proper emotional atmosphere for getting ready for the change. However, once denial of future difficulties and over-idealization of the new environment distorts reality testing of the immigrant family, the outcome will be increased potential danger for future maladjustment.

Coping stage of immigration

This period has to be divided into three consecutive developmental stages, namely *impact, rebound* and *coping level.* The impact level is experienced at the moment of arrival to the destined new environment. It is characterized by elation, relief and feeling of fulfillment. This level is relatively quickly followed by a rebound reaction, after having encountered the reality of the new environment. It manifests itself by expressions of disappointment which is often followed by anger or mere depression. It can be considered the psychological and social equivalent of the physiological «flight or fight» reaction. The clinical manifestations in this sub-stage can be either an expression of acting-out of anger or complete withdrawal and avoidance of involvement with the new environment.

The coping level comprises the process of learning and mastery. The family improves the modes of communication with the environment which is also reinforced by learning the language. This stage of adjustment also comprises the development of familiarity with the support system by learning the potential of the environment for offering understanding and help. Strenghtening emotional ties through adjustment of children and relatives, enhances the development of the feeling of trust and increased security.

Settlement stage

The process of positive adjustment reaches its climax in the stage of settlement. Readiness of the family to accept compromises with the new environment plays a major role. Once the family feels it is understood by its surroundings, it will also be more prepared to understand and accept the demands of the outside world towards them. Identification with the common cause of others (when the family feels a part of the world around them) brings about a feeling of belonging.

Summary

Introducing the concept of crisis in the understanding of the acculturation process of new immigrants, points out the necessity of accepting the developmental approach in dealing with migration and migrants.

It seems that no migration can be carried out without emotional and often physical stress and traumas which expose the individual migrant and the immigrant family to somewhat predictable but often unexpected additional stress factors. This process can be compared with the natural development of grief reactions. This approach advocates that a natural course of reactions must be experienced before reaching the state of emotional and social stability following immigration. A similar condition exists in individuals and families who are confronted with stressful and often life-threatening situations (like major catastrophies, floods, earthquake or even war).

The process of acculturation of migrant families, therefore, can be better understood when approached with a multidetermined bio-psycho-social concept. This dynamic process reflects the continuous between individual, family and socio-cultural environment.

By learning more of the facts concerning psychological, medical and socio-cultural aspects of the migration process, one hopes to learn better not only how countries of immigration can help newcomers, but also how recipient communities can be prepared for better coping with the problems encountered.

Additional research, therefore, must continue not only to relieve and prevent migrants from emotional disturbances, but to aim at the reduction of intergroup tensions and the promotion of a more stable and healthier society.

Bibliography

1 Bar-Yosef, R.W.: Social absorption of immigrants in Israel. In: David, H.P. (Ed.): Migration, mental health and community services. American Joint Distribution Committee, Geneva, 1968.

2 Berger, L. (Ed.): The battle of Israel's social front in the 1970's. The Jewish Agency, Jerusalem, 1970.

3 Bergman, R.: Professional absorption in Israel of nurse-immigrants from the USSR. Int. J. Nurs. Stud. *12,* 73 – 80, 1975.

4 Born, D.O.: Psychological adaptation and development under acculturative stress. Soc. Sci. & Med. *3,* 529 – 543, 1970.

5 Brody, E.B. (Ed.): Behaviour in new environments. Sage Publications, Beverly Hills, California, 1970.

6 Champion, Y.: Social-psychiatric aspects of migration. In: David, H.P. (Ed.): Migration, mental health and community services. American Joint Distribution Committee, Geneva, 1968.

7 David, H.P.: Migration, mental health and community services. American Joint Distribution Committee, Geneva, 1968.

8 David, H.K.P.: Involuntary international migration. Chapter 3. In: Brody, E.B. (Ed.): Behaviour in new environments. Sage Publications, Beverly Hills, California, 1970.

9 Davies, A.M.: Migrants and their children in Israel. Isr. J. Med. Sci. *7,* 12, 1344 – 1347, 1971.

10 De Sole, D.E., Singer, P., Roseman, J.: Community psychiatry and the syndrome of psychiatric culture shock – The emergence of a new functional disorder. Soc. Sci. & Med. *1,* 401 – 418, 1968.

11 Eisenstadt, S.N.: The process of absorption of immigrants in Israel. In: Frankenstein, C. (Ed.): Between past and future. The Henrietta Szold Foundation for Child and Youth Welfare, Jerusalem, 1953.

12 Eitinger, L.: Concentration camp survivors in Norway and Israel. Universitetsforlaget, Oslo, 1964 – 1965.

13 Erikson, E.H.: Identity and uprootedness in our time, uprooting and resettlement. World Federation for Mental Health, Geneva, 1960.

14 Ex, J.: Adjustment after migration. Martinus Nijhoff, The Hague, 1966.

15 Fabrega, H., Jr.: Social psychiatric aspects of acculturation and migration: A general statement. Compr. Psych. *10,* 314 – 326, 1969.

16 FRANKENSTEIN, C. (Ed.): Between past and future. The Henrietta Szold Foundation for Child and Youth Welfare, Jerusalem, 1953.

17 HARTEG, J.: Transcultural aspects of community psychiatry. Ment. Hyg. 55, 35 – 44, 1971.

18 HERSKOVITS, M.J.: Acculturation: The study of culture contact. Peter Smith, Gloucester, Massachusetts, 1958.

19 HERTZ, D.G.: The problem of «reverse» culture shock. In: Boroffka, A., Pfeiffer, W.M. (Eds.): Fragen der transkulturell-vergleichenden Psychiatrie in Europa. Westfälische Wilhelms-Universität, Münster, 1977.

20 HERTZ, D.G.: Families in transition and the problem of symptomformation. Paper given at International Congress of Ethnomedicine. 14 mimegr. p. Heidelberg, 1977.

21 HERTZ, D.G.: The pleasure and pain of returning home. (Adjustment problems of immigrants and returning residents in Israel.) Abstract, VI World Congress of Psychiatry, Honolulu, Hawaii, 1977.

22 HERTZ, D.G.: Remigration. In: Pfeiffer, W.M., Schoene, A. (Eds.): Transcultural psychopathology. Ferdinand Enke Publishers, Stuttgart, 1980.

23 KOSA, J.: Land of choice. University of Toronto Press, 1957.

24 KUSHNER, G.: Immigrants from India in Israel. University of Arizona Press, 1973.

25 LEIGHTON, A.H., HUGHES, J.R.: Cultures as causative of mental disorder. In: Causes of mental disorders: A review of epidemiological knowledge. Milbank Memorial Fund, New York, 1961.

26 MEZEY, A.G.: Psychiatric aspects of human migration. Internat. J. Soc. Psych. 5, 245 – 260, 1960.

27 MURPHY, H.B.M.: Social change and mental health. In: Causes of mental disorders: A review of epidemiological knowledge. Milbank Memorial Fund, New York, 1961.

28 REDFIELD, R., LINTON, R., HERSKOVITS, M.J.: Memorandum for the study of acculturation. In: Beyond the frontier: Social process and cultural change. Natural History Press, Garden City, N.Y., 1967.

29 SANUA, V.D.: Immigration, migration and mental illness. Chapter 13. In: Behavior in new environment. Sage Publications, Beverly Hills, California, 1969.

30 SHEBA, CH.: Jewish migration in its historical perspective. Isr. J. Med. Sc. 7, 12, 1333 – 1341, 1971.

31 SCHMELZ, U.O.: The demographic evolution of the Jewish population in Israel. Isr. J. Med. Sci. 7, 12, 1348 – 1363, 1971.

32 SHUVAL, J.: Immigrants: On the threshold. Atherton Press, Prentice Hall, New York, 1963.

33 SHUVAL, J.: Patterns of integration over time: Soviet immigrants in Israel. Israel Institute of Applied Social Research, Mimeographed 42 pp. Jerusalem, 1975.

34 STOLLER, A. (Ed.): New faces: Immigration and family life in Australia. Melbourne, Cheshire, 1966.

35 Teller, J.L. (Ed.): Acculturation and integration. American-Histadrut Cultural Exchange Institute, New York, 1965.
36 Weinberg, A.A.: Migration and belonging: A study of mental health and personal adjustment in Israel. Martinus Nijhoff, The Hague, 1961.
37 Weintraub, D.: Immigration and social change. Israel University Press, Keter, 1971.
38 Wolstenholme, G.E.W., O'Connor, M.: Immigration: Medical and social aspects. Churchill, London, 1966.

Chapter 5

Feeling «at home»:
Immigrants' psychological problems

Leo Eitinger

Introduction

What are the problems with which the individual migrant is confronted, and how does he experience his situation? What does a newcomer think, feel, understand and experience when he arrives in the country in which he will settle down for a while − or forever? How do these conditions influence his mental health, and how does the situation appear to the various members of the family? Similar questions arise and will briefly be considered in the subject pertaining to the members of the established minorities.

This presentation is based upon actual experience, studies of literature, conversations, interviews with two to three thousand newcomers in several countries, and on a number of investigations through questionnaires. The systematised interviews are centred on psychiatric problems which brought the persons in question to me (often concerning compensation) because of incapacity caused by a stay in a Nazi concentration camp. The general background, and in particular the psychological situation of the subjects, was a necessary condition for an adequate evaluation in every case, and was therefore always discussed very thoroughly. With such a one-sided dealing with only «sick» people, or people who had had to consult a psychiatrist because of problems of compensation, one might easily obtain a slanted impression of the questions and the problems that occupy «normal», «healthy» migrants. A succession of conversations of a less systematic nature with «non-patients» was necessary to complete the impression.

Contrary to many other psychological-psychiatric problem areas, it is not difficult to get relevant information from migrants in various countries when entering into their relations towards «the new surroundings», if one can only document that one does not oneself belong to these new surroundings. To have these general but somewhat unsystematised impressions from conversations further substantiated, questionnaires have been used. I do not intend to render here any tables or figures, but will only summarise the general results.

Who are the newcomers?

Who are these newcomers, migrants, members of minority groups actually? As a very superficial, outside observation, they would appear as a homogenous mass «not Norwegian or Swedish or etc.». In reality they are an extremely complex group of people with utterly different religious, political, ethnic, national, emotional and motivational background, attitudes and experiences. They could be people who had actively opposed a regime and had fled in fear for their lives, or they could be people the said regime merely disliked and had tried to dispose of. They could have just shown their dissatisfaction of the governing body, or they could have heard that the economic conditions were superior in some other country, and on these grounds chosen to become «refugees». They could be people who had consciously taken the decision to leave their homeland for purely economic reasons to seek, temporarily or permanently, a better existence: that is, immigrants in the true meaning of the word. Finally, they could be people who, during or after the Second World War, had been in prisons, penitentiaries, forced labour or Nazi concentration camps, who had endured all the wellknown sufferings and who, deeply scarred and isolated, had tried to find a refuge where they could «live in peace for the rest of their lives».

To define all these various newcomer categories with one label cannot be considered unproblematic. The question of whom should be considered emigrant (respectively immigrant), whom «seasonal labour», «guest worker» or tourist, is difficult to answer and is not only of theoretical interest.

One definition, that an emigrant is, in principle, a person who, without any intent of returning, leaves his homeland to seek work and permanent domicile in another country, can hardly be applied to many of our present day migrants. All the previously named categories deal with voluntary migrants, without reference to force. If one should consider force, with all its nuances, from brutal persecution to the more subtle feeling that the political or socio-economic conditions do not permit the adequate development of life's possibilities, the situation becomes considerably more complicated.

Hardly any sharply defined description can fully cover all the different categories of people who, since the second world war, have become migrants, and the somewhat diffuse name «newcomer» perhaps best expresses the conditions outlined above. These very dissimilar backgrounds and the different motives that have led one to become a «newcomer» also gives very different starting positions and varying degrees of preparedness when it comes to adaptation and adjustment to new conditions of life.

The significance of motivation

The psychological fact that human motivations are extremely complex is very important in this connection. Only in extremely rare cases is there only one isolated motive that decides our actions.

As a rule there is a rich co-operation of dissimilar, at times parallel, but often very conflicting factors of motivation. For the total situation of the adjustment regarded from the outside, *all* factors of motivation are, of course, significant. Experience has shown that a newcomer with a strong and positive motivation has a relatively high level of frustration tolerance, that is he can withstand the most serious hardships. On the other hand, a newcomer with a weak motivation e.g. a person who left his homeland with only a vague conception of what he really wanted, or because discontent is an integral part of his character, has a low tolerance threshold, i.e. a poor ability to cope with new difficulties. Therefore these persons easily react to this new and problematic milieu with neurotic or other (somatic) symptoms of illness.

Background

Assimilation – Integration

In spite of their dissimilarities and differences, the newcomers have something in common. They have all, either consciously or sub-consciously, brought with them a bit of their old culture. Totally independent of how many of their earthly possessions they had to leave behind or how many they may have brought with them, however rich, however poor they may have been, they brought with them a set of values, rules of conduct and experiences that no-one had been able to take from them. They know, or propose to know, what is right and what is wrong. They know which days of the year are high days and which are holidays – and know how they should be celebrated. They know their God and how to honour him. They know songs and fairytales their mothers or grandmothers taught them when they were young. Some have read works by the poets and authors of their countries, have learned to prize them and can quote pertinent passages at the appropriate times. Some know only proverbs, to be used as the occasion demands. They know, or propose to know, what relationship there should be between an adult and a child, a man and a woman, between different members of the family group. They know, or propose to know, what their attitude should be towards their neighbours, their colleagues, their bosses, towards their grocer or their hairdresser. They know which expressions one can or should use on which occasions. They know which food is good and how much alcohol should be drunk on an everyday occasion or at a party. They know «how a proper person should behave» – or they propose to know. And now, having finally arrived at this new place, where they will settle down and eventually put down roots, they are told that everything they, until then, had considered a matter of course, «natural», standard-creating and correct, is suddenly no longer valid. No-one knows, or is interested in their national holidays, in their poets or authors, in their association with their fellows or with their God. No-one knows anything about the cultural inheritance that they, until then, had considered a central point in their lives. They are expected to put all that behind them. They must be «assimilated», be «completely Norwegian, completely Swedish or completely American or Australian» etc. If the local people are asked what the newcomer must do to avoid difficulties and isolation, most of them will, rather unreflectedly, reply that «adjustment» probably is the best course. They must be Norwegian or Swedish in «mind and body». This would be «the most straightforward, the simplest, the easiest, the most natural». But for whom – the resident or the newcomer? In the press one will often find the demands clearly formulated – it is important that the newcomers should be «assimilated» or «integrated» as quickly as possible. And here we must first clear up a comparatively frequent misunderstanding – the equalizing of two terms which have somewhat different meanings. To be assimilated means actually to be changed and to «disappear» completely in the new surroundings like for instance food does when it is eaten and assimilated to become part of the eating organism. The term assimilation is also used in linguistics where it means that one letter changes completely and becomes like the following one. Integration on the other hand means that the individual part remains basically unchanged, but becomes an «integral» part of a larger unity cooperating in it and with the other individual parts in harmony.

Contrary to the permanent population, the newcomers

have no ready-made opinions as to «what is best for them». Their opinions on integration or assimilation are considerably more differentiated and they change with length of residence and with the experiences they undergo. In the first flush of enthusiasm they would love to be «completely» Norwegian, Swedish, Danish, Australian or American, as most of their countrymen suggest. Actually, these are not the most pressing problems. For refugees it is most important to feel safe, not persecuted, while economic immigrants are more interested in securing their social existence with employment and place of residence. There are also many clear exceptions, especially amongst immigrants who had been politically active and would wish to return to their homelands as quickly as possible. These have no wish to «fit in».

It cannot be denied that both newcomers and permanent residents must contribute towards the primary adjustment if it should take place without overlarge problems or difficulties. By weighing the demands one can make on the individual newcomer, by reducing unnecessary stress-situations and by showing acceptance, one can make giant strides in the right direction. Strong or imperative demands to denationalize or assimilate can be interpreted as a significant serious additional stress, and can lead to a complete breakdown, with a protracted mental illness as a consequence.

Isolation and the adoption of roles

Speaking about a newcomer as if he were an isolated individual is only an abstraction − an important, but also erroneous abstraction. The absolute and completely isolated individual is not, practically speaking, to be found in our daily life. Perhaps he could exist as the consequence of a shipwreck, or on an arctic expedition, but it is such an exceptional condition that it cannot tell us anything about the meaning of isolation in normal psychological experience.

It is totally false to look at people as completely isolated entities. A person who once held a certain position can never be regarded as completely divorced from it. And everyone has at some time held a definite position — not only those prominent in community life, those in positions of trust, but each and every one. Each and every one has had his family, his social circle, his friends, his colleagues. He has meant something to all these people, and they to him. But this coming to a new country, either as a voluntary or involuntary immigrant, a new country with a new environment and new people, also means, perhaps first and foremost, being severed from his social contacts, his significance to other people, or as described by the sociologists: from his role in a group. It is, of course, in and through a group that one first attains knowledge of language, gestures, roles, aspirations, opinions of oneself and others. It is through and in a group that one first becomes a responsible and integral part of a whole. This same adoption of a role in a group, the fact that some attitudes are assumed automatically and not reflectively, is of great importance. It gives the individual security and protects him from mental stresses. The fact that one does not need to take a new stand towards one's surroundings every minute of every day, that one's behaviour, one's way of existence, one's expectations, etc., are «parts of one's being» contributes greatly towards the liberation of mental energy for other activities. The individual does not constantly absorb new stimuli from his surroundings, to which he should, in one way or another adapt himself. We execute most of our daily actions without undue reflection. This mechanism in our psyche can freely be compared to the mechanization which characterises part of our physiological being. We walk, we stop, we move in traffic etc., without having to unduly consider the mechanisms of these. A good chauffeur reacts «automatically» to everything that is going on in the traffic, without being clearly aware of reading the brake pedal or changing gears. If we should, instead of reacting mechanically, send all stimuli to the cerebrum, deal with them there, consider reactions and, eventually, execute them, our lives would be very complicated. Mechanization, automization, is a tool for relief and protections in both psychological and physiological reactions.

With the transplantation to a completely new milieu, the former customary mechanization and automization are rendered useless. Far more serious than this «technical» insecurity, is the unsureness one feels towards the people one meets and towards the new social situations one is exposed to. As one's «role adoption» from the former group is of no help, one must first improvise and later learn new roles. The worst is, one is never sure how individuals or the new group will react at one's improvization. Security in the old group came not only from knowing what actions were expected, but also from knowing what reactions one's own actions would stimulate in the group. This continual insecurity contributes to a rise in the number of situations to be consciously considered, to be judged, on which to take a stand. In other words: not only the number of stimuli confronting an individual, but also the number of decisions to be taken, are manifoldly increased. If the individual has sufficient resources at his disposal, or if he is confronted with groups and situations not fundamentally different from those previously known, the development will not suffer insurmountable difficulties. On the other hand, situations can be regarded as insoluble when one can find no relation whatsoever between the old group formation and the new. Here one must learn new «roles» in all areas, process all new stimuli, and as their numbers can be overwhelming for the less elastic personality, one can be exposed to a situation which could be called «flooded with stimuli», as situation which could be difficult to master. The result could be a «total collapse» of the personality.

Psychological problems of migrants

There are many indications that the increased morbidity amongst migrants and especially among refugees is chiefly caused by the pressures brought about by the migration itself.

If one should try to schematically classify the serious mental diseases (psychoses), according to the perhaps somewhat disputed principle of mainly inherent factors as opposed to those caused by the «external» factors far more numerous in a migrant society than in the indigenous population. More thorough observations based on migration group studies over several years [7] show that the situation-caused mental illnesses are much more frequent only in the earliest immigration years. When the migrant has established himself, the difference between the two is considerably reduced.

A detailed investigation of individual case histories show, with a fairly large concurrence, that there is a crystallization of two factors of significance in the rise of situation-caused mental illnesses. The first is that he/she is torn from his/her group interdependence, does not belong, feels isolated, does not know how to play his/her role in the new group formation to which he/she has been transplanted. One never knows exactly what the others expect of one, and here we meet the second factor — the feeling of insecurity. This isolation and feeling of insecurity is caused by the overwhelming, urgent and dominating need for contact that most of these people have. If this need for contact is not adequately satisfied, they will feel hurt and, in individual cases, increase the mental intrapsychic insecurity and liability to illness. Every effort made to reduce newcomer's adjustment problems must, therefore, take the above-mentioned central factors into consideration. In the following we shall see how this affects the daily life of the newcomer.

The significance of the family

Shortly after the Second World War, when Europe's Displaced Persons refugee camps were flooded with an almost limitless mass of people, many immigration countries were willing to accept these hundreds of thousands of homeless, both on humanitarian grounds, and not less so because of their policies on population. Selection criteria were often very rigorous, and most countries would try to ensure that they received the «best human material». This led to young, unmarried people being preferred. Families with numerous children of school-age, or even those with members who were ill, were put in a secondary category, or were completely denied immigration. However, it was very soon noticed that this process of selection did not give the expected results. Frequent failures to adjust and mental disturbances, together with re-emigration, were conspicuos in the optimistically regarded «good groups» [11]. On the other hand, it was shown that married workers with responsibilities for, and an anchorage in a family, showed considerable stability in their work, something that should have been thought of beforehand. They showed fewer complications than the single individual.

Despite all the changes it has undergone, the family is still the most important link between people, and it represents the central primary group formation. It is therefore not surprising that, at a comprehensive UNESCO conference held in Havana in 1956 [2], which dealt with the problems of migration, it was concluded that any form of meaningful migration must be based on the family unit. This meant that any country accepting migrants must be willing to deal with the problems that ALL members of the family might encounter, and not concern themselves only with individuals who may contribute to the productivity of the country.

The father, who is most often the breadwinner, will be the adult with most contact and inter-action with the new environment, become acquainted with the production apparatus, and eventually with his employers and colleagues. He is in touch with realities, but these do not always conform to the ideal ways in which one would wish foreigners to be handled. The circle of a man's experience is not regulated by the international conventions agreed to by the government. Neither by the often very beautiful and erudite articles written in some of the country's better newspapers, especially in connection with international meetings and treatises — articles which contribute little to an individual's private experience of life. Unfortunately, neither is the self-sacrificing work of many well-meaning and interested organisations, the decisive factor. Our experiences are determined by the people we meet every day — on the way to work, in the press of a crowded bus, in the queue for the underground, while we shop, and not by any means least, at work. Thus the father very often has the largest plane of contact. The attitude of his colleagues will play a decisive role in how effectively he will adjust. If they will accept his early attempts at making himself understood, accept him as a work-mate, his knowledge of the country's language will increase without undue stress. He will slowly slide into the ways of the new environment, get to know attitudes, political views and lifestyles in general. Unfortunately, it is only infrequently that the period of adjustment is that free of friction. Even when one is theoretically «free of prejudice», «liberal», «open», aware of that «people can be different», willing to accept that «minorities also have rights», completely convinced that all discrimination based on nationality, race or religion is wrong, the situation is totally changed when one is personally exposed to such a minority. Old and ingrained prejudices are difficult to uproot. The conviction of the superiority and excellence of one's own habits, foods, ways of proceeding and work tempo, is so ingrained that «the other must be slightly backward» not to realize this at once.

Under these conditions, the integration into the new environment can become somewhat difficult. But even under the most ideal circumstances it would be meaningless to expect that all earlier experiences in a mature adult should be eradicated. The earlier feeling of identity, personality, character, world of thought, must be expected to continue for many years. Even with intensive efforts to learn the language of the new country, adults almost never acquire the «language-melody» and will, therefore, nearly always speak in a «broken or accented» way. That means that no matter how much they believe that they have been assimilated, they will always reveal themselves as «newcomers».

Integration is not a one-sided process which can be determined by the individual newcomer or employee. This applies to speed, efficacy and progress. It is, in any case, a two-sided process, where the attitudes, understanding and expectations of the environment are of the greatest importance.

Mothers have the easiest, as well as the most difficult time of it. She will not often take outside employment, but will continue to care for home and children. This means that, to a large extent, she continues her former role which represents a continuation of the emotional atmosphere. On the other hand she has but modest contact with the new milieu. Too little attention has been paid to this factor when considering a meaningful integration and to the central role women play in the internal life of the whole family. The problem can be especially serious in relation to the internal harmony of the family. The mother falls out of step with her children in both trivial matters, fashions, taste and clothes, and in serious questions concerning identity and basic values.

The problems of the children

The children of the family are those most often exposed to the greatest change, and their conflict situations are therefore the most prominent. The development of their personalities has not been completed, and the influence of the environment will therefore have a larger impact on them than on adults. These influences pull in different directions, and no matter at which age or at which stage of development the child, family, school, street and place of employment will all exercise their changing and equally conflict-filled and conflict-creating influences. With children generally, the identification with parents, and all they represent, is seen as the most important form of unconscious and natural education. On the contrary, migrant children live in a continuous conflict, where the parent's milieu and the new stand in sharp contrast to one another.

Usually children learn in school what they learn at home. They can, therefore, as far as adult influence is regarded, identify with both teacher and parent, without creating conflict. The teacher will usually support the parent, and vice versa. With migrant children it is not that easy. At school they are encouraged in a thousand different ways to learn the new language, to acquire the new cultural values, and the better they manage, the larger the rewards — both in the form of teachers' approval and acceptance and in the form of good marks. While the parents themselves will consciously express the wish that the children should succeed at school, it means the children will thereby remove themselves from the world of the parents. Unconsciously the parents would wish the children not quite so capable of forgetting all that is of importance to themselves. After all, it is not an insignificant part of their working day the children spend at home. Who can imagine what problems are caused by the inability of the children to communicate with their parents? And at school the children are exposed to a cruel discrimination that only their peers are capable of practising. They are scorned for their clothes, their habits, their way of speaking, perhaps only for their name or appearance stamped as «different». They cannot fullfull the great need for conformity that children have, and are cold-shouldered. But at home children seldom complain about their defeat. They expect no understanding from their parents, who themselves represent everything their companions laugh at, make fun of, debase.

It is important to realize that children *should not be forced to deny their parents,* their language, their values, and with that, their own identity, just as they are beginning to accept the values of their new environment and to integrate these in an adequate manner. Experiences in many countries have shown that such a solution is possible, but unfortunately, these problems are usually underrated. One can even meet direct attack against the mother-tongue and the child's right to use it. Such thoughtlessness can have tragic consequences. This situation is even more serious when the children are near or undergoing puberty.

It is usual for the migration stream to flow from a country with a more conservative, traditional and autocratic way of life, to one with a more liberal pattern of behaviour, where family life is built less on father's unquestioned authority and more on democratic discussions and decisions. It is natural enough that the generation conflict experienced in all families can lead to conflict between the old way of life represented by the parents, and the way of life represented by the young, the new industrialized and individualistic society [6]. The ideas and opinions of the parents are fought with enthusiasm and energy. They are not only thought old-fashioned, but also inferior. The youngsters are ashamed of them and avoid taking friends home in case they should notice how «hopeless and impossible» the parents are. This often unfolds in the direction of self-hate. The primary development is contempt towards everything to do with the old traditions, the old nationality or religion. Later the hate can be shifted from its own, and aggression be directed against the community as a whole, resulting in serious maladjustment in the form of juvenile delinquincy. The initial form is described in depth by EISENSTADT et al. [5] in Israel. They found that in families where there were the largest differences between the norms of the parents and those of the environment, the children had a high rate of truancy and the youth were amongst the most unreliable of employees. Several studies from the years between the two world wars, show that there had been a conspicously large degree of criminality amongst the youth from the migrant milieu [3, 8, 13] in the USA, while reports from Australia can only confirm this phenomenon to a small degree [14, 16, 17]. It is natural to assume that the different contributions made by these two countries were the decisive factor in the different results. On the other hand we have information in the literature showing that youth can react differently to outside influences. Too much pressure on young migrants, demands for their assimilation for their relinquishing of identity, individuality and national background, can lead to an exaggerated chauvinistic display of all values, habits and customs seen as characteristic of all old traditions [1]. When considering the psychology of migration problems in a somewhat wider perspective, it becomes clear that it is the harmonious adjustment of the child to the new circumstances which plays the central role.

Problems of contact

Good and bad experiences from different countries have shown that integration of migrant families is a slow process, that it can only develop gradually and must be aided by an understanding and sympathetic attitude from the new surroundings. Forced assimilation will usually fail. In Norway for example it was tried, for practical reasons, to place single individuals or families in villages or small rural towns, but the strong pressure from the milieu led to considerable complications, in some cases even to the point of endangering the mental health of the new arrivals. There was a longing to occasionally speak their own language, to participate in the religious services of their childhood, to be able to discuss «the good old days». And everyone knows that the older one gets, the better become these «good old days», and even better when they are far away, not only in time but also in distance. Such a longing can be overwhelming, but this problem has even graver aspects. The religious and national education of the children becomes a serious and urgent question for the family. The parents have a basic need to exchange experiences with someone they can rely on without reservation, often meaning someone with the same background. The decisive factor is not necessarily seeing the problems in the same manner, but that one has confidence in one another and can speak out to each other. Psychiatric and psychological research has shown that people who cannot exchange experiences with someone else, easily develop misunderstandings, misconceptions and finally, paranoid reactions. Newcomer families therefore need contact with a group formation which is not foreign to them, otherwise they can be threatened by pathological developments. Especially convincing are the discoveries made by TAFT [16] amongst immigrants in Australia. He could show that newcomers living in smaller towns were in all respects less integrated than those living in larger cities, in spite of the fact that the latter had more occasion to come in contact with large groups of their countrymen. For further information also see KORANYI's chapter in this book.

In countries where one systematically tried to achieve a meaningful integration of newcomer families [10, 13], it is shown that contact in both directions is essential. Newcomers generally wish to live amongst their new countrymen, but at the same time close enough to the old group to facilitate contact if and when desired. Such possibilities of balanced contact with both the old and the new is important to mental hygiene. It reduces the tendency towards isolation in individuals as well as in groups. It also reduces the mental tension to a bearable level. It must, however, be noted that the contact discussed here must, to the highest degree, be a valuable interpersonal acceptance of one another. An oversensitive soul very soon notices the least sign of charity or/and expectation of gratitude.

Every re-adjustment takes time and the larger the difficulties and the wider the gap between the old and the new values, the longer the period of adjustment. The higher the level of expectations and the more the development is left only to the newcomer, the worse the end result. Also TAFT [15] sums up his research by pointing out that a socially accepting attitude and respect towards the immigrants professional and cultural background and aspirations is the key to a satisfactory adjustment. On the other hand, a forced education in language and social habits can only be of limited benefit.

The positive aspects of migration

It must be obvious that migration does not only have negative aspects. JENNER [9] has shown that migration can, at times, be of large economic benefit to the recipient countries. Here we will only bring out two of the other positive aspects — on the one hand, the significance of a selective migration on the cultural development of a country and, on the other hand, the phenomenon of «The Marginal Man». After the Nazis took over Germany, the American congress adopted a somewhat liberalized immigration for a number of persecuted intellectuals. DIMONT [4] maintains that as a consequence of this the number of Nobel prize winners in the USA and Germany changed basically. During the years 1901 – 1939 only 14 Americans were awarded the Nobel prize in physics, chemistry and medicine, while the 13 year period from 1943 – 1955 produced no less than 29. For Germany the situation was exactly opposite. During the first 30 year period there were 35 prize winners in the above-mentioned categories, while in the latter 13 year period only 5.

The phenomenon of «The Marginal Man» was first mentioned by PARK [12] already in 1928. Subsequently, several authors have dealt with the subject. Migration, with its cultural collisions, conflicts and infiltration of people, seen as one of the decisive forces in the history of mankind. The essence of migration, whether collective or individual, is the breaking of old habits and the exposure of more people to different ideas and associations, to new worlds of thought. One of the consequences is that many migratory people must live in two different cultural circles with dissimilar values. In this way the personality, called «The Marginal Man» by PARK is formed: a person in whom there has arisen a synthesis of the different cultural values and cultural worlds to which he has been exposed during his migratory life. Such persons learn to see the world from which they come, in which they were born, and in which they were brought up, with almost the same selective eyes as «an Alien». An «Alien» is a free man in both theory and practice. He scrutinezes his relations with a fresh, often critical gaze. He is less prejudiced, subjects everything to a new and objective evaluation. He is not as confined by the old habits or representations as in the general population – he is «cosmopolitan». For society, this person on the border of two cultures will have a stimulating effect on both sides, and will inspire the progress of human development.

Established minorities

It is from this point of view that one can best understand or should consider, the question of minorities that are established as such. When one regards the historical development of minority groups in Europe, America, Australia, one finds a fairly similar pattern. So-called national minority groups are assimilated in the course of some generations, depending on the receptiveness of the adopting country, and on the fact that the numbers of newcomers are relatively small and that they are willing to accept the «cultural superiority» of their hosts. Many Scandinavian emigrants to the US may serve as an example of this, but here one also notes that compact minorities able to shape an autonomous «infrastructure» i.e. own schools, own newspapers, own cultural centres, etc., will appear as well-established groups with no small part of national characteristics intact during several generations. The situation is somewhat different when concerning the religious minorities. The religious life seems to be anchored considerably deeper. Immigrants will usually continue to practice their religious mores, independent and uninfluenced by the religions practiced by those surrounding them. Religious authorities and schools which accent religious education will, therefore, soon be established. Because of religion's deep psychological roots, these institutions have a tendency to last, to be continued through generations, even though the practicers of a minority religion, in other respects, seem well integrated and hardly discernable from the majority group.

In a special category we find those minorities which are differentiated from their surroundings by way of skin-colour or by other outward appearances. Prejudice and inherent opposition to the mixing of races is still so over-whelming that any attempt of complete integration is condemned to fail from the beginning, and this minority will continue to be separate group, with or without its acquiescence. It is this latter form of involuntary and lasting formation of minority groups which has to a large extent characterized the standard way of thinking surrounding the question of minorities.

People are «condemned» to belong to a group that is different. The conceit and feelings of superiority of the majority will not primarily be dealt with here. Neither is it possible to discuss thoroughly the majority's need to use the minority as scapegoats for their aggressions. On the other hand it must be pointed out that people who scorn or hate others in a blind and unthinking manner, take from themselves the ability to think or feel in a differentiated way. The first to point out this in modern European cultural history, was Thomas Masaryk, the first president and greatest teacher of Czechoslovakia. Already in his earliest writings he fought energetically against anti-semittism, not because of some romantic love for Jews, but because hate and prejudice poisons people. If one judges people according to colour of skin, their ethnic, national or religious association, and not according to individual merits, one will enter a spiritual dead-end which can be as dangerous for the persecutor as for the persecuted. Masaryk's prophetic words have found confirmation in today's situation in Europe, America and Africa. But race hatred and hatred of foreigners need not neccessarily take the extreme form we know from the war years. Even countries officially friendly to foreigners and as unprejudiced racially as the Scandinavians, develop problematic situations when individual inhabitants are closely confronted with race problems. That is the problem of the majority.

But how does the minority develop in its relations with its surrounding world? After the minority has established itself its own religious and/or cultural and/or social institutions, based on its cultural heritage, they will represent a «foreign body» in the new community even after its members have become integrated into the new world. If the majority can understand and accept that new conceptions, different life-styles and cultural values can be meaningful to themselves, the result will be satisfactory. Such an adjustment can contribute to the widening of the horizions of both groups and have a stimulating effect on both cultures. A harmonious form of symbiosis, with mutual respect, should develop. A majority group which, on the other hand, is totally convinced of its own excellence, and which regards anyone coming from outside as inferior, will naturally enough feel scorn, if not complete disdain, for the minority group and its members. These negative sentiments will not remain without psychological consequences on those towards which they are directed. A permanent degradation of everything to do with the minority will eventually set its stamp on the minority itself. The majority will influence their norms, and even if they cling to their cultural heritage and their cultural values, they will easily begin to regard themselves as inferior. Thereby the first tragic step is taken on the road to self-denegration. People who do not value their own culture, lose their creative ability, become reduced and, in extreme cases, disintegrate. Doubting one's cultural values, one begin to doubt one's own value and that of one's background identity. If the most elemental human rights, both legal and humanitarian, are offered to minorities as charitable gifts from the majority, and not as a natural matter of course, it will soon have a crippling effect on the member's evaluation of what is obviously due to them. The same people who, in their own circle, can be noble, clear-thinking and creative representatives of their people's traditions, can come to feel insecure, inferior and cowed by the «master population». National costume is a small but telling example. The majority use national costume as a «party dress» at festive occasions, but laugh at the minority's «peculiar» clothes. Therefore it is not long before they disappear.

The significance of a minority in a democratic community

The minority group should be aware of its own worth. It is very important that they should know that their culture is in no way inferior, nothing to be ashamed of. They will grow with the awareness that they can be, in the true meaning of the word, as worthy and as deserving as the majority of the country. Only when one can preserve this feeling of inner merit and equality, can one avoid very unfortunate psychological extremes. On the one hand, underestimation of self, and on the other the reaction which leads to over-evaluation of ones background. This over-evaluation which is not based on reality, only leads to empty nationalistic and chauvinistic words and phrases without meaning.

The majority is also best served by minorities calculatingly and openly demand their rights. They will often act as the touch-stone of a country's democratic temper. That minorities should be seen, valued and experienced as people with the same worth, and in all ways equally deserving, is the essence of a vital democracy. The field of tension between large political questions and the regard for the rights of the individual, not only for those of the governing or ruling majority, but also for the minority, is a vital necessity in a democratic community. Such a community can only exist if all its citizens have the possibility of critisizing — that is, have the outside framework and the inner security to do so. Frightened, cowed, unsure, subjucated «subjects» are not fellow citizens in the real meaning of the phrase. They are subservient and as such, not worthy of a democracy. It is natural that members of an established minority have better possibilities for practising democratic and critical activities than any other. Their vulnerable position makes them more sensitive towards undemocratic actions and eventual injustices. It is always the weakest to first feel the strain of these undemocratic actions, and to feel themselves unable to cope with them. In a true democracy it is the weakest who has the particular duty to speak up the moment he notices that the basic democratic values are threatened. Therefore, he must have security to enable him to do this without fear of losing his livelihood or his rights. In addition to this, the members of a minority group have a further advantage over those of the majority. The knowledge that they, having accepted and integrated the norms of the community, also have another set of values which are of significance to them, give them a somewhat more detailed attitude, as well as a broader outlook. Both are of significance in a dispassionate evaluation of communal phenomena, and thereby for a positive and constructively-critical attitude towards them.

Both on the grounds of mental hygiene and of democratic political judgments, will psychologically strong, aware and critical minorities be seen as a positive effect that a democratic community hardly can be without.

Bibliography

1 BANCHEVSKA, RACHELLE: A new way of life. In: Stoller, A. (Ed.): New faces. Melbourne/Canberra/Sydney/London, 1966.
2 BORRIE, W. D. et al.: The cultural integration of immigrants. A survey based upon the papers and proceedings of the UNESCO conference in Havana, 1956, Paris, 1959.
3 CHILD, I.: Italian or American. The second generation in conflict. New Haven, 1943.
4 DIMONT, M. I.: Jews, God and History. New York, 1962.
5 EISENSTADT, S. N., BEN-DAVID, J.: Intergeneration tension in Israel. Int. Soc. Sc. Bull. 8, 54, 1956.
6 EITINGER, L.: Psychiatric investigations among Refugees in Norway. Universitetsforlaget, Oslo, 1958.
7 EITINGER, L., GRÜNFELDT, B.: Psychoses among refugees in Norway. Acta Psychiat. Scand. 42, 315, 1966.
8 GLUECK, S. & E.: Family, environment and delinquency. London, 1962.
9 JENNER, P.: Some speculations on the economics of immigration. In: Wolstenholme, G. E. W. (Ed.): Immigration: Medical and social aspects. Ciba foundation report. J. & A. Churchill Ltd., London, 1966.
10 KERN, K. K. L.: Immigration and the integration process. In: Stoller, A. (Ed.): New faces.
11 MURPHY, H. B. M.: Refugee psychoses in Great Britain. In: Flight and resettlement. UNESCO, Paris, 1955.

12 PARK, R.E.: Human migration and the marginal man. Amer. J. Sociol. *33,* 88, 1928.

13 SELLIN, T.: Culture, conflict and crime. New York, 1938.

14 STOLLER, A. (Ed.): New faces. Melbourne/Canberra/Sydney/London, 1966.

15 TAFT, D.R.: Does migration increase crime? In: Stoller, A. (Ed.): New faces.

16 TAFT, D.R.: From stranger to citizen. — A survey of studies of immigrant assimilation in Western Australia. Tavistock, 1965.

17 ZUBRZYCKI, J.: Settlers of the Latrobe Valley. Canberra, 1964.

18 ZUBRZYCKI, J.: The immigrant family. In: Stoller, A. (Ed.): New faces.

Chapter 6

Uprooting and settling:
The transplanted family

RACHELLE BANCHEVSKA

Setting the scene

Absorption and integration of immigrants have played a
major role in the settlement and development of Australia.
From the first landing of reluctant, unwilling prisoners,
transported to a distant country not merely in order to
banish them from their homeland, but to populate a new
colony, the problem of «fitting» people to the new environment remained significant throughout Australian history.

While greater or smaller waves of immigrants continued
to arrive, at no time did Australia find itself in the situation
in which it is now, when about one quarter of the total
population has lived in the country not much more, or
possibly less, than one quarter of a century. The massive
intake of the immediate Post World War II period continued until the early sixties and to date there is a steady,
though much diminished trickle adding to existing ethnic
groups and creating new ones.

The old policy of absorption no longer could cope with
the numbers arriving, nor with the diversity of nationalities with the accompanying variety of cultures and languages; the newcomers became too visible to be ignored
and too numerous to be disregarded. Assimilation did not
provide a fast enough remedy. The early expectations of
instant conformity were proven quite unrealistic, particularly in view of the type of immigrant that Australia was
encouraging: the unskilled, often semi-literate, poverty
stricken peasant, who would be prepared, willing and able

to work on the large developmental projects in the outback, or on the conveyor belt assembly in large factories.

The more educated, often skilled, displaced persons from post war camps, gradually integrated into the community. In gathering material for this exercise, it was realized that there were no government social workers or welfare officers for fairly large ethnic groups, such as the Poles, Latvians or Lithuanians for example. The same observation could be made about the western and northern European communities, whose members were among the educated and skilled. True, all these groups have national organisations, some more, some less active, but all concerned mainly with cultural and religious matters, extending in some cases only to welfare work with their compatriots [2].

The inability of integrating in the same manner the great mass of immigrants from the Mediterranean regions, the deep attachment of all groups to their past, have forced, in a way, the development of a policy of multi-culturalism.

Australia is the second or third country in the world, with the largest number of ethnic groups; this is a fact that is obvious to even a casual observer. Various languages are spoken in the streets, on public transport, in shops and places of amusement; restaurants and cafes serve food from all corners of the world; newsagents sell papers printed in many tongues; there are advertisements in many languages on the back of taxis and on street boards. It is inescapable – people of many ethnic origins inhabit Australia and make their presence felt and seen.

The question to ask is how is the multi-cultural climate affecting the older settlers and what does it provide for the newer ones. It must be stated at the outset that it did not prove a panacea for all problems nor did it smooth away all the difficulties of starting a new life in a country, in almost all cases, quite dissimilar to the native land.

It may be impossible not to encroach on the territories of other contributors to the book, but perhaps the very fact of the overlap may add significance to the issues.

When one writes about maladaptations, as experienced

by immigrants, it would seem important to distinguish between problems which would have beset the individual wherever he/she lived and those which arose as a result of immigration. In this category one could include difficulties in communication, due to ignorance of language and customs, the loosening of social controls leading, for example, to breakdown in family bonds, lack of emotional support from one's own ethnic group, lack of acceptable models as expressed in the behaviour of longer settled compatriots and finally and overall, lack of economic security, the awareness that there is no one to help in time of need, that one is alone, a stranger in a strange land.

Mention must be made also of the difficulties which rural dwellers must face of necessity when transferred, at jet plane speed, without any preparation, to a large metropolis, full of unfamiliar people and objects. It would be true to say that the rural to urban transition would constitute a problem also in an internal migration; how much greater is it, when added to the new environment is a feeling of great distance from one's kin and community, of bewilderment and confusion, when all is alien.

To some extent, the first shock of arrival is cushioned by life in a hostel, where all is provided, including accommodation, board and, at present, also orientation and crash courses in English as well as advice regarding employment, housing, health insurance etc. On the minus side, hostel life is often too sheltered and is followed by an even greater shock when one is exposed to the hurly burly of life in the community, where the responsibility for all decision making is one's own. In many ways, hostel life is institutionalized to a high degree, thus depriving family members of their traditional roles and inducing apathy and boredom.

In discussing the settling-in process, the building of a new life and the efforts to maintain an intact family, it is important to pay attention to the longer settled persons, as well as to the new arrivals.

The immigrant family

There is a need to apologise for grouping all nationalities under the one heading of immigrants. Any attempt to discuss migrant families as such is an obvious generalisation which will leave out important features, gloss over others and attribute undue significance to some that may be applicable only to specific ethnic groups; it is impossible, however, to expand on each separately.

The western style family

Since it is assumed that the North American, Eastern, Western and Northern European, South African and British families follow much the same patterns as the so-called Australian families, little attention will be paid to them. This does not signify that these families do not experience problems of translocation, it simply implies that their problems do not centre quite so strongly round the family structure and the roles which are seen as appropriate for members [2].

On the whole, people from these loosely called «western» countries, came with better skills, sometimes with employment pre-arranged, often with some knowledge of English. They came mostly from urban settings and were used to the hustle and bustle of big cities. Many of those who came from rural areas, settled in country towns, some on the land, after they conquered their apprehensions caused by great distances, sparse settlement and the ensuing isolation. Perhaps their main problems arose from unmet expectations and unfavourable comparisons with the remembered status quo at home. Many cut their losses and returned home, often to come back and, having faced realities, to settle happily.

As mentioned earlier, one does not come across welfare provisions, tailored to their specific needs, aimed at their group members. The reply of one experienced worker why this occurred, was a simple «they conformed, or they perished». Even less than 10 years ago, that was true to a considerable extent. The immigration from Eastern and Western Europe was greatest in the early post World War II period; since then, there has been only a trickle coming, often for family reunion, and the communities were able to absorb the newcomers. The ethnic organisations pursue the work of maintaining the cultures and traditions of their homelands, they provide a social outlet and support for their members, with the longer settled serving as models to the more recent arrivals.

The Mediterranean family

Not so long ago, one would have titled this section the Southern European family. With the advent, in the last few years, of many from all the shores of the Mediterranean Sea, the appellation has changed, but it is still possible to generalise, with some degree of accuracy, about the people.

On the whole, it would be true to say that the Mediterranean family is hierarchical, authoritarian and paternalistic. The roles of family members are clearly defined and the rules firmly fixed and expected to be obeyed. There is a great deal of pride attached to the correct behaviour of members and an insistence that, at all cost, appearances must be preserved. The «face saving» mechanism operates under many names — the Italian «la bella figura», the Greek «filotimo» and so forth. There is a well maintained closing of ranks to protect the good name, the reputation of the family and of the ethnic group. When a Greek welfare officer disclosed in a daily newspaper that many of his compatriots treated their wives as second-class citizens, as servants and sex objects, he brought the wrath of his whole community on his head. Although no-one really disputed the facts, he was accused of disloyalty, almost high treason, by men and women alike. One does not wash one's linen, whether dirty or clean, publicly.

In the permissive, egalitarian atmosphere of Australia, the traditional Mediterranean family is subject to many pressures and onslaughts, both from within and without, giving rise to many problems and affecting the daily life and the pattern of interactions of their members.

The head of the family

There is no need even to state that the undisputed head of the family is the man; he is regarded as such even in the liberated families, even if he retains the name only, without much power. The Mediterranean family recognizes fully the dominance of the husband and father and admits that decision making, management of family affairs, remain his domain; the admission, however, is no longer undisputed and that is where trouble starts [2].

He is no longer the only breadwinner, he must rely on the earnings of his wife and children if he wants to achieve some financial security: buy a house, a car, furniture etc. He needs their earnings for the family's well-being, but he expects to receive them as his right, whether there is need or not. It was interesting to hear a Maltese professional man, brought up in Australia, disclose that when he worked as a schoolboy and later as a university student in his holidays, it never occurred to him that he should keep his wages. He handed them over as a matter of course; he comments that he was repaid a thousandfold, but that does not change the principle.

The majority of the Southern European, Turkish and Arabic speaking immigrants, came from rural areas, remote villages and from among the dispossessed proletariat of the large cities. They brought no skills, except their strength, a healthy body and a preparedness to work hard to earn a living. What they did not know is how different and monotonous the work would be and how very different the conditions in which they would have to spend long days: factories, often sub-standard, echoing with the noise of strange machinery. Nothing in their previous existence was like it.

When, therefore, they fell victim to an industrial accident, the trauma they suffered was much greater than it would have been for others. They saw themselves as maimed for life, deprived of their only asset, a healthy body, unbelieving that they could be cured and returned to the work force. Apparently, the word «rehabilitation» does not exist in Greek and welfare officers have much difficulty in conveying this concept to their clients. The «Mediterranean back» has become the subject of much discussion, investigation and even derision. The facts speak for themselves: at one community health centre of 200 Turkish patients, 80% came because of industrial accidents. Of one hundred back injuries, about one or two improved in the case of Greeks; the recovery rate for Anglo-Saxon Australians is ninety-two. The facile explanation and diagnosis of «compensation neurosis» needs to be amplified and put into the context of the meaning of an accident to a worker, who sees his usefulness at an end, who is put into an invalid role and who is shunted from doctor to doctor, in some cases, as many as fifty different health professionals, in order to fight for the final outcome, the nebulous, non-existent pot of gold which will liberate him and his family from drudgery.

Although two ethnic groups have been mentioned, many more can be added to the list. Many accidents occur soon after arrival and commencement of work and, obviously, are due to inadequate briefing, lack of training in safety procedures and in the operation of machinery, and, first and last, to lack of good communication in the worker's native language, which would ensure that all pertinent issues have been understood.

The injured immigrant worker, sitting at home hopelessly and helplessly, often disabled at the final outcome of litigation, unable to find a «light» job, particularly in times of unemployment, not only sees himself as deposed, but is seen by his family as bereft of authority [8].

The skilled immigrant has his own hurdles to clear, particularly was this the case in the past, when the need for manual workers, on the one hand, and the difficulties in having his skills acknowledged and recognized by the appropriate trade or professional bodies, on the other hand, resulted in a loss of status and occupational standing and led to unskilled work, as the only available means of earning a living. It is painful to accept a down-grading with its accompanying loss of status.

Apart from the internal familial and the work situation, the male migrant faces another problem in a society, where women are taking part in the affairs of the community and are occupying positions of authority in employment, government and welfare. To ask a woman for help, for permission to act, is a novel and not a pleasant experience for many. Thus some like to think of their sojourn in Australia as a temporary one, only long enough to save for a life of ease at home. The Turkish immigrants, in particular, used to the concept of guest workers, live for the dream of returning. Often their troubles really start when they realize that it is not easy to turn the clock back.

The migrant woman

For many women, the decision to emigrate may have been reached without any knowledge on their part, or consultation. From the sheltered, restricted environment of her home, family and community, she is transported to a strange land, where more often than not, she has no relatives, friends or even acquaintances, where she cannot understand others, nor be understood by them; everything she touches is strange, unfamiliar. More often than not, she has to leave her children and seek work in a factory, at machines she does not understand, in an environment that is bewildering and anxiety-rousing. When she returns home tired, she has all the house chores to do – cook, wash, clean, provide for husband and children, with no help from the males of the family, sharing the burdens only with her daughters, many too young for the task [2].

On the other hand, the awareness that she is a financial contributor, that but for her the house, or the car would not be bought, brings her a new pride and a feeling of worth, which she lacked in her home country. Seeing women walking around freely, standing up to the authority of their husbands, chastising their sons, as well as the daughters, imbues her with a courage to demand a better deal. Many cultures permit the husbands to chastise their wives, often to beat them brutally and the women submit meekly and suffer in silence; to whom can they complain? In Australia they learn about women's refuges, about lawyers and courts, and their ethnic welfare workers. They complain, they protest and sometimes walk out, a thing unheared of in their country of birth; marital disputes, many concerned with wife-bashing, figure high on the case lists of welfare, legal and personal counselling agencies.

The comments made about the men's work situation, can be repeated about the women's. Again the incidence of industrial accidents and disabilities is high, particularly with injuries to arm, wrist, hand and fingers. Apart from pain, there is fear of disfigurement, of permanent damage. Daily work also means leaving young children without proper care and supervision, a worry which is uppermost in the mind of every mother.

Yet in some ways, the working woman is better off than the one left at home, isolated, lonely, unable to communicate with others for lack of language, a permanent stranger in her environment; she even lags behind her family, unable, as she is, to share their experiences and their new world. The children at school, the husband at work, all gradually learn some English, acquire some understanding of the surrounding world and accept changing life-styles. The woman, at home, often forbidden by her culture to venture out, is bypassed by the learning process and left alone. She becomes depressed and often has to seek psychiatric treatment; her inability to speak English and her great isolation loom high on the list of factors contributing to her illness.

Many husbands like to think that they have progressed and adjusted to Australian mores. In fact, the changes are less than superficial, as disclosed by the Greek welfare worker already quoted. A young Syrian was quite adamant that his wife could do as she pleased, within reason of course, which meant she could do anything, provided it brought him no shame. A cursory inquiry ascertained that very many things would bring shame on him, therefore his wife could not dance or talk with other men at a social gathering, which both attended; she could not ask his male friends to wait in the house if he was not there. Many object to their wives going out at night without them, even when it is to professional, work-related, or educational events. This restrictiveness is deeply ingrained in many cultures and cuts across social and educational standards.

There is much room for improvement in the lot of the immigrant women and at last, many injustices are discussed in public. One of the most difficult areas to comprehend and accept, is the mystery and mystique of the health services. Although interpreters are becoming more available in hospitals, they are not on a 24 hour shift, nor do they cover the many languages in the community. The difficulties of communication are the same for men as women, but women, particularly of child bearing age, make more frequent use of the hospital services. It is shameful to admit that very distressing, almost ludicrous, often tragic incidents occur, simply because no one understands the patient's problem [6, 7, 9, 10].

At a conference on «Language Learning for Migrant Women», one of the speakers told of a pregnant migrant woman, who, unable to explain her condition, was given tablets for her nerves by the doctor. A few days later she was taken to hospital with septicaemia, her unborn baby dead inside her.

A Turkish woman gave birth on the floor of her house at two o'clock in the morning, as her frantic husband could not convey to anyone that he needed a taxi.

At a conference on «The Immigrant Woman and the Hospital», a lecturer quoted the story of a Turkish woman who kept pointing to her abdomen when she came to casualty. She was sent from hospital to hospital, told she could not be helped, until the taxi driver delivered her baby on the back seat of the cab [9]. The trauma and indignity of it!

In the matter of contraception, the language barrier is as great as the cultural one for many. Thus the Family Planning Clinics don't see many migrant women, but they figure high on the list of abortions.

Perhaps the fact itself that the plight of the migrant woman is discussed, is a ray of light, a precursor of change. To give a very minor example, the Health Commission of Victoria, at the time of writing this, is finishing the production of a 60 second television film, to illustrate the plight of the isolated, home bound woman, without any knowledge of English, or the country's customs, and appealing to her to make use of existing counselling and educational services. It will be made in seven languages, the languages of the most needy groups. Graphics from the film will be used for posters on public transport on routes in areas densely populated by migrants. The message will be the same, in a language appropriate to the locale, giving the address of the nearest centre.

The aged migrants

Since the great waves of immigration have started in the late forties and early fifties, many immigrants are reaching retirement age. Many came at a fairly advanced age to join their families; many elderly parents are still arriving. Frequently their lives are mapped out by their children, even in the case of long-settled migrants; since they are not working any longer, it is their duty to help their working children by minding the grandchildren. They look after the babies, they feed and dress the older ones, they take them to school and bring them back home. They also look after the house and cook the meals. It may give their lives a purpose, but it taxes their strength and restricts their freedom. Some would like to go to their native country to visit or settle, but feel unable to desert their grandchildren.

Sometimes mothers are brought to Australia for that

purpose and their lives remain completely divorced from the outside. At a group for elderly migrants, a woman who spent more than two years in the country, confessed that she spoke not one word of English, has never been to a shop and never visited the city centre. Her daughter did all the shopping, she bought clothes for her mother, whose task consisted of minding the baby and looking after the house. Attendance at the group was her first social outing, apart from family events.

A worse plight awaits the childless aged, migrant or those whose children live too far to be of assistance. Some ethnic organisations are planning to establish homes for their aged, while a few have already done so.

The child

The immigrant child, particularly if it's the first in the family, is born disadvantaged. The young mother, deprived of advice, support and help of her female relatives, is often unable to cope and sometimes rejects the child. A typical example is the story of the young Maltese woman, who developed a psychotic illness, refused to accept the new born baby or return to their newly bought home. The distraught husband had no choice but to sell the house and take his wife and child back home to her mother. After several months in the bosom of the family, the couple are back in Australia and coping well. Many mothers, find the new ways of caring for a young baby strange. Infant welfare sisters complain of inappropriate diet and of dehydration, which babies suffer as a result of over heating under too many clothes and blankets.

Some, forced by term payments and hire purchase commitments, have no choice but to return to work when the child is still very young. Unable to afford licensed child minding services, and often mistrustful of strangers, they look for women from their own group or other migrants to mind their children, unaware that the lack of facilities, lack of stimulation, affect the child adversely. Because the nursery school and the kindergarten do not provide full working time care, the working parents cannot place their child in them and thus further deprive him or her of intellectual stimulus [4].

No wonder then, that a preliminary study, carried out by Dr. Margaret Nowotny of the School Medical Service, Health Commission of Victoria, on children of school entry age (approximately 5 years old) indicated that Turkish children, as well as their controls from deprived and disadvantaged non-migrant families, all living in high rise Housing Commission apartments, performed poorly in English. The Turkish children performed poorly also in their mother tongue. In contrast, a similar group of children, living in more advantaged suburban area of Melbourne, were functioning at an age appropriate level, or beyond [11].

It is easy to continue, the stage having been set, with a story of difficulties at school, due to a variety of factors; of these, the very important ones are insufficient knowledge of language and a culturally influenced, different system of concepts. While many children of migrant parents succeed greatly, are ambitious and diligent, many more fail, often not because of lack of innate ability. Although some schools are introducing ethnic teachers' aides, special language teachers and are attempting to make the child feel at ease and even proud of his/her heritage, there are still many more, where the children meet with hostility and prejudice on the part of peers and staff [4].

The Australian school with its permissive atmosphere and fairly lax discipline and a curriculum which includes many non-academic subjects, is incomprehensible to migrant parents. Although many are ambitious for their children and exert pressure to make them study in the hope that they will continue with a university education and finish in a profession, many more, due to ignorance at times, but more often because of economic necessity, are glad when the children can leave school at 15, start work and bring some money into the household. At present, because of the large unemployment, especially among the young and more particularly those from migrant families, they stay at school longer, but with doubtful academic benefit [3].

The adolescent

Much has been written about adolescents, whom this writer, in a previous publication, called «dead end» kids. While some issues have changed due to the greater awareness of needs, many inadequacies remain in both the educational and vocational system, which are particularly disadvantageous to the adolescent migrant. Having learned little at home, he has little chance to learn much in the new country, especially if, on arrival, he/she is near school leaving age and the economic pressures on the family require the financial contribution of each member. While the upper age limit for apprenticeship training has been extended, the poor knowledge of English and the low level of educational achievement, leave the migrant adolescent out of a very competitive race [2].

A few years ago jobs were available for these young people — monotonous, dirty, noisy, unskilled work, but paid work. It led nowhere, to a dead-end of poverty and ignorance, but for the time being it brought a little money into the family. At present, because of high unemployment, these jobs do not exist and many adolescents find difficulty in filling empty, meaningless days.

Many leave school speaking a kind of English, but unable to read or write, or even follow more sophisticated speech. The younger arrival, or even the child born in this country of non-English speaking parents, often finishes with similar results, as teachers at times over-look the language inadequacies in the early primary grades and provide no basic instruction in the 3 R's (reading, writing, arithmetic) in the higher grades [2].

It is also in adolescence, the time of turmoil and rebellion for all, that the migrant finds him/herself in greatest conflict with the parents. It is argued that the Australian born, or Australian reared youth, are in even greater conflict than the newly arrived adolescent, who had a chance to assimilate to some degree the values of the native country. Sons are still subject to strict control by fathers, who usually take all their earnings, give them little pocket money above that required for acknowledged necessary expenses and expect them to account for their movements. Sons are expected also to take responsibility for their mothers and sisters, often to the detriment of their personal life styles. Taught that women are inferior, they have problems in accepting female authority in school, in recreational clubs or at work.

The daughters fare much worse, as they are restricted severely in their movements, kept segregated from the opposite sex and expected to obey parental injunctions. In their rebellion, some run away from home, engage in deceit or openly defy the parents. Since parents believe it is their duty and right to control all aspects of their children's lives, they oppose associations which they fear may endanger their children's morals. The permissive upbringing of Australian youngsters is often seen as a dangerous influence and such friendships are strongly discouraged. In the case of the girls, they are not allowed to go out, even with a chaperone, with boys from other ethnic backgrounds, sometimes even from other regions of the parental homeland. Ex-nuptial pregnancies are considered to be the ultimate disaster. While attempts may be made to kill the boy, the girl is kicked out of the house and forbidden to return, sometimes even if she marries the father of her child.

If the parent-child relationship is basically a good one, if the family functions well and the bonds between the members are strong, these adolescent crises are weathered and survived. Where, however, there is serious dysfunction, the worst often happens and a complete break between parents and children occurs. It must be pointed out that well intentioned professionals, teachers, youth and welfare workers, unappreciative of the strong traditions and ties, which are ingrained even in the rebellious youngsters, encourage them to follow the new ways and may even suggest separation from home as a solution to conflict.

They fail to understand that to a young person closely sheltered within a family group, warned throughout their lifetime of the terrible dangers lurking in the outside world, leaving home is the worst possible solution, particularly when it is accompanied by a certainty that they are doing the wrong thing and that retribution, when it catches up, will be terrible. No matter how much they resent their parents, they see a break with the family as an equally great evil as submitting to parental orders. The sensitive counsellor will encourage the young to compromise, will try to interpret parental values and persuade that acceptance may be best.

On the other hand, counselling of parents has often led to some loosening of the restrictions, a better understanding of the protests and sometimes to a conditional modification of rules. It was quite startling to find that many young married women from the Mediterranean region still harbour a deep resentment of their parents, yet others still living at home, now in their twenties, accept the conduct values as beneficial and appropriate, if they are to retain their good name and find a suitable marriage partner.

An interesting sideline on the adolescent rebellion and culture conflict issues, are the self confessed attitudes of the young adults, especially women, who impose similar restrictions on their children, even if they do it under a more democratic guise. They plead the dangers of city life, the anonymity of a metropolis, the permissive environment, the difficulty in resisting the example of immoral peers, but, in the end, agree that they are stricter with their children than their parents were with them, particularly if they were brought up in their country of origin.

The communication gap

On deeper consideration, it would seem that immigrant problems can be summed up under four major headings, randomly listed hereunder:
the need for economic security;
the need for emotional support;
the breakdown in social and moral traditions and conduct rules;
the language and culture gap.

For the non-English speaking migrant, the greatest hurdle is the inability to understand and be understood, not only because of a lack of language, but also because of an inability on one hand to explain, on the other to understand the differences in behaviour, in attitudes, in appropriate expressions of feelings, even in modes of reasoning. Such differences quite obviously exist between the various ethnic groups leading to further misunderstandings, particularly when the views of one group are interpreted by members of another group. The wisest counsel, if inappropriate and unacceptable in the terms of one's culture, is worthless; while the knowledge of the language helps, it is not the complete answer to a full understanding [3].

Mention was made of the plight of migrants when confronted by medical emergencies. The embarrassment, nay the humiliation, of mothers dependent on the language skills of their young children need not be elaborated, nor is there need to comment on the loss of prestige of a father who takes his young child as an intermediary to any transactions. The large number of legal disputes in which migrants are involved, mainly concern hire purchase, house and car purchase agreements. They don't understand the contract, they don't understand what the salesmen tell them, they have no previous experience of buying on time payments, they overcommit their limited resources, and consequently, they sign disadvantageous, crippling contracts; they mortgage themselves and their families, body and soul.

The newest arrivals can benefit from the post-arrival

settlement, language and orientation programmes, mainly centred on hostels. They are given information on the law of the country, housing, employment, availability and ways of seeking it, on social security entitlements, medical insurance and when they leave, some hints about the neighbourhood to which they are moving. Outreach welfare workers, employed by the Commonwealth Department of Immigration and Ethnic Affairs, are located in areas of migrant residential concentration and are available to the perplexed. English classes are available to children and adults. Those who wish to attend full time crash courses receive a living allowance, equivalent to the unemployment benefit [5].

Little, if anything, however, is available for the longer settled migrant with hardly any knowledge of English. The backlog is great and remains untapped − a virtual mass of people, middle aged and elderly, often condemned to a life of isolation, because, through no fault of their own, they had no opportunity to learn a language, which is essential for communication. Whatever arguments there are for the introduction into education and daily use of the, so-called now, community languages, the need for English remains undiminished. In fact, the greater the number of ethnic groups in Australia, the greater the need for a lingua franca, a universal means of communication. No one would argue that English is not the natural choice, for this continent at any rate.

A very distressing, but unfortunately true side effect of the striving for better English to help in the obliteration of their «differentness», has been the frequent rejection of their mother tongue by the children. Brought up with a poor knowledge of their own language by parents too busy to talk to them, often minded by people of a different ethnic group and language, they refuse to speak anything but English, even when it is far from perfect. The tragic result is an alienation of children from parents, an inability to communicate with each other beyond basic daily needs, quite inadequate to bridge the normal generational gap and the very difficult, ever widening, cultural gap.

To round off the picture, one must add the already mentioned total lack of appreciation of the finer nuances of each language, of the varying dialects; as a result, multilingual speakers, or speakers of basically the same language, but spoken in different countries or areas, may be unable to convey meanings with any degree of accuracy.

The significance of ethnic organisations

It is now an accepted axiom that new settlers, new arrivals, need the emotional support of their own kind; they need the warmth, the understanding and also the example of those who have mastered the initial shock of adapting to a new country. The often maligned «ethnic ghettos» are a necessary adjunct to a process of gradual adjustment, a shelter offering relief from the continuing stress of coping with the unfamiliar [1].

In discussing various ethnic groups and the ability of their members to relate to the wider community, one comes across such statements: «they are alright, they participate in the social activities, they are well organized in their own right», or «no, they never join; they are split into little factions, they trust no one, even not one another, they are not organised», or «they present with many psychological problems, they have no ethnic organisation».

These statements are not an exaggeration and leading members of ethnic groups work hard and consistently to establish viable religious, social, educational and communal activities to present to the world outside a unified and culturally significant front and to give to their compatriots a visible and supportive centre for recreation, for friendly interaction, and for the expression and satisfaction of personal needs. Some groups, in doing so, have had to overcome regional allegiances and create a feeling of national unity [12].

The existence of strong, active ethnic organisations provide their members with a sense of reassurance about the continuity of their national entity, a hope of retaining the

interest and loyalty of the younger, especially the Australian born, generation and a place of contact with others of
the same kind. It may be said that they provide salvation
for many isolated, depressed individuals, for whom they
constitute an escape-hatch from psychiatric ill health.

The silver lining

Much is said about the traumas of immigration and the accompanying maladaptations. In all fairness, something
should be said of the ways undertaken to alleviate the
crises, inadequate and few though the solutions are. Sus-
tained efforts are being made in various directions to give
credibility to the concept of multi-culturalism, to cushion
the period of transition and to engage in truly participatory
interaction. Although the list of services may look impressive, it needs to be remembered that one can have a long
list with a meagre substance.

The introduction of interpreters and a 24 hour telephone interpreter service are gradually making inroads
into the health care and legal areas. Notices in many languages alert their speakers to events in the community and
warn them of dangers. The ethnic press is growing in
number of publications. Municipal libraries are establishing sections of books in various languages. Neighbour-
hoods organise national fêtes and cultural events in which
everybody can participate and where the community at
large has an opportunity to learn about the host group.
Restaurants and cafes serve food and drink of every nationality resident in Australia and some serve as meeting
places, social clubs, particularly for men. Community languages are spoken in some department stores. A radio station, part of the government controlled network, presents
only ethnic programmes, often planned by representatives
of ethnic organisations. Trials for an ethnic television
programme have been carried over the past few months.
Migrant Resource Centres are offering a full range of services, advice, information, practical assistance and educa-

tional material in English and in the language of the inquirer. Only a few weeks before this was written, a newly elected member of Parliament, made his maiden speech in his native tongue and declared his intention to do so again.

The most significant change, however, is to be seen taking place in educational institutions. Community language teachers' aides, bilingual kindergarten aides, overseas trained teachers working in local schools, are but a modest beginning to prevent educational failure and to ensure good language development. Some schools have managed even to break the barrier, separating and excluding non-English speaking parents, and have encouraged, nay persuaded them, to participate in school activities and to join school councils. The introduction of community languages into the curriculum and the inclusion of information relating to the history and culture of the countries of origin of many school children, have helped in restoring a pride of belonging and have even eased communication problems in the home.

It is happening, but it is only a small silver lining on still overcast skies. It is to be hoped that with the current recognition of the importance of the mother language and of the basic culture to the healthy development and adaptation processes of the individuals, there will be a continuing growth of facilities, even at the time of a very unfavourable economic climate in the country, which militates against the employment of new specialist staff, the expansion of existing and the creation of new services.

A new type of migrant

The strict limits put on the number of immigrants currently being admitted, were followed by stricter selection procedures. Apart from those arriving under the family reunion scheme, the remainder are chosen for their occupational skills, in line with the prevailing needs of the economy. Thus, many migrants coming to Australia nowadays, are urban, middle class, educated and skilled.

Their chances of having their qualifications recognized are better and though many have to serve an apprenticeship and submit to examination, the system is made known to them and the opportunities exist. Because of their background, they are more energetic, have greater initiative and settle reasonably well in a much shorter time. Their occupational and social mobility is great, they are better able to reach their goals. Among the new arrivals to whom these statements are applicable, are the Russians and the South Americans; one of their greatest problems appears to be a need to reach their former social status and establish contacts with people of their kind.

They are critical of the social workers, who, they say, think in terms of the help needed by the great numbers of unskilled, ill-educated, rural immigrants. They claim that they need housing, an opportunity to learn English and patience, until they can find a suitable job, not just any job. They go to full time language courses, enabled to do so by a living allowance, they send their children to tertiary educational institutions and aim to re-establish themselves. On the whole, the recent arrivals, whether immigrants, quasi refugees or refugees, find employment more quickly and, at least superficially, they adjust better. The less skilled, being less choosy, also manage to secure employment, even at a time when it is difficult to obtain.

The refugee

Many arrivals in Australia could have been classified as refugees, because they left their homeland as such. By the time they come to Australia, however, they arrive with immigration visas and therefore, are not classified as refugees; to this category belong the refugees from USSR, Chile and from Czechoslovakia and Hungary a few years ago. At present, the term refugee is applied primarily to those from Indochina, the boat people from Vietnam, Laotians and Cambodians.

They enlist the sympathy of charitable organisations

and, for reasons of political expediency, the help of the government. They receive a great deal of help and they respond with gratitude and appreciation to their hosts, content to be safe. Like the new migrant described above, those who manage to escape, in the majority, are people with initiative, with money, with education and with survivor skills. They come determined to settle and to achieve. They are largely from middle-class background, the young are students or would be tertiary students and they aim to re-establish themselves at a similar level. Although they are worried about relatives and friends left behind, they are forced to concentrate on their own well-being.

Studies of refugee adaptation, from whatever part of the world they come, indicate that early satisfaction changes to discontent as time proceeds. They start missing their country, relatives and friends. They dislike the food and the social and recreational facilities available to them. They become aware of prejudice, discriminaton, unpleasant work conditions, of their inadequacies in coping with the system. They perceive the behaviour of Australian, English speaking youth as too permissive, undesirable and see it as a threat to their own children. They worry about their children's education, their manners and their values. Although it is too early to make assessments, it would appear, however, that the knowledge that there is no chance of returning, makes them more flexible, more ready to adapt.

The truth about discrimination

Even though every fourth person in Australia was either born overseas, or was born of overseas-born parents, there is still a great deal of discrimination against those who appear to be «new» Australians, even if they have lived in the country for most of their lives; a «foreign» appearance, a «foreign» accent, no matter how good the English, can be a distinct disadvantage. In spite of recognition that this is a multi-lingual country, one finds resentment of languages other than English. «They get together in their clubs and shops and they jabber in their own lingo. Why can't they speak English?». There is hostility and intolerance, even if it is not as open as it used to be [1].

Recent surveys conducted in several States in Australia, indicated that migrants were endowed with many negative characteristics. They were thought to be arrogant, deceitful, greedy, over-emotional, hot tempered, etc.

A recent news item in a daily newspaper told of a young woman who was refused a job as a typist/receptionist, for which she was fully qualified, because she spoke with an accent and could not pronounce «th» correctly. It reminded the writer that about thirty years ago she was refused a position in an international organisation because of her foreign surname and a slight accent. Thirty years in the history of immigration is obviously not enough to eradicate prejudice. It must be stated, however, that there are probably no areas of human endeavour, which migrants have not entered as of right and to which they have not contributed.

A sad twist to the story of prejudice, must be attributed to the desire of minority groups to be identified with the powerful majority. The fear of once again becoming the cynosure of all eyes, of once again commiting the crime of not knowing, turns the longer established against the new arrival, leads to a refusal of help, a denial of the whole relationship. It has happened in the past, it is happening at present and, no doubt, will continue to occur as long as one cowers in the uncertainty of personal identity and defensively shouts: «Am I my brothers' keeper?» [2]

There is great need to implement a better programme of education for the non-migrant population, however it may be defined, to eradicate senseless prejudice; there is great need also for a programme of education which will obliterate old hatreds and lead to harmonious co-existence [3].

Who is an Australian?

In the text of this chapter, the word Australian was used in the sense of a WASP, a white, Anglo Saxon, not necessarily protestant, locally born and, of course, English speaking. This is a completely incorrect use of the word, as it should refer to all permanent residents of Australia and they are by no means as the first definition would have it. The terminology is not an important issue in its own right; it is important by implication because of the changes which are occurring, because of a necessity to change stereotypes, attitudes, concepts, even nomenclatures.

There has been no really satisfactory term to describe arrivals to these shores and descriptive phrases are too cumbersome for daily use. The bronzed Anzac, if he ever represented the Australian of pre-World War II days, no longer depicts the average inhabitant of Australia. Calling languages foreign, meaning other than English, has been euphemistically replaced by the expression community languages, but they remain alien to a great number. Whether a migrant is called a «refo», a new Australian, or a new settler, to omit the more obnoxious names, the fact remains, that he is not yet called simply an Australian.

It will be interesting to hear how the question «who is an Australian» is answered in the year 2000.

Epilogue

The material for this chapter was gathered from interviews with a great many workers in the field, who gave generously of their time and knowledge; although they are too numerous to be mentioned by name, the writer wishes to acknowledge their contribution most gratefully.

Appreciation is expressed also to the Mental Health Division, Health Commission of Victoria, for the assistance given.

Bibliography

1 BANCHEVSKA, R.: A «new way of life». In: Stoller, A. (Ed.): New Faces – Immigration and family life in Australia. Cheshire, Melbourne, 1966.
2 BANCHEVSKA, R.: The immigrant family. In: Krupinski, J., Stoller, A. (Eds.): The family in Australia. Pergamon Press, Australia 1978.
3 Commissioner for Community Relations: Annual Reports 1976, 1977, 1978, Community of Australia.
4 COX, D. et al. (Eds.): An uneasy transition – Migrant children in Australia. Commissioned for the 9th International Congress of the International Association of Child Psychiatry and Allied Professions. Melbourne, 1978.
5 GALBALLY, F.E.: Review of post arrival programmes and services to migrants. Canberra, A.G.P.S. 1978.
6 HARPER, J.: The immigrant woman speaks, presented at «The immigrant woman and the hospital» seminar. Melbourne, October 1978.
7 KEAM, R.G.: If you can make my voice heard – Satisfaction with health and helping services and perceived health/welfare needs in the inner suburbs of Melbourne. Health Services Research Group, South Melbourne, 1979.
8 LLOYD, J., STAGOLL, B.: The accident victim syndrome: Compensation neurosis» or iatrogenesis? A social perspective, to be published in «New Doctor», Workers' Health Issue, 1979.
9 MARSH, G.: Communication in a not so multi-cultural system – presented at «The immigrant woman and the hospital» seminar. Melbourne, October 1978.
10 Migrant Women Speak – A report to the Commonwealth Government by the National Women's Advisory Council, April 1979.
11 NOWOTNY, M.: Children of the High Rise – Language problems of the Turkish migrant child at school entry. Proceedings of the Australian Speech and Hearing Association Jubilee Meeting, February 1979.
12 UNIKOWSKI, R.: Communal endeavours – Migrant organisations in Melbourne, A.N.U. Press, Canberra, 1978.

Chapter 7

Children of immigrants

Vivian Rakoff

Murphy [8] proposed a «general hazard theory» to explain the apparent vulnerability of many immigrants to psychiatric illness. He was anticipated by Hippocrates who remarked that movement to another country was always followed by «terrible perturbation». And in the list of problems compiled by life stress investigators, displacement or disruption of expected context constitutes the greatest single common factor [9]: change of home, change of work, loss of familiar people, physical illness, (indeed even pleasant changes such as promotions are experienced as stressful). The immigrant experience is often a compendium of many of these factors and the immigrant is almost in the situation of someone who has suffered a profound physical loss of capacity such as a cerebral vascular accident: having to learn again, to walk, speak and work. Perhaps most crucially, the immigrant has to learn to relate anew to other people in terms of his altered resources: the sustaining aspects of the previous familiar culture having been largely lost.

However, immigration is not a unitary experience and the reactions of the immigrant are modified by many factors. Morrison [6] offered a model of «intervening variables» which in their different combinations affect the degree of stress or adaptation in the immigrant.

This author proposes a further intervening variable which is of significance for the population under consideration in this paper, namely, the capacity of the *family* as a system to mediate the accumulated shocks of the immigrant experience: to negotiate the stresses in the «general system».

It is against this background of the general stress syndrome, Morrison's intervening variables, and the experience gained in numerous studies of migrants and immigrants in general that one has to consider the adaptation of the children of immigrants. Unfortunately, there is a relative paucity of studies in this area, but those that do exist suggest that children as well as adults are responsive to the same disharmonies.

MINDE & MINDE's [5] study of Asian children in Canada is one of the few reports of a global assessment of adjustment in the target population. For that reason and for the light it throws on the problem in general, it is useful to examine it in some detail. Their sample consisted of children who had fled with their families from Uganda to Toronto after the expulsion of Asians by the then president, Idi Amin. They included all newly immigrated Ugandan Asian families with children attending primary schools in Metropolitan Toronto and through the intermediary agency of a member of the Ismaili community they made contact with 51 out of a possible 55 families. They attempted to gain as wide as possible a picture of the background of each family historically, and at the time of the investigation. They collected data pertaining to the type of family, the number of siblings, past education, the medical and psychological history of the children, the parents, social information, related to income and amenities both in Canada and Uganda, experiences during the forced exodus and the assimilation to Canada, the general likes and dislikes towards Canada, the perception of food, work, the countryside, people at work and at play, schools, and hopes and fears regarding the future.

The children were interviewed separately and asked about family, school friends, occupational choices and their memories. In addition they answered a questionnaire based on similar questionnaires that had been used in both British and non-British populations [15, 16, 17]. In addition the mother's emotional status was rated against a malaise inventory derived from the Cornell Medical Index Health Questionnaire.

After the home visit three clinical ratings were performed involving the total family unit, and the child's school teacher. The level of psychiatric disturbance of the target child was assessed using the methodology of RUTTER and GRAHAM [17].

The global assessment of psychiatric disturbances in these children found 60% without abnormalities in behaviour; 14% showed moderate abnormality of mood or social relationship and 10% of all children were scored as being moderately disturbed in all three areas, 16% demonstrated a severe disturbance in at least 2 of the 3 areas examined. In school performance the Ugandan children were significantly retarded in areas requiring language skills. No other academic subjects distinguished between the local children and the Ugandan children although it should be noted in fairness that over a period of a year the Ugandan children improved their school performance quite dramatically.

Regarding the families as a whole the psychiatric assessment gave the following results: 47% were seen as functioning well, showing only minor conflict in one of the areas of cohesion, communication or discord in the parental roles. 27% showed minor or moderate problems in one or two areas of functioning primarily related to the financial situation of the family in Canada. 8% had experienced moderate to severe psychological conflicts in Uganda in two or more areas which continued in Canada and *on examination 18% exhibited severe problems which had apparently not been present in Uganda.*

Probably the most crucial variable underlying family unhappiness was the drop in income of those fathers who had been well off in Uganda compared with Canada, and the present economic position, that is the position of the families at the time that the study was undertaken, was correlated with the ability of both parents to speak English well. While most men were fluent enough to find employment, many women were not.

These women were also disadvantaged in other areas. They had few contacts outside their immediate families and their social isolation was much greater than that of the men who worked outside the home.

Connections with the host society were relatively poor for the families as a whole. They specifically found the weather difficult and inimical and they missed their community life.

The parents were concerned about illnesses and tragedies of people they knew and loved; and 60% expressed concern about the racially discriminatory encounters they had experienced. These had frequently involved the children at school. Few children had ever brought a non-Asian child to the house and of the 59% who had done so there was little repeat visiting. About half of them had been invited to white houses. The essential picture that emerged was of cultural isolation. The families were unable to mobilize themselves to visit the local sights. They were in short lonely, sad and alienated from the host society.

The general level of disturbance found by the Mindes in their study, is confirmed in its broader aspects by the more specific work done by RUESCH [13] who found an increased rate of delinquency and psychological abnormality among children whose parents had been born abroad compared with children whose parents had been born in the United States. And Rorschach responses of Spanish refugees in the United Kingdom compared with those of English children [21] revealed a higher proportion of aberrant responses in the immigrant children. Furthermore, studies of West Indian children [2] referred to psychiatric clinics discovered not only an over-representation of children of immigrants, but a distortion of the usual sex distribution. In contrast to the usual preponderance of boys and girls in child psychiatry or child guidance clinics, these studies found boys and girls equally represented and «all West Indian children despite matched socio-economic background variables presented more antisocial symptoms than did their English peers». Similarly RUTTER et al.'s survey of 2043 West Indian parents, and 34% of the West Indian girls scored within the abnormal range as compared with 24% of the English born boys and 12% of the indigenous girls. YULE et al. [23] found similar difficulties their studies of the children of West Indian Immigrants in London. The immigrant children studied by RODRIGUEZ [14] in Geneva were also seen to have reading and other adaptational difficulties. The problems in the Swiss studies were not as severe or statistically significant as the English studies.

However, there is a risk of overinterpreting the results of the studies cited above, and a cautionary note is necessary: in contrast to the specific difficulties related to reading and conduct in the West Indian children's group RUTTER et al. remarked that there were no differences between them and the indigenous children in behaviour such as marrying, being anxious, stuttering or thumbsucking. And more forcibly, KALLARACKAL and HERBERT 1976 [4], using the same teachers' questionnaire as the RUTTER group to investigate children of Indian immigrants to Britain, discovered that the rate of maladjustment among the English children exceeded that of the children whose parents were born in India. They suggested that this provided evidence that the nature of the Indian family may have mediated the tensions of immigration. And in 1979 COCHRANE [1] compared rates of psychological disturbance in children of Indian, Pakistani, West Indian and British parents and on this occasion the Rutter teachers' questionnaire revealed that there were no differences of any great significance between any of the three ethnic minority groups and the British group with regard to conduct or emotional deviance, or indeed for total deviance.

In terms of MORRISON's intervening variables the Israeli experience with children of immigrants is particularly significant in supporting the finding that the immigrant experience does not need to be pathogenic [3]. Far from being an unwelcome alien, the immigrant in Israel is for the most part perceived as «family» of the host community. Of course this is a statement of an ideal which in particular circumstances breaks down; and the individual immigrant or family will encounter the same suspicion and hostility as in any other society. MORRISON specifically cites the relatively benign progress of the immigrant in Israel. His observations have been anecdotally confirmed by the contrast of the relatively high rate of psychosis found among Jews in post-war Holland and Belgium, and the much lower rate in Israel [18]. Commenting on these observations SANUA remarked «We could assume that whatever trauma was incurred by Jewish refugees was tempered by the feelings of returning to Zion.» TOULIATOS and LINDHOLME [20] found that in America, too, effects of migration are not necessarily always present, and indeed in certain populations may not be found at all. Their findings are similar to those of OSBORNE who found little or no evidence that native-born whites tested by the Bell Adjustment Inventory differed from their sample of foreign-born highschool students, of whom about one-half were of Mexican descent and about one-quarter were of Protuguese descent.

In their study TOULIATOS and LINDHOLME examined 2991 children who were native born and white, and 97 children whose parents were foreign born. Sixteen of the «foreign» children were of European descent, 19 of Latin American descent, 20 of Indian descent, and 42 were of other Asian parentage. They obtained general information and ratings on a behaviour problem checklist from teachers and they took into account age, sex, social class in terms of father's occupation, and the ethnicity of the children, their grade in school and whether or not they were residing with their biological parents.

The findings in this study are so at variance with most others that they have to be carefully assessed. (In spite of the few studies cited which support a non-pathogenic view of immigration, most studies and common sense reinforce the sense of the disruptive nature of the immigrant experience for both parents and children.) The authors themselves think that the procedural differences between various studies would have to be ironed out to make sense of it. They also note that the definitions of psychopathologies changed in various studies. In addition, they feel that the ratings from teachers' questionnaires and problem checklists might reflect stereotypic beliefs about minority groups. They write: «It could be argued that findings of superior adjustment for Asian Americans in this study might have been influenced to some degree by the positive stereotype of this ethnic group held by teachers.» «Among these stereotypes are strong family obligations, restraint of intense feelings, obedience, conformity, respect for authority, formality in interpersonal relations and high academic achievement.»

It is possible, as suggested earlier in this paper that TOU-LIATOS and LINDHOLMES' phrase, «strong family feelings» may hold the key to the differences found between the children of immigrants in their study and most other reports. Furthermore, the characteristics of the family vary not only in terms of individual characteristics, ethnicity and the host society, but also according to the stage of immigration of the family.

SLUZKI [22] has written, «there is a unique drama that characterizes migration in each case. In fact, this drama often becomes part of the treasured heritage of each family». Allowing for the tremendous variability of each particular immigration, he proposed a set of normative stages which have to be taken into account to understand what happens in the process of migration, whether it be internal or from one country to another. These are:
1. the preparatory stage,
2. the act of migration,
3. the period of overcompensation,
4. the period of decompensation,
5. the trans-generational phenomena.

He proposed that each step has distinctive characteristics, triggers different types of family coping mechanisms, and as he puts it, «unchains different types of conflicts and symptoms». In the author's experience SLUZKI's structures have been remarkably apposite and are particularly useful when they are compared and considered with Morrison's intervening variables.

It is during the preparatory stage that the first «up and down» pattern of expectations appears. The second stage of the immigrant process is the act of migration. As SLUZKI points out, «Migration is a transition with little or no prescribed rituals». This process is probably more dependent than any other upon the antecedent circumstances of the move, and the receptivity of the host society. Flight or voluntary movement to a better life clearly differentiates the degree of composure or distress affecting the entire family. Openness or secrecy, money or poverty, knowledge of language or unfamiliarity, the social status and educational experience which allows the family to respond to officialdom in a way that expects either cooperation and help, or intimidation and impersonal authoritarianism. During this phase a pattern of strong bonding and association may be set up in groups who share a common experience during the act of migration. Some families burn their bridges and the act of migration is the character of something final and unchangeable. Others have a fantasy (or perhaps a real perception) that their immigration is «only for a while» regardless of the unlikelihood of a return.

The period of overcompensation: During the period immediately following migration there is often a time during which the participants are apparently unaware of the stressful nature of the experience and of its cumulative impact. In fact it is a period when a «heightened task efficiency» is seen. It is often characterized by a strong increase in the split between instrumental and affective roles within the family, in the service of the basic need for survival and adaptation in the new culture that is to a greater or lesser extent, alien. There is a strong denial of the alien aspects of the new culture. This «cancellation of dissonance» is maximal precisely at the period in which the bombardment by dissonant experiences is also maximal. It is as though the difficult task of adaptation gives a supporting structure to the family. Although some families experience the greatest stress during this period, this is not the rule «during this period immediately following migration». However, one way or another the period of «apparent calm and overcompensation» gives way some months or even years after it started to an era of major crisis: one in which the «long range responses» to migration take place.

SLUZKI labelled this latter time: *the period of decompen-*

sation or crisis. Now the principal task of the recently migrated family is enacted. It must reshape its new reality and must preserve its continuity in terms of identity and its compatibility with the new environment. The whole collective task is «complex, painful and unavoidable». During this stage the generational tensions frequently become manifest. It is as though the parents and children have a non-synchronous immigration: while the children tend to catch up with the new culture and the new language (verbal and non verbal) much more quickly than their parents do. The children tend to adapt the mores of the host culture. They truly change countries, while the parents tend to remain fixed psychologically in the «old country». The most difficult task is that the family must recognize «rules about the changing of rule». Sexual mores, patterns of filial duty, the hierarchical relationships of the generations are all altered. There may be a rise in intrafamilial factions and many families that fail in their coping mechanisms experience a rise of factionalism between the generations, or even between various alliances that were established between parents and particular children. «In fact in order to deal with or express accumulated stress, tension, pain, conflict, family members will frequently activate the socially acceptable and interactionally powerful pattern of the «somatic complaint» or the psychiatric problem. And occasionally the socially less acceptable pattern of «social deviant» (for example as a juvenile delinquent).

Stage 5. *Transgenerational Impact.* During this phase there is an increased degree of attachment to past values and a period of idealization and nostalgia vis-a-vis the homeland that has been left behind, and the capacity to assimilate or change towards the new values of the host society produce strains in the family. «Whatever has been avoided by a first generation will appear in the second one, generally expressed as a clash between generations.» «In many cases the clash is intercultural rather than intergenerational.»

While MORRISON's intervening variables and SLUZKI's normative stages may account for anecdotal and epidemiological variations, an additional model may be required to account for those forms of behaviour that are characteristic of maladaptive migration: school difficulties, sociopathic behaviour and intergenerational tensions. «Why is it,» one may ask «that change of context is so stressful»?

In another place [10] this author has developed the thesis that the shared myths and social structures of language, history, food habit and religious beliefs, etc. of a particular culture facilitate the movement of the child, from the intimate context of the family — the «ecos» — to the public context of the «polis». Moreover, the shared structures and the sense of membership in the polis are essential components of the ego. Society and civilization are not in this sense inimical to the individual, but as is commonly agreed, an essential component of identity. The lack of this shared structure, this amputation or agenesis of the social limb of the psychic corpus, underlies the experience of anomie and alienation with its attendant pathology: suicide as its extreme manifestation, and the lesser, but intensely debilitating sensations of loneliness and geographical restlessness. Perhaps, too, it may account for that feeling of non-identification with the group which permits vandalism and delinquency: since there is no investment of the self in the society, the property of the society becomes «fair game» for the venting of destructive and aggressive impulses; and the laws of the society are perceived as alien at best, and more seriously as non-applicable to the newcomer, or member of an incompletely welcomed minority.

In addition the loss of old networks and the failure to re-establish effective new systems of support beyond the nuclear family may generate excessive mutual attachment within the family: The appropriate movement of adolescent away from intense parental and sibling relationships may be perceived as threatening by both generations. In the instance of children of Jewish concentration camp survivors the hypercathexis occasionally produces a frequently described syndrome: The children are fearful of separating from the parents who may be both resented and viewed with intense and inappropriate protectiveness, while the parents impose excessive expectations on the children. In this tragic instance the children are expected not only to compensate for the lost homeland, but for entire families murdered during the holocaust of European Jewry [11, 12, 19].

In less intense form the turmoil of intergenerational strife described by SLUZKI as so characteristic of the period of transgenerational impact, may be re-interpreted. It may not only be due to a clash of values – of old versus new – but also the transgenerational expression of the mutual fear of separation. For the children it is closer to the normative stage of the specific struggle of adolescence in the direction of autonomy and identity, but for the adults it contains elements of the fear of abandonment. It is, in some ways, a re-evocation of the intense loneliness of the first arrival in the new country. The family welded together like a small fighting unit during the period of physical travel and displacement has in these instances *become* the country, and sustaining community – a tiny capsule representation of an entire history and ‹polis›. Its disruption represents a profound crisis.

Social and therapeutic responses need therefore to take into account the unique pattern of intervening variables for each family, the stage of immigration and the essential need for sustaining shared historical and social structures. SLUZKI emphasizes the therapeutic usefulness of making the family aware of the stereotyping or normativeness of the process of immigration. He writes, «It may be pertinent to add that the specific culture notwithstanding, the introduction of certain amounts of future orientation and planning may be particularly useful in families stunned and confused by the experience of migration. Also, an effort towards differentiation may prove very beneficial in enmeshed families, and contrariwise a certain amount of de-differentiation and intimacy may be favoured in extremely dissociated families. In disorganized families, in turn the acknowledgement and reinforcement of generational patterns may be most valuable».

At both the social and individual level the sustaining aspects of association with the native culture of the immigrant family should be recognized. In Canada the psychiatric and social expression of migration and displacement — anomie and suicide, is at its greatest in the highly mobile and uprooted population of the prosperous Western states, and at its least among the poor, but communaly stable, communities of Nova Scotia. And H.B.M. MURPHY [7] has reported the supportive function of a functioning Chinatown community, which seems to lessen psychiatric hospitalization. The retained connection of the family with its roots, appears to act as a decompression chamber during the transition to new country and new community. It facilitates the movement of children toward the host culture, and gives the older generation a source of support and satisfaction other than the achievement, closeness and compliance of the children.

Conclusion

Immigration places the entire family at risk. It carries with it the psychological and social threat of alienation, loss of identity and financial insecurity. And even while it promises escape from a poor, or oppressive homeland, the accompanying perturbation is more or less inevitable. The children of immigrant families need to adapt to the changed behaviour, and (often) status of their parents, while they accommodate to the demands of the host society. Frequently they adapt more completely than their parents and they may find themselves in the paradoxical position of being more accomplished in the new society: they may become parents of their parents.

They are frequently excessively cathected by the parents, and the burden of expectation and nurturance, may on occasion be pathogenic. As a consequence separation is often more stressful and threatening than usual: At its extreme it can be perceived as disloyalty and abandonment. If adaptation does not occur because of the family or society and the host society remains alien, it may generate diminished academic achievement, anxiety, and/or delinquency. Yet in spite of these burdens and difficulties the majority of children of immigrants do adapt and display no more pathology than comparable indigenous children. Indeed it would be remiss, in a paper of this kind, not to mention the positive aspects of the immigrant experience: the increased family closeness; the clear articulation of life goals; the aspiration (and frequently optimism) that may generate energy and creativity, which becomes the stuff of family legend in later generations.

Bibliography

1 COCHRANE, R.: Psychological and Behavioural Disturbance in West Indians, Indians and Pakistanis in Britain: A Comparison of Rates Among Children and Adults. British Journal of Psychiatry *134*, 201 – 210, 1979.

2 GRAHAM, P.J., MEADOWS, C.G.: Psychiatric Disorders in Children of West Indian Immigrants. Journal of Child Psychology and Psychiatry, 105 – 116, 1967.

3 HOECK, A., MOSES, R., TERRESPLSKY, L.: Emotional Disorders in an Israeli Immigrant Community: A Comparison of Prevalence Among Different Ethnic Groups. Israel Annals of Psychiatry *3*, 213 – 228, 1965.

4 KALLARACKAL, A.M., HERBERT, M.: The Happiness of Indian Immigrant Children. New Society, 422 – 424, February 1976.

5 MINDE, K., MINDE, R.: Children of Immigrants: The Adjustment of Ugandan Asian Primary School Children in Canada. Canadian Psychiatric Association Journal *21*, 371 – 381, 1976.

6 MORRISON, S. DAVID: International Journal of Social Psychiatry *19*, 61 – 65, 1973.

7 MURPHY, H.B.M.: The low Rate of Mental Hospitalization shown by Immigrants to Canada. In: C.A. Zwingman, M. Pfister-Ammende (Eds.): Uprooting and After. Springer, New York, 1973, pp. 221 – 231.

8 MURPHY, H.B.M.: Social Change & Mental Illness. Millbank Fund, Quaterly *39*, 385 – 439, 1961.

9 RAHE, R.H., HOLMES, T.H.: The Social Readjustment Rating Scale. Journal of Psychosomatic Research. Vol. *11*, 213 – 218, 1967.

10 RAKOFF, V.: History of Transitional Object. Adolescent Psychiatry. Vol. *8*, 1980.

11 RAKOFF, V.: A Long Term Effect of the Concentration Camp Experience. Viewpoints *1*, 17 – 22, 1966.

12 RAKOFF, V., SIGAL, J.J., EPSTEIN, N.B.: Children and Families of Concentration Camp Survivors. Canada's Mental Health *14*, 24 – 26, 1967.

13 RUESCH, J.: Acculturation and Illness. Psychological Monograph *62*, 1 – 40, 1958.

14 RODRIGUEZ, R.: Difficulties of Adjustment of Immigrant Children in Geneva. Medicine and Hygiene *845*, 1 – 6, 1968.

15 RUTTER, M., YULE, W., BERGER, M., YULE, B., MORTON, J., BAGLEY, C.: Children of West Indian Immigrants – 1. Rates of Behavioural Deviance and of Psychiatric Disorder. Journal of Child Psychology and Psychiatry *5*, 241 – 262, 1972.

16 RUTTER, M., TIZARD, J., WHITMORE, K. (Eds.): Education, Health and Behaviour. Longman, London, 1970, pp. 339 – 343.

17 RUTTER, M., GRAHAM, P.: The Reliability and Validity of the Psychiatric Assessment of the Child, Interview with the Child. British Journal of Psychiatry *114*, 563 – 579, 1968.

18 SANUA, VICTOR D.: In: Brody, E. (Ed.): Behaviour in New Environments. Sage, California, 1970, pp. 291 – 342.

19 SIGAL, J.J., RAKOFF, V.: Concentration Camp Survival: A Pilot Study of Effects on the Second Generation. Journal of the Canadian Psychiatric Association *16*, 393 – 397, 1971.

20 TOULIATOS, J., LINDHOME, B.W.: Behavioural Disturbance in Children of Native Born and Immigrant Parents. Journal of Community Psychology *8*, 28 – 33, 1980.

21 TULCHIN, S.H., LEVY, D.M.: Rorschach Test Differences in Groups of Spanish and English Refugee Children. American Journal of Ortopsychiatry *15*, 361 – 368, 1945.

22 SLUZKI, CARLOS E.: Migration and Family Conflict. Family Progress *18*, December 1979.

23 YULE, W., BERGER, M., RUTTER, M., YULE, B.: Children of West Indian Immigrants II. Intellectual Performance and Reading Attainment. Journal of Child Psychology and Psychiatry *16*, 1 – 17, 1975.

Chapter 8

Bilingualism and educational adjustment of immigrant children: A case study of Lebanese families in Ontario

Jim Cummins and Ali Abdolell

In this paper we will examine the educational adjustment of immigrant children from two perspectives: first, we will analyse factors which appear to differentiate immigrant and minority language children who succeed in majority language schools as compared to those who experience school failure. This analysis will lead us to suggest that ambivalent attitudes towards both their own identity and the majority group may be an important factor in explaining the poor school performance of some groups of minority children. We will then examine the role of this «bi-cultural ambivalence» in a case study of Arabic-speaking Lebanese families in southern Ontario, Canada.

School failure among minority language children

The rapid increase in immigration brought about by the economic expansion of the 1960's resulted in an influx of culturally and linguistically diverse immigrant children into the school systems of Western Europe, North America and Australia. These school systems were generally ill-prepared to adapt to meet the needs of immigrant children, both because there was little research documentation as to what these needs were, and also because coherent societal policies regarding ethnic and linguistic diversity had not been worked out. Consequently, it is not surprising that educational failure has been widespread among many groups of immigrant and minority language children. For example, according to the European Commission [5] there are currently about two million immigrant[1] students attending schools in the European Economic Community and more than half of these (100 000 each year) fail to obtain any job qualification (academic or vocational) at the end of compulsory schooling.

It is possible to identify three distinct phases in the assumptions which school systems have made regarding immigrant and minority language children. The first approach, which in the first half of this century was almost universal, involved no attempt on the part of the school to adapt to minority children's educational needs. This approach has been termed «submersion» or «sink or swim» by COHEN and SWAIN [1]. The school failure which many minority children experienced was viewed as reflecting genetic, cultural or linguistic deficiencies within the child.

The second phase coincided with an increasing concern among educators in the early 1960's for the equalization of educational opportunity. The educational difficulties which minority language children encountered were viewed mainly as a function of their deficiency in the language of the school combined with the cultural mismatch between home and school. Thus, specialized teachers were employed to help children acquire skills in the language of the school, and efforts (often only token) were made to broaden the cultural base of the school system and to generate respect for cultural diversity.

The third phase which is currently controversial in many countries concerns the extent to which minority children's mother tongue should be incorporated into the school curriculum. In many countries, the assumptions underlying the second phase of remedying the child's language deficiencies by specialized teaching have not been supported. Despite intensive teaching many groups of minority children still tended to perform several years be-

[1] The term «immigrant» is being used to include «migrant».

hind native norms in academic skills [8, 9]. Many investigators [1, 2, 8, 9] have argued that the educational difficulties of minority children are due to the fact that schools try to replace the linguistic, conceptual and cultural patterns that the child brings to the school rather than using these patterns as a basis for expansion of the child's skills. To this end, these investigators have argued that children's mother tongue should be used as a major medium of instruction in schools.

The intial results of such «language shelter» or «bilingual education» programs appear to support this argument. For example, HANSON's [6] longitudinal evaluation of a language shelter program for Finnish immigrant children in Sodertalje in Sweden has shown that children taught mainly through Finnish, with Swedish taught as a second language from grade 3, perform close to Swedish children in Finland on both Finnish and Swedish academic skills. This represents a considerable improvement on Finnish children's performance in Swedish-only programs.

A second example comes from ROSIER and FARELLA's [8] evaluation of the bilingual program for Navajo students at Rock Point in the United States. Prior to the institution of the bilingual program in 1971, students in the Rock Point school were two years behind US norms in English reading by the end of elementary school despite intensive teaching of English as a second language. The bilingual program involved delaying English reading instruction until Navajo reading skills were well-established and using each language for approximately 50% of the time in subsequent grades. By grade 6 the students in the bilingual program were performing slightly *above* US norms in English reading despite considerably less instructional time through the medium of English.

These are not isolated results. CUMMINS [2, 3] and TROIKE [11] have reviewed a variety of other studies showing similar effects. However, it should be noted that not all groups of minority children appear to need instruction in their first language to «survive» educationally. For example, CUMMINS [3] has reviewed studies carried out in Toronto, Canada in the late 1960's which show that most groups of minority language students born in Canada tended to perform *better* academically than native unilingual English students. The major exception to this trend was the Franco-Ontarian group whose academic performance (in English-only programs) was considerably inferior to that of unilingual English students.

It is clear that it is not possible to account for the academic failure of minority children in terms of home-school switching or lack of school system sensitivity *per se* because different groups exposed to similar educational conditions react in very different ways. Thus, there must be an interaction between the affective or cognitive characteristics which children bring to the school and the educational conditions.

An examination of the socio-cultural characteristics of minority groups that tend to perform poorly in school situations suggests that the attitudes of these groups towards the majority group and towards their own identity may be an important factor in interaction with educational treatment. Specifically, groups such as Finns in Sweden, North American Indians, Spanish-speaking children in the US, and Franco-Ontarians in Canada may tend to have ambivalent or negative feelings towards the majority culture and often also towards their own culture. This pattern has been documented for Finnish immigrants in Sweden by SKUT-NABB-KANGAS and TOUKOMAA [9]. For example, they quote HEYMAN's [7] conclusion:

«Many Finns in Sweden feel an aversion, and sometimes even hostility, towards the Swedish language and refuse to learn it under protest. There is repeated evidence of this, as there is, on the other hand, of Finnish people – children and adults – who are ashamed of their Finnish language and do not allow it to live and develop.»

The same pattern of ambivalence or hostility towards the majority cultural group and insecurity about one's own language and culture is found, to a greater or lesser extent, in other minority groups that have tended to perform poorly in school. For example, many Franco-Ontarians tend to regard their own dialect of French as inferior and to show low aspirations for social and economic mobility in the majority anglophone culture. In contrast, minority groups that do well in school tend to be highly motivated to learn the majority language and often (though not always) have a strong sense of pride in their own cultural background.

How does the pattern of parental ambivalence towards home and majority cultures get translated into school failure among minority language children? First, obviously, these same attitudes get transmitted (probably unconsciously) to the children so that they may not be strongly motivated either to maintain their original language or succeed in school. Teachers may contribute to this pattern either through low expectations of the child's ability to learn their mother tongue or through insensitivity towards the child's cultural background.

However, a second way in which the home environment affects the child's school performance is through the linguistic stimulation (or lack of it) that children receive at home. Because parents are ashamed of their cultural background or feel they speak an inferior dialect of their own language, they may not strongly encourage children to develop their verbal skills in the home. For example, they may communicate with the child only when necessary or use a mixture of their own and the local language in the home. Thus, children's abilities (i.e. the development of concepts and thinking skills in their mother tongue) may be poorly developed on entry to school. This leaves children without a conceptual basis for learning the local language in school and consequently they may achieve only low levels of proficiency (e.g. reading skills) in both languages. According to this interpretation, the success of language shelter programs derives from the fact that children and parents are encouraged to take pride in their own language and culture as well as from the fact that schools try to build on the cognitive and linguistic abilities which children bring to the school.

In the second part of this paper we will examine the relationship between children's school success and parents' ambivalence towards home and majority cultures in the case of Lebanese Arab families in southern Ontario, Canada.

A case study of Lebanese families in Ontario

This study was not a stringently controlled empirical study but rather relied on more or less informal interviews with parents and children as a source of information on attitudes towards Lebanese and Canadian cultures and languages as well as on interpersonal proficiency in Arabic and English. A sample of 30 children of Lebanese origin living in either Toronto or London, Ontario was chosen randomly from a group of about 90 of the Lebanese community. Only one child from each family was chosen. Parents were contacted and asked for permission to interview the child in both Arabic and English as part of a research project being undertaken by one of the authors (A. A.) at the Ontario Institute for Studies in Education. Four verbal tasks were devised to assess children's proficiency in Arabic in an interpersonal situation. The tasks were designed to minimize cognitive demands since the focus was on interpersonal Arabic skills. The four tasks were as follows:
1) The description of the plot of a story pictorially represented
2) Giving directions from the house to a familiar place
3) Oral translation from Arabic to English and from English to Arabic
4) Discoursing in Arabic for a minute about one of the following topics:
   a) why I like/dislike school
   b) my favourite sport or hobby
   c) my plans for the future.

These tests were administered informally, in the form of a game at the informant's home — to encourage spontaneous expression in a relaxed and natural setting, with parents providing the necessary moral support. The questions were formulated in Lebanese Arabic, and the children were instructed to use this dialect, their mother tongue, in solving the verbal tasks. All children were fluent in English and thus the English component of the third test presented no difficulty to them.

Performance on these tests was evaluated by the interviewer according to accepted criteria with a maximum of *five marks*. Scores on the four tasks were strongly related to each other.

Parents were extremely co-operative and anxious to discuss their children's progress in school as well as their own adaptation to Canadian life and their plans for the future. Usually parents spontaneously invited the investigator to examine the children's school report cards and to interpret the grading system used to assess and evaluate the academic achievement of the particular child. Notes were not taken by the investigator during the interview with parents as this would have interrupted the flow of conversation; instead, notes were written up after each interview according to preordained categories. Children's school progress (as judged from the report cards) was categorized on a five-point scale. Information was also entered on parents' and childrens' attitudes towards Lebanese and Canadian culture, language spoken at home, parents' competence in English, leisure time activities, educational level, year of arrival in Canada. We recognize that the information obtained in this informal way depends to a certain extent on the subjective interpretation of the interviewer; on the other hand, more formal methods of investigation would likely have elicited a much more cautious and possibly uncooperative response on the part of the parents.

Results

Before considering differences between children whose school progress was satisfactory and those who were performing poorly in school, we can note certain general

153

trends in the data. A large majority of parents (97%) had positive attitudes towards learning the English language but negative attitudes towards Canadian culture (83%). Many (57%) had made attempts to resettle in Lebanon but had returned to Canada. In contrast to their parents the children had positive attitudes towards both the Canadian culture (90%) and English language (100%). Most of the parents had a relatively low educational level. Only 30% of the fathers and 13% of mothers had received more than an elementary (grade 6) education. Watching television, visiting, and playing cards were the predominant leisure time activities of parents. Only nine of the children and three of the parents included reading among their leisure time activities. About half the parents had arrived in Canada within the past ten years, and about one of four within five years. A large majority (87%) of parents used Arabic predominantly at home while the remainder used both Arabic and English. Almost half (47%) the children used Arabic predominantly at home; the same percentage used both Arabic and English while the remainder used only English. Forty-three percent of the fathers and 26% of mothers had fluent English skills, 47% of fathers and 37% of mothers had restricted English skills and 10% of fathers and 37% of mothers had very inadequate or zero English skills.

In order to investigate which factors were associated with success in school, children whose school reports were average or above were compared with those whose reports were below average or unsatisfactory. Clearly no causal inferences are justified on the basis of differences between these groups *per se*. The causes of school failure among minority children are very complex indeed.

The data analysis showed that the «school success» group was significantly more likely than the «school failure» group to
— be female
— be Canadian born
— include «reading» in their leisure time activities
— have fluent Arabic proficiency
— use Arabic predominantly at home

- have positive attitudes towards the Arabic language and culture
- have parents whose attitudes towards the Arabic language and culture are positive
- have parents who are fluent in English
- have parents with more than an elementary education.

There were no differences between the groups in present age, parents' attitudes towards Canadian culture, parents' language at home, number of parents' attempts to return to live in Lebanon.

The pattern of results outlined above is generally consistent with that predicted on the basis of our analysis of school failure among minority groups in the first part of this paper. There it was suggested that ambivalence both towards the majority language and culture and the home language and culture was a major factor in the school failure of some groups of minority children. Although there was little variance in attitudes towards the English language and Canadian culture either among children or parents in the present sample, there was a clear relationship between children's school success and several variables related to confidence in Arabic identity. Also, parents' attitudes towards the majority society are probably reflected in their English proficiency and here again there were clear differences between the «school success» and «school failure» groups. The predominantly negative expressed attitudes of parents towards Canadian culture are probably directed at specific aspects of the culture and may stem from intergenerational conflict since a large majority of children expressed positive attitudes towards Canadian culture.

The finding that girls were more likely to maintain fluent Arabic proficiency than boys is consistent with TAFT and BODI's [10] results and is probably due to the fact that the girls tend to remain home with their mothers whose English skills tend to be relatively restricted and who thus use Arabic predominantly. It was also found that children living in the relatively large and concentrated Arab community in London tended to perform better in

Arabic than these living in isolation from Arab communities.

Another interesting finding was that 7 out of the 11 children not born in Canada showed poor Arabic proficiency (as well as poor school performance) despite the fact that according to their parents they spoke fluent Arabic upon their arrival in Canada. The fathers of all of these children showed either negative or ambivalent attitudes towards Arabic language and culture and all but one child and two mothers showed a similar pattern of attitudes.

The interplay of different factors in determing minority children's school success can be illustrated by four case studies. We have chosen two children who were performing well in school and two who were performing poorly.

Case studies of individual children

1. Mohamed. Mohamed was two years old upon arrival from Lebanon and is now seven. He was retained in grade 1 because of poor progress. He is the youngest of three brothers and four sisters who all, like him, are performing poorly in school. Mohamed's spoken English is somewhat restricted and Arabic proficiency is non-existent. The parents speak both Arabic and very restricted English at home and Mohamed speaks English only. His only leisure time activity is watching T.V. Father's attitude towards Arabic language and culture is negative while the mother's attitude is positive; however, she is dominated by the father. Mohamed's attitude towards Arabic language and culture is negative to the point of wanting to be called «Mike».

Both parents are unskilled and have low levels of education. Initially they were motivated to emigrate by poverty in Lebanon. Both were receiving minimum wage in Canada and were forced to work long hours; the father often worked at two jobs. Chronic fatigue on the part of both parents led to marital tension. This was made worse by crowded living conditions. Upon arriving in Canada they had no money and lived with relatives; this involved 20 people in a house designed for five. Currently, the family of 10 are living in a small two-bedroom house.

The parents' roles followed traditional lines; the husband was free to go drinking and dancing whereas the mother was expected to do housework and take care of her eight children in addition to working in a factory.

2. Hamid. Hamid was born in London and is seven years old. He is the oldest of a family of three boys. His school progress was «below average». Arabic is spoken at home.

The father emigrated in 1960 at the age of 18, motivated by poverty at home. He has a grade 9 eduation. Initially unskilled he is now a hair stylist and works 12 hours a day seven days a week. His objective is to get rich before he is 40 at which time he intends to retire in Lebanon. He tried to return to live in Lebanon on three previous occasions but always returned to Canada. His English is fluent; watching T.V. is his only leisure time activity.

The mother is 25 years old with very little education and virtually no competence in English. She emigrated in 1970 at the time she married, aged 16. She feels frustrated and isolated from the world because her husband is seldom at home and she must stay alone with the children. The result is tension and conflict at home.

3. Leila. Born in London, 14 years old and doing extremely well in school. She has an excellent command of spoken Arabic and speaks Arabic at home. She has positive attitudes towards both Arabic and Canadian language and culture. She enjoys reading, music, and theatre.

The father is 47 years old and emigrated in 1958. He has a grade 9 education. Initially an unskilled labourer he became a carpenter. He reads a lot, plays chess and spends most of his leisure time at home. He takes his family with him when he visits. He is proud of Arabic language and culture and encourages his children to be likewise. His attitude, towards Canadian language and culture is positive.

The mother is also 47 years old. She has a grade 5 education and emigrated in 1962 when she married. She is a dress-maker but stays at home and weaves in her spare time. Marital relationship is excellent and mother participates in every decision. She would like to return to live in Lebanon but is content to wait.

4. Khawala. Born in London, Khawala is now 11 years old and doing very well in school. She has an excellent command of spoken Arabic as well as reading skills in Arabic developed as a result of instruction from her mother. She seemed relaxed and happy.

The father is 32 years old. He emigrated in 1968 one year after his wife who sent for him. He has a grade 5 education. Initially unskilled he is now a welder. He works hard but always stays cheerful and plays with the children and takes them places. He is concerned about their education and proud of their academic achievement. Marital relationship is excellent. He allows wife to run the affairs of the household and respects her decisions.

The mother is 39 years old and has a grade 5 education. She has continued her self-education and is mentally sharp and confident. She manages to run a type of nursery of babysitting service in her house. She is proud of Arabic language and culture and communicates this enthusiasm to her children. The family had some initial problems of adjustment to Canada but overcame these and now own their own house. Both parents' English skills are somewhat restricted.

These case studies illustrate the fact that the same factors that determine children's educational adjustment in a unilingual majority language setting are also operative in an immigrant setting. Harmonious family relations and parents who spend time interacting with their children are important factors. However, in an immigrant setting the economic, socio-cultural and linguistic adaptation problems of parents often militate against harmonious marital relations, with consequent detrimental effects on children's adjustment.

The families interviewed in the present study gave ample evidence of isolation and loneliness deriving both from their inability to gain full entry into Canadian society (as a result of linguistic and cultural factors) and their lack of integration into a cohesive Lebanese community. As a result of this isolation immigrants often begin looking for an escape route. The only escape route they find is a return to Lebanon and thus they plan to work hard for several years to save enough money to live a comfortable life in Lebanon. However, in order to earn this money it is often necessary to hold two jobs. The chronic fatigue and psychological pressure that results from this overwork negatively affects marital relationships and this familia tension engulfs the children and disrupts their emotional and educational development. In addition, the fatigue of parents affects the quality of the time they do spend with their children. Thus, children will often be exposed to relatively little linguistic or intellectual interaction in the home.

The children who do well in school are those whose parents overcome their own adjustment problems to living in Canada and who spend the time to encourage children to perform well in school. These parents also tend to encourage their children to maintain Arabic language proficiency and to identify with the Arabic culture. These children give the impression of belonging to two cultures whereas those who are failing in school give the impression of being between two cultures and belonging to neither.

Helping immigrant children's educational adjustment

Many of the factors affecting the educational adjustment of recently-arrived immigrant children derive from the economic and social difficulties that parents face in adjusting to a new country. The ability of school personnel to alter these economic and social determinants is naturally limited. However, our analyses have suggested that an additional factor in the school adjustment of minority children is the «bicultural ambivalence» which many parents and children experience. School personnel have in the past contributed directly to this ambivalence by undermining children's confidence in their own identity and by trying to eradicate their proficiency in their mother tongue. Despite the fact that these abuses are now widely acknowledged, more subtle versions are still prevalent in many school systems.

In terms of the analysis presented in this paper, school personnel should attempt to reinforce children's and parents' pride in their own cultural heritage since children with low self-esteem also tend to have little confidence in their learning ability. Parents should also be encouraged to spend time communicating with their children in order to promote conceptual development.

In summary, although broader economic and social determinants of minority children's poor educational performance are largely beyond their control, school personnel have an important role to play both by encouraging children to take pride in their own language and cultural background, and also by advising parents of the *educational and cognitive advantages* of strongly promoting children's linguistic development in the home. A major effort should be undertaken by educational authorities to correct the misconceptions of teachers, psychologists and parents regarding mother tongue maintenance for minority language children since these misconceptions can contribute directly to the bicultural ambivalence which is associated with children's school failure and bad mental health.

Bibliography

1 COHEN, A.D., SWAIN, M.: Bilingual education: The immersion model in the North American context. In: J.E. Alatis, K. Twaddell (Eds.): English as a Second Language in Bilingual Education. TESOL, Washington, D.C., 1976.

2 CUMMINS, J.: Linguistic interdependence and the educational development of bilingual children. Review of Educational Research 49, 222 – 251, 1979.

3 CUMMINS, J.: The language and culture issue in the education of minority language children. Interchange, 1980 (in press).

4 CUMMINS, J.: Psychological assessment of immigrant children: Logic or intuition? Journal of Multilingual and Multicultural Development, 1980 (in press).

5 *European Commission.* Activities for the education and vocational training of migrant workers and their families in the European Community. Contribution to the Standing Conference of European Ministers of Education, 1978.

6 HANSON, G.: The position of the second generation of Finnish immigrants in Sweden: The importance of education in the home language to the welfare of second generation immigrants. Paper presented at the symposium on the position of the second generation of Yugoslav immigrants in Sweden, Split, October 1979.

7 HEYMAN, A.: Invandrarbarn: Slutrapport. Stockholms Invandrarnamd, Stockholm, 1973.

8 ROSIER, P., FARELLA, M.: Bilingual education at Rock Point – some early results. TESOL Quarterly 10, 379 – 388, 1976.

9 SKUTNABB-KANGAS, T., TOUKOMAA, P.: Teaching migrant children's mother-tongue and learning the language of the host country in the context of the socio-cultural situation of the migrant family. The Finnish National Commission for UNESCO, Helsinki, 1976.

10 TAFT, R., BODI, M.: A study of language competence and first language maintenance in bilingual children. International Review of Applied Psychology, 1979 (in press).

11 TROIKE, R.: Research evidence for the effectiveness of bilingual education. NABE Journal 3, 13 – 24, 1978.

Chapter 9

The invisible ones:
A double role of women in the current European migrations

Mirjana Morokvasić

There is a considerable literature in various disciplines on the ‹temporary› European migrations[1]. Yet the migration of women has attracted the interest of relatively few researchers and not until recently. Indeed, in the beginning, the migratory movements were predominantly male and the slightly unbalanced ratio has persisted in some receiving countries. Women who emigrated mainly from the countries of the Mediterranean basin (but also in the case of the UK from former colonies overseas, the West Indies and the Indian subcontinent) were considered to be dependants, accompanying the male migrants. They have been referred to implicitly either as wives or mothers. These, however, were supposed to be within the framework of labour migration and its temporary character, less important and more trivial issues than, for instance, matters concerning the employment and development to which the issue of migrant women was seldom related. Thereby only their reproductive function was either directly acknowledged [23] or indirectly considered to be of relevance to the possible stabilization of migrants in the receiving countries (i. e. by transforming the temporary migrations into permanent ones [8]). But migrant women remained invisible (or not

---

[1] By ‹temporary› migration I mean the flow of workers in the 60s and 70s mainly from Europe's periphery to the centre. For a substantial number of these workers migration has become permanently temporary in character: i. e. a permanent life style and long term enterprise, with the insecure status of an officially temporary or guest-worker.

visible enough) as economically active protagonists of the migration of labour.

Migrant women may legally be «dependants»: the head of the household according to the legislation or the mores in most countries is a man[2]. I want to stress, however, that legal or customary dependency does not necessarily entail economic inactivity. In the case of migrant women it is rather the opposite: married migrant women are those who have been increasingly economically active.

Though the official statistical evidence is deficient, I shall try in this chapter to draw attention to what the specific feature of immigrant women in contemporary Europe is: their combined productive and reproductive function and thereby their double contribution to the countries of immigration, demographic and economic. From the woman's own perspective this is often called «a double burden» and many people would argue that women in the receiving countries are in the same situation. This is only overlooking the nature of the double burden for immigrant women, forgetting that they live in conditions rarely shared by the indigenous population and work in sectors and jobs where only a minority of indigenous women accept. There is also statistical evidence that native women manage to a greater degree to leave the labour market for some time in order to bring up their children[3] (see graph 3).

The conditions under which migrant women work and live make them more vulnerable and more prone to bear the consequences of overwork, and very often isolation. I shall give an account of these conditions as evidenced in current research on migrant women and briefly point to some of the effects on women as individuals.

[2] Which leads to sex discrimination at various levels. One affecting migrants in Britain is the present regulation which does not allow foreign born women to bring in their husbands or fiancés.

[3] One has to point out, however, that by leaving the labour market for a few years women are, in the long run, losers. A professional break means difficulties of reintegration, diminished chances for upgrading and maintenance of low wages. Women are being penalized for performing the most essential function in the society, the reproductive function.

1. Sources of information

This is a subject in which stereotypes and clichés often tend to replace knowledge and where emotions override facts, and it is even more difficult for a researcher to find appropriate evidence because its lack and insufficiency were precisely two of the reasons for stereotyping. In research on migration of women one has to combine information from various sources: official statistics, i.e. stock and flow data on the subject[4], other research on the subject or related subjects, direct accounts of migrants' lives as they themselves experience it. All these sources suffer from inadequacies and deficiencies.

A deficiency like under-numeration has been pointed to in a recent official document on Labour Supply and Migration in Europe [24]. It refers to studies by DRETAKIS [13] and SOPEMI [37], which both indicate the under-estimation of the number of migrants in the two principal immigration countries, Federal Republic of Germany (West Germany) and France. It is most likely to affect the female migrants who, if they immigrated outside the rather strict regulations for family reunion, would be the most inclined to conceal their presence.

The official Annual Reports of the OECD on labour migration (SOPEMI) do not mention women except in connection with families and children. In the outline for specific country reports women appear only under a separate sub-heading: ‹special categories: youths, women, frontier and seasonal workers›.

The French statistics on flows of migrants split up only demographic information by sex, while the professional information is not broken down by the sex of the migrant [3].

A very interesting labour survey [38] can be doubly use-

---

[4] Flow data provide information on the numbers and characteristics of the migrants at the time of migration; census stock data show the numbers who have remained in the country up to the time of the census and their characteristics after having resided in the country for some time.

less for locating migrant women professionally: information is not broken down by sex and covers only industrial and commercial firms of 10 persons and more, i.e. the organized sector of the economy where migrant women are less likely to be found. The definition of work and employment in that survey is in itself revealing of the status and consideration women's work officially has. In some sociological and other literature on migration, women are hardly mentioned [5, 19], or are presented in a stereotyped way [11, 12, 29].

Many researchers have, within the general topic of migration, dealt with female migrants too [28, 10], particularly in the FRG, but little attempt was made to analyse and define the specificity of female migrants as opposed to male migrants. And even now there is not much consensus on whether research on migrant women should be carried out separately [25].

Increasingly more attention has been paid to female migration since the mid-seventies onward[5]. Some draw attention to the until then little analysed topics of work [4, 30] or struggle [4, 44], hardly mentioned before in connection with migrant women. In two recent articles SHEILA ALLEN has analysed the condition of immigrant women in Britain [1, 2] and AMRIT WILSON has described the condition of the same women in a recent book based on indepth interviews [44]. Her account, as well as the extremely well documented survey by TABOADA and LEVI [39] focus on culture and tradition within the new context, the framework that has always been considered the most appropriate as an approach to the study migrant women. There is other research now being carried on or not yet published [9, 31]. The role and position of migrant women has been studied in relation to issues of development [12] and a theory of female migration in developing countries has been suggested [42].

There is much debate about whether «women» can be a category of analysis or not [25]. It is certain however, that

[5] The research and publications mentioned here are examples only.

unless migrant women are studied and approached separately, many issues considered traditionally to be related more or less exclusively to them, would remained unanalysed and unanswered. These issues, however, in the end appear to be universal and therefore of concern to both genders. Besides, the totality of their experience would not be apprehended otherwise. This does not mean that women would be viewed as isolated individuals independently of their social context (i.e. class or ethnicity or their relationship to man). On the contrary it is precisely within that social framework that the condition of women − in this case immigrant women − has to be assessed.

2. The presence of women and their double function

The presence of women and the sex specific migration flows depend on a number of factors which never function disjointly. Though individual motivations of migrants have received much attention in literature and have served as a basis for a number of typologies [39, 41], migration cannot be understood and analysed in terms of individual motives only, but also in terms of the operating social forces which create conditions in both the rich capitalist countries and in the developing areas that are becoming increasingly dependent on them. Labour demand and wage differentials, followed by various immigration policies can encourage or restrain the migration of women. But the relative impact of economic factors on emigration of women has to be balanced against other social forces stemming from the specific conditions of social reproduction in the emigration areas, often involving, for women, sexist oppression and hard, unremunerated labour. These are the conditions that many migrant women flee from, joining the cities where for the first time they can have cash in hand and often more control of their lives and their work.

There is no doubt that migrants and frequently women experience their own emigration as an individual decision (or as an individual decision of their husband or of their family), originating in outstandingly specific and personal situations. These have, however, little explanatory value for the analysis of migratory movements when they reach their current size and importance in Europe.

About one third of all the immigrant population in Europe are women. A rough estimate would be about three million [43], if one relies on the official figures of the beginning of the seventies (which are thought to be underestimated, as we have shown above).

2.1. Demographic contribution[6]

The knowledge of the demographic structure, i.e. age and relative proportion of married versus single persons of each sex is of more importance (than the global size) for understanding the possible impact of migrants on the overall population structure. For example, an overall excess of males, if single, would complement the structure of the native population, which everywhere in the west has an excess of females over males. ‹This would allow some native women to marry who otherwise would not› [24]. On the other hand, the presence of immigrant women of reproductive age will have implications for the fertility rates and for the natural increase of the population.

The data in the table below are extracted from the above-mentioned UN Report on Labour Supply and Migration in Europe [24] and represent the proportion of married persons per sex, country of migration and citizenship (Table I).

Compared with data a decade earlier, based on census figures around 1960, French and Swedish data on aliens' marital status show little change, while German and Swiss data show an increase in the proportion of married persons

[6] Only one aspect of the reproductive function will be presented here: the production of human beings, child bearing and thereby reproduction of the labour force. It is understood, however, that reproduction includes the socialization of the children and the maintenance of the members of the household by the accomplishment of unpaid labour in the household. It will be discussed later.

Table I. Married persons per sex (%), 1970.

	Males		Females	
	Citizens	Aliens	Citizens	Aliens
France (1975)	65	66	53	62
Sweden	61	62	53	67
FRG	71	68	60	64
Switzerland	64	67	59	62

of both sexes. This means that the situation at the beginning of the 70s, when migration started getting stabilizied, is very much the same in the four countries: *the majority of migrants of both sexes are married.* These are the average ratios for all nationalities. However, they can vary greatly across the countries between nationalities and for one and the same nationality. For instance, there are twice as many married Yugoslav women per 100 married Yugoslav men in Sweden as in Germany, (89 and 41 respectively). The

Table II. Birth rate and natural increase of citizens and aliens 19660 – 1975 (rates per 1000 population).

Country and period		Birth-rates		Natural increase	
		Citizens	Aliens	Citizens	Aliens
France	1962 – 1964	18.2	14.4	6.9	4.4
	1965 – 1969	17.3	13.9	6.2	4.6
	1970 – 1974	16.9	13.4	6.1	5.9
Germany, Federal Republic of	1961	18.0	20.3	6.8	14.5
	1967 – 1969	15.9	23.4	3.5	20.4
	1970 – 1974	10.7	24.3	– 1.7	21.8
Sweden	1967 – 1969	13.8	28.0	3.2	25.4
	1970 – 1974	13.1	25.2	2.4	22.5
Switzerland	1960 – 1964	17.3	26.4	7.1	21.4
	1965 – 1969	15.3	30.1	5.0	26.1
	1970 – 1974	12.0	25.9	2.0	22.3

Source: Labour Supply and Migration in Europe, UN, ECE, Geneva, 1979, Table II.32, p. 126.
Note: In France the definition of alien at birth is quite different from other countries and had it been the same as in the FRG the birth rate among aliens would have been 19 instead of 13.9 in 1969.

meaning of that discrepancy can be understood once the non-married persons are defined[7].

Because of their favourable age structure immigrants have low death rates and high crude birth rates[8]. In each receiving country immigrant women have thus contributed to compensating for the falling or stagnating birth rates [24] (Table II).

The figures for foreigners represent children who at birth acquired foreign citizenship, usually if both parents are alien. But the table indicates that these birth rates are sometimes double that of the citizens'. The more favourable age structure cannot however explain this discrepancy completely. Comparison per age of mother for different nationalities, in Sweden and the FRG, shows that migrant women have children earlier than the Swedish or German, but those nationalities with particularly high birth rates, Turks and Greeks, continue having children at a later age than the native women (see graphs 1 and 2 below).

This information is to be linked with data on the economic participation of women, which will be discussed in the next section. Graph 3 indicates clearly the discrepancy in activity rates of German and foreign women. The latter remain active during their reproductive age.

2.2. Economic activity of migrant women in Europe

The comparative data for all immigration countries are based on the population censuses of the 1970s. The table below is extracted from the above-mentioned UN Report, for the population of age 15 and over (the more recent data

---

[7] This could be an indication of the presence of migrants *with their spouses* in Sweden, while in Germany it is usually interpreted by the presence of a large number of single Yugoslav women [24]. However non-married persons are not all single and the category ‹other than married› includes in the FRG also a large number of separated and divorced persons, always higher among migrant women. They could be heads of families remaining in Yugoslavia, mothers whose children are in Yugoslavia, or single mothers.

[8] The number of live births per 1000 persons.

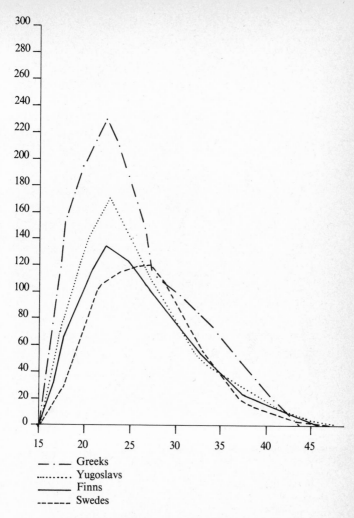

Graph 1. *Sweden 1976.* Age specific birth rates by citizenship.

Source: Befolknigsförändringar DEL 3, 1976, SCB, Stockholm.

are available for some countries but their comparability is questionable on the European scale).

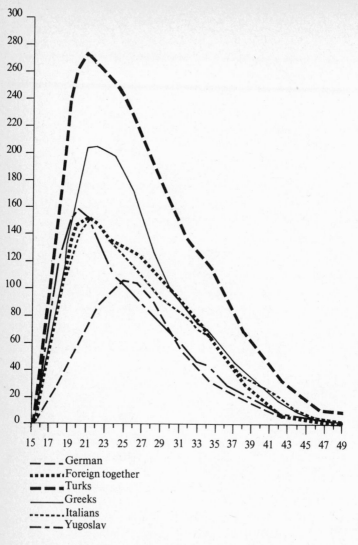

Graph 2. *FRG 1976.* Age specific birth rates by citizenship. (Rates per 1000.)

Foreigners have higher birth rates than the Germans.

Source: Ausgewählte Strukturdaten für Ausländer 1976, Statistisches Bundesamt, Wiesbaden.

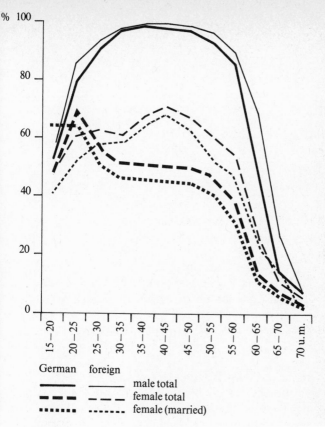

Graph 3. *FRG 1976*. Age specific activity rates of Germans and foreigners per sex.

Married or not, immigrant women do not drop out of the labour force during their reproductive age.

Source: Stand und Entwicklung der Erwerbstätigkeit, Statistisches Bundesamt, Wiesbaden.

It is well known that immigrants have much higher activity rates[9] than the native population. It is however

[9] Activity rate is the number of persons employed per hundred persons of the same group.

Table III. Activity rates of alien and citizen women in % (aged 15 and over).

Country of residence	Alien women		Citizen women	
	1960	1970	1960	1970
Austria	33.4	58.9	45.4	38.7
Belgium	26.4	30.9	25.5	28.0
France	27.9	31.1	36.4	39.0
FRG	50.6	71.6	41.0	37.3
Luxembourg	35.3	33.1	26.0	23.1
Netherlands	25.5	33.9	22.9	25.7
Sweden	48.9	43.2	32.3	36.9
Switzerland	70.0	64.3	31.4	37.8
United Kingdom	43.2	47.2	37.2	42.3

usually understood that this discrepancy concerns men only or men in particular. Indeed, differences between migrant men and indigenous men exist and they vary from as low as 2% only, as in Belgium or the UK, to as high as 17%, as in West Germany, where migrant men's activity rate is 94.4% versus 77.8% for German men. However, the differences in activity rates between foreign women and native women are even higher, as shown in Table III below.

The figures in this table suggest the following comments:

— In some countries like the FRG and Switzerland immigrant women have double the activity rate of the native women (so that they are even more economically active than the German or Swiss population, both sexes taken together). In other countries like Austria and Sweden differences are still considerable.

— The activity rates of migrant women in Austria and the FRG, two important immigration countries, have substantially increased over a period of 10 years, while in the same time native women's activity rates have decreased the most in these two countries.

— In all other countries the increase is equal for both migrants and natives except in Luxembourg where they both decreased and in Switzerland where a very high activity rate of migrant women decreased from 70% to 64%.

- The outstanding exception is France, where immigrant women have lower participation rates than French women. This is usually explained by the French migration policy, more favourable to family migration than to the migration of workers, whereby the family members (‹personnes à charge›) were understood to be *inactive*. In other words, ‹family› and workers are supposed to be two necessarily separate entities and alternative, exclusive statuses for migrant women.
- It is interesting that this increase in economic rates in Europe covers the period characterized by increased ‹family reunion› of migrants, in particular in Germany where, for instance, the number of married persons registered increased considerably (as we have shown above in Table II).

This leads us to question the nature of the so-called ‹family immigration›[10], and define thereby one of the reasons for under-estimation of migrant women's activity rates in certain countries. Other reasons are in the structure of the labour market and the place migrant women occupy in it rather than in the migration process.

Before immigration to France was stopped TAPINOS [40] drew attention to the ‹profound transformation› of family immigration and suggested that a number of entering spouses were becoming active in the labour force. MOROK-VASIC [32] analysed the French flow data and concluded that there was an increase in the activity rates of *married* migrant women. The fact that the French government had temporarily suspended family migration in 1977, because family members increasingly applied for a labour permit,

[10] In France the family immigration channel is open to ‹spouses of migrants residing in France, their daughters under 21 and their sons under 17›. Another immigration channel is ‹permanent workers›. The denomination of those two channels suggests that immigration to France was supposed to be permanent in nature and family in character, which in reality it was not. Family reunion applied more to migrants of some origins and less to others. As for its permanent nature, the French government had brought both channels to a halt in 1974 and 1977 and introduced measures for inciting migrants to return (bonus schemes).

is an indirect proof that family migration in France became a cover-up for the immigration of labour, and this precisely in those sectors where it could without much difficulty remain invisible.

This is one source of possible under-estimation of the activity rates of migrant women in France. There are others. Speaking of activity rates, two other points are not clear: it is not always known or considered how many hours one has to work to be recorded as employed. Thus in the UK, for instance, it is well known that about half the women economically active work part-time. This is not the case for migrant women in the same country, who are more likely to work full-time, as shown by SHEILA ALLEN [2]. This author also gives evidence of the proportion of women of child-bearing age at work, which is higher for immigrant than for native women.

In France, a study carried out by TABOADA and LEVI [39] on migrant women indicates a 53% activity and in my study of Yugoslav women 93% were active in the labour force. Data in my study of Yugoslavs indicate that half of the women in France are in the informal sector while only two-thirds in Germany and Sweden are in this sector. And it is in France that the activity rates of Yugoslav women are officially registered as the lowest of the three countries — though the highest among the immigrant women there.

Many forms of economic activity are excluded from official definitions: this is the case with family business, homeworking, working in services, subcontracted firms etc. In some parts of the informal sector men can also be employed illegally but there are many others, completely ‹feminized› (and dependent on foreigners) which escape recording. In domestic service in France, for instance, there is an estimate that about one third of the workers are not declared [15]. Women working in several types of production, a few hours in each, are also excluded from being recorded. A cleaner working a few hours at several places may remain all her life officially a dependent housewife. It is generally assumed that ‹she does not work, she only cleans›. 20% of my sample of Yugoslavs had two or three

174

jobs while only *one* was declared. In the garment industry in France in small sweatshops based on sub-contracting, a man is usually declared while his wife (and possibly a daughter or a visiting cousin) are employed as well. In this case the unpaid labour of the female family members (as in other types of family business) is necessary to meet the tight profit margins (or to increase them)[11]. This sexist division of labour in the production units can easily remain invisible because it only reproduces the division of roles in the family, where the man is the breadwinner and the woman a dependant, and which is accepted as a *norm* in the society. The reality is often different however.

This information may run counter to some widely spread stereotypes about migrant women as ‹inactive› and dependants. In spite of that and for the above mentioned reasons it is necessary to consider the data in Table III as an *under-estimation* of the size of the participation of migrant women in the labour market.

The usual interpretations of migrant women's alleged inactivity in terms of ‹cultural› and ‹traditional› constraints on some women on working outside the home may play some part in perpetuating the stereotype. But the real influence of tradition and culture is, however, very uncertain, and a necessity to work may be given priority regardless of cultural norms. This occurs in particular when kin and other community ties are not revived in the new setting because of scattered housing accommodation. In fact, precisely these women, Algerians in France, Pakistanis in Britain are most likely to be allocated to invisible work. The options for jobs being more restricted for them, they will get those that will enable them to maintain intact, or disrupt the least, the norms of ‹good mother and wife›.

In reality, they combine home-work, housekeeping (‹concierge›, ‹Hauswart›), various cleaning jobs, with child

[11] A recent study [17] in Germany indicates that one out of ten women working with their husband in a family firm has no contract (while he has). Immigrant women enter this kind of situation to a much greater extent, proportionally.

care and maintenance of their own household. Because they, in fact, never leave the family cell to work outside, they are bound to have less control over the returns of their work and the value of their work is considered lower.

There are, of course, women who genuinely do *not* work outside their household. In some national groups they are the majority. Again it is not the cultural background that entirely determines whether they will work or not. These women are dependants or ‹supported persons› from the administrative point of view. The unpaid labour they perform at home and the upbringing of their children is not considered as productive work and women are in economic dependence on their husband. In this respect, theoretically there is no difference between migrant women and native women [18]. However, the experience of migrant women is different: many studies have pointed to the complete isolation and lack of movement of these women, confined to their overcrowded flats and with little knowledge of the outside world [34]. They have the constant responsibility of their young children which, back in their home villages, was shared by other kin or neighbours. This makes their physical isolation worse. As AMRIT WILSON [44] points out: «Weakened by the separation from their families, suffering often the loss of mother, sisters and close friends, these Asian women find themselves in a strange, unknown society. The realization that this is a racist society . . . accentuates their loneliness and their isolation makes it harder for them to fight against racism» (p. 21).

Some of these women, however, become increasingly aware that their role and function in the countries of immigration is not that of mere dependants, as expressed by this Algerian woman in France: ‹Work outside the home, impossible! When you have 4, 5, 6, 9 children! I bring them up. For whom? Not for myself, for them (the French employers). *They* will need them. I make them big and strong, so that they can work hard . . . And if one day I do not feed my husband, if I don't wash his clothes — he will not go to the factory. *They* will need him. It is the work I do for *them. They* should pay me, too› [14].

3. Working and living conditions

It was argued above that migrant women's specific feature was the «double burden», their combined economic and family role. It was suggested that the combined exercise of the two roles was much more frequent among the immigrant than among the native women. Now we shall see in what circumstances and in what conditions this double function is being performed.

Migrant women in the European countries live and work under conditions closest to those of the working class. But the constraints on the choices open to them are so great that they often appear to be marginal to it.

It is impossible to engage in an analysis of the conditions in which they live. Only the most characteristic features will be briefly outlined here.

3.1. Housing conditions

Bad housing conditions affect women more than men because they either spend more time at home − if not all the time − or they must cope with the limited space and few utensils at their disposal. A recent book by BERTIEN VAN MANEN is the most vivid presentation so far of the constraints women have to cope with at home [27]. In my study, the worst housing conditions appear to be in France and the best in Sweden. Some families lived for years in one single room without any sanitary facilities: ‹The worst for me were the winters: everything was so damp and I had to heat water in a pot on a little gas stove and give the children a bath in the cold kitchen in front of the electric fire, which we could not leave on for long because it was so expensive.›

There are studies indicating that migrants live in worse housing conditions than the natives and still pay higher prices [16]. The rent for a damp, smelly room in a Parisian ‹hotel meublé› for foreigners was higher than a better lodging in better parts of the town.

But some migrants may not have their own place at all.

Married couples used to live in hostels provided by the firms and meant to house single workers. A husband and wife could thereby be separated for years while still working in the same town. Usually very strict rules are observed in these hostels and visits are not allowed. Residents have hardly any privacy because they share rooms with one or more other women. How disruptive for the life of the family or couple or a single person this can be is obvious and one need not search for evidence in scientific studies. This evidence exists [26]. Some authors however offer cultural explanations for psychological disturbances and even assume a ‹pre-morbid› condition in the homeland [6].

For home-workers and workers in garment sweatshops, home and workplace are on the same premises. D., a Yugoslav woman in my study, worked all day long in a laundry on the outskirts of Paris. She lived with a married couple of Yugoslavs who had a little workshop in a little two-roomed flat. Three machinists were working there and when D. came home she joined in and worked until after midnight. ‹Even if I wanted to rest I couldn't: my bed was there with the machines.›

3.2. Working conditions

Migrant women enter those sectors of the economy which traditionally employ women, like services, textile and garment industries, the modern electronic industry. Because of no skill, low or inadequate skill they are assigned to jobs at the bottom of the hierarchy with little prospect of promotion or they are employed in jobs where upgrading is virtually impossible.[12] Because they are also migrants their situation is unstable, subject to fluctuations in the economy, and like their male counterparts they are considered as interchangeable commodities in the process of production.

Yugoslav women work longer hours than men. 20% of

[12] Once they master the fastest way of doing a routine task, they may be put on another similar routine task, but there is no mobility upwards.

them hold two, even three jobs and still their wages are much lower than men's. The majority approve of these differences in wages because they consider men's work as harder and more difficult than women's [31]. Only in Sweden is sex differential in wages negligible as regards equal jobs. These facts are confirmed by the official German data on wages: Repräsentativuntersuchung [33], for instance, indicated that in 1972 65% of migrant men earned 1200 DM and more while only 15% of migrant women did, and that 52% of migrant women earned less than 1000 DM while only 9% of migrant men did (see also [30]).

This wage differential has persisted over the years since in 1976, for instance, foreign women were still right at the botton of the wage ladder and only 1.8% reached the level of *1800* DM and more per month against 26.7% of German men, 10.3% of foreign men and 5.7% of German women [36]. (The lower wages of the latter were due to their part-time employment.) Provided that German women work part-time (the reason usually given to explain the high sex wage differential in that country) and knowing that migrant women work full-time, this puts the latter even lower on the wage ladder than is officially observed.

Bangladeshi women in the garment industry could earn as low as 17p per hour in 1979 [21] or 25p a piece [44].

The low wages are due to no skill, low skill, inadequate or unrecognized skill and to the allocation of migrant women to those sectors which are historically feminine and where the wages have always been low.

In France over a third of migrant women are in services, a third are mostly unskilled workers in industry and others are employees. In the FRG, services account for less than one third and industry for more than one third. In Sweden, 31.2% work in services, 35.2% in factories and the rest are divided between office work and ‹other› (which could be, for instance, work in hospitals).

‹In the UK, migrant women are more definitely concentrated than native women into a narrow range of jobs as cleaners, hospital domestics, canteen assistants, semi- and unskilled work in manufacturing industries and among the

179

lowest paid women with poor working conditions and often shift work> [2].

The migrant women I surveyed often started, both in France and Germany, at below the minimum wages mentioned in their contracts. The employer usually justified this by a period of apprenticeship which could go on for several months for a ‹skill› that could be picked up in a few hours. There was little women could do about it because they were tied by a short-term contract which they expected to extend. Any complaint on their part could seriously endanger the prospect of extending their stay in the country.

Low wages and piecework combined are the best incentives to working long hours. 25% of the women in my sample declared working over 12 hours a day, some up to 14 – 16 hours. This mostly applied to workers in hotels and restaurants in Germany or in the garment industry and services in France. Many worked on Saturdays to complement the low wages [31].

Some who were put on a ‹shorter week› relied on occasional prostitution to complement the low wages, always hoping that this was just temporary and that they would be able to lead a normal life again when they found another job.

Working full-time and overtime can then be considered to be the dominant pattern among migrant women and not exceptional. Again, long working hours are the characteristic of sectors where legislation is difficult to implement and control impossible. 66% of the Portugese domestic servants in France work more than 60 hours a week, which is much above the legal upper limit [4, 15]. The working conditions of some of these domestic workers in France are not very different from those of their predecessors in the 19th century [22].

A recent study of immigrant women in France shows that not only do they work full time (40 hours a week) but some, because they work at several places, work 60 – 80 hours a week ([39] p. 98). Their alternative is cleaning or factory work, both hard and tiring. The authors stress that they accept it with resignation and as a necessity. Only the housekeepers are satisfied ‹because it enables them to remain with their children›.

‹I lived in a tiny room which was no more than a bed and cupboard. Sometimes I used to work 90 hours a week. I would go up at midnight, fall on my bed and wake at 7 o'clock with the alarm. I had the impression I had not slept at all, telling myself you should get undressed and get into bed. I was so tired. I was no more a person, but could be anything ... ([39] p. 159).

In her study of Asian women in Britain, WILSON [44] points to the humiliation to which these women were subjected by their white employers. The wages they got were lower than those of white women for the same job. More often no white women worked in those jobs: «You don't want to come and work here, love, we won't be able to pay the sort of wages that'll keep you here» (English girls are being told by employers [44] p. 64).

WILSON quotes from an official report about work conditions in a factory: «. . . conditions in the factory constitute definite health and safety hazards. All the machines were archaic with no proper safeguards, e.g. guillotines, spring making machines and other similar machines with a cutting edge had no automatic stopping device . . . The machines in the spring department gave off choking fumes and a grey pall seemed to hang over the department . . . about 90 per cent of the work force are coloured, many of whom cannot speak English . . . I was not allowed to speak to the workers. It seems that their trade union membership is not allowed by the management» ([44] p. 53).

Conclusion

Women from the underdeveloped parts of Europe and the Indian subcontinent came to Western European countries either as single workers or following their husband's migration or most often they took part in a joint economic project of migration.

It was argued in this paper that, whatever their official status, these women cannot be considered as ‹supported› or ‹dependants›, as they often are in research and in policy, where reference is made to them in the framework of the family. With their high fertility rates they contribute to the natural population increase in the countries of immigration. They bring up their children without any kin support, often in isolation and in appalling housing conditions. These children will in turn replace them and their husbands in the years to come in the labour market of the immigration countries. There is evidence that a large proportion of second generation immigrants do not get any qualifications at all.

These women remain active in the labour force during their reproductive years to a much greater extent than the native women do. Their economic activity often takes place in sectors where they largely remain unrecorded and invisible.

Though a large proportion of migrant women live isolated lives and confined to their ‹four walls›, the majority faces the constant contradictions and difficulties of combining their family and their social-professional role. Some resolve this conflict by separating themselves from their children for several years, as shown in recent surveys of the Yugoslavs [7, 31], but further conflicts then arise in strong feelings of guilt and psychological problems aroused by the separation. Others could take advantage of day care facilities, were these sufficiently provided. But this is not the case and children are left to members of kin, child-minders, neighbours and even alone.

Migrant women are overworked, they have the lowest wages, the worst housing, they work in bad conditions and without safety and often have no job security or other fringe benefits.

It can be argued that the specificity of migrant women's condition lies in *combination* of their status of woman, of a worker and of a migrant. They carry a tripple burden of their sex, their class and their ethnic origin. This means that *as women* they perform the unremunerated work at home but as immigrants they are more isolated, face hostilities and racism or to say the least indifference. Because they are immigrant *and* working class they mostly live in the conditions that indigenous working class rarely share. *As workers* they are disadvantaged by being in the same time female and immigrant: they are at the bottom of the wage scale and their jobs are the most insecure, with the highest risk of accidents. Finally *as immigrants* they share the precarious status of their male counterparts, but again their sex is their disadvantage.

Consequences for their physical and mental health are inevitable. There is evidence in a number of studies of psychological disturbances due to the constant stress under which they live.

Though the situation of migrant women is best defined as one of ‹multiple negatives›, I would like to stress that the conflicts and contradictions that migrant women are exposed to daily can be precisely a ground for consciousness raising and increased awareness of their role in society and its functioning.

A number of strikes in which migrant women participated (or which were led by them) showed that there are migrant women who are less and less likely to be acquiescent in all the conditions imposed on them [20]. Entry into social production makes women aware that they are not isolated. Migration and paid labour offers only a *potential* for mobilizing and organizing. This again depends upon the degree of isolation in which they work and other forces tending to preserve their subjected status intact even though they are wage-earners. However they are still a minority, rarely organized, and are in sectors to which the unions are indifferent or openly hostile. The provision of job opportunity though often stressed as a necessary condition for women becoming more independent is not *in itself* liberating because there is nothing emancipating in bad conditions, low wages, humiliation, discrimination and overwork.

Bibliography

1 ALLEN, SH.: Perhaps a Seventh Person? Women's Quarterly International. Forthcoming, 1980.
2 ALLEN, SH.: A Triple Burden. Paper presented at the Women's Anthropology Group Seminar. The Transnational Institute, Amsterdam, 1. 12. 1979.
3 *Annuaires de l'ONI* (Office National d'immigration), France.
4 ARONDO, M.: Moi la Bonne. Stock, Paris, 1975.
5 BERGER, J., MOHR, J.: Seventh Man. Penguin Books, 1975.
6 BLUM: Über eine Anfallsepidemie bei einer Gruppe jugoslawischer Arbeiterinnen. Nervenarzt *43,* 192 – 198, 1972.
7 BOCH, C., TIEDT, F.: Befragung jugoslawischer Haushalte in der Bundesrepublik Deutschland. Institut für Sozialarbeit und Sozialpädagogik, Bonn, 1978.
8 BÖHNING, W.R.: The economic effects of the employment of foreign workers. OECD MS/M/404/415, 1973.
9 BRETTEL, C.: The Migration of Portuguese Women to Paris. (PhD thesis). Brown University, USA, 1978.
10 CASTLES, S., KOSACK, G.: Immigrant Workers and Class Structure in Western Europe. IRR, Oxford/London 1973.
11 *Collectif d'Alphabétisation.* Maspéro, Paris, 1972.
12 Continuing Subordination of Women in the Development Process. Special issue of IDS bulletin, April 1979, vol. 10, no. 3, University of Sussex.
13 DRETTAKIS, E.G.: Données sur les migrations et sur la croissance démographique en Allemagne Fédérale 1950 – 1972. Population, no. special, INED, March 1974.
14 *Les Femmes Immigrées Parlent.* L'Harmatanc etim, Paris/Génève, 1977.
15 Femmes immigrées au travail: Bulletin du Comité Médical et medico-social d'Aide aux migrants, no. 4, 1975.
16 FENTON, M.: Asian Households in Owner Occupation. A study of the Pattern, Costs and Experiences of Households in Greater Manchester. Working papers on ethnic relations, no. 2, SSRC, 1977.
17 Frankfurter Allgemeine Zeitung, 12 March 1980: quotes the results of a study carried out by ‹Forschungsgruppe Bonn› of Institut für Mittelstandsforschung, Bonn, 1980.
18 GARDINER, J.: Political economy of Domestic Labour in capitalist society. In: Barker, L.D., Allen, Sh. (Eds.): Dependence and Exploitation in Work and Marriage. Longman, London, 1976, pp. 109 – 120.
19 GRANOTIER, B.: Les travailleurs immigrés. Maspéro, Paris, 1971 and 1979.
20 GRUNWICK: Race and Class. XIX (3) 1978 (also summer 1977).
21 GUARDIAN: 19. 10. 1979: The untouchables of the labour market.
22 GUIRAL, P., THUILLIER, G.: La vie quotidienne des domestiques en France au XIX siècle. Hachette, Paris, 1978.

23 HÉMÉRY, S., RABUT, O.: Contribution des étrangers à la natalité en France. Population 6, 1063 – 1077, 1973.

24 *Labour Supply and Migration in Europe* (Economic Survey of Europe: Part II) ECE, UN, Geneva, 1979.

25 LEEDS, A.: Women in the Migratory Process: A Reductionist Outlook. Anthropological Quarterly 49, 69 – 76, 1976.

26 MAČEK, O., MAYER, B.: From a study on mental hygiene and social problems of Yugoslav workers in an Austrain textile factory. In: Verhaegen, P. (Ed.): Mental Health in Foreign Workers. ACCO, Louvain, Belgium, 1973.

27 VAN MANNEN, B.: Vrouwen Te Gast. Feministische Uitgeverij SARA, Amsterdam, 1979.

28 MEHRLANDER, U.: Soziale Aspekte der Ausländer Beschäftigung. Verlag Neue Gesellschaft GmbH, Bonn, 1974.

29 Minces, J.: Les travailleurs étrangers en France. Paper presented at the CEE Conference on Migration Problems. Louvain-la-Neuve, Feb. 1974, mimeo.

30 MOROKVAŠIĆ, M.: L'immigration féminine en France: Etat de la Question. Aimée Sociologique 26, 563 – 575, 1975.

31 MOROKVAŠIĆ, M.: Yugoslav Women in France, FRG, Sweden (Study Report, mimeo, 1980). CNRS, Paris, 1980.

32 MOROKVAŠIĆ, M.: Les femmes immigrées. Yugoslaves en France et en RFA. Hommes et Migrations, Paris, 15. 11. 1976.

33 *Repräsentativuntersuchung* 1972.

34 SAIFULLAH-KHAN, V.: Purdah in the British Situation. In: Leonard Barker, D., Allen, Sh. (Eds.): Dependence and Exploitation in Work and Marriage. 1976, pp. 224 – 247.

35 Stand und Entwicklung der Erwerbstätigkeit. Statistisches Bundesamt, Wiesbaden, 1977.

36 SAIFULLAH-KHAN, V.: Pakistanis Villagers in a British City. (PhD thesis.) University of Bradford, 1974.

37 SOPEMI: Continuous reporting system on Migration. OECD, 1977 Report, p. 47.

38 Statistiques du Travail, Suppl. au bulletin mensuel, no. 31, 1975.

39 TABOADA, I., LEVI, F.: Femmes et Immigrées. Documentation Française, 1979.

40 TAPINOS, G.: L'immigration etrangère en France. Cahiers de l'INED, PUF, 71, 115 – 117, 1975.

41 TAYLOR, R.C.: Migration and Motivation. A Study of Determinants and Types. In: J.A. Jackson (Ed.): Migration. Cambridge University Press, 1969.

42 THADANI, V., TODARO, M.: Towards a theory of female migration in developing countries. The population council, center for policy studies. Working Paper, May 1978, mimeographed, 36 pages.

43 WIDGREN, J.: Migration to Western Europe: the social situation of migrant workers and their families. UN Office, Geneva UN SOA/SEM/60/WP2.

44 WILSON, A.: Finding a Voice. Virago, London, 1978.

Chapter 10

Psycho(patho)logical Reactions among foreign labourers in Europe

W. BÖKER

I. Introduction

Ever since the end of World War II the rapidly growing European industry has absorbed many millions of labourers coming in search of work from the less developed European countries, as well as from North Africa and Turkey.

However, due to the worldwide economic recession, there has been a reduction in the labour migration, beginning with 1974.

In 1973 the total foreign resident population in Western Europe was estimated at 9.5 to 11.5 millions [13].

In 1973 the immigration into the Federal Republic of Germany (FRG) was at the peak with a total of more than 2.3 millions of foreign workers, equal to more than 10% of the total, not self-employed, working population. The main quotas of foreign labour were supplied, in 1973, by Turkey (22.5%) and Yugoslavia (19.8%), followed by Italy (17.5%), Greece (11.4%) and Spain (7.6%). These immigrants consisted to more than 70% of un-skilled or semi-skilled workmen coming from rural areas with poor education. About half of these people were merely able to make themselves understood in German or had no knowledge of German at all. In comparison to the German population there is a striking preponderance of the age group 20 – 40 years.

About two thirds of these immigrants were married [17].

In most cases the migration was stimulated by recruitment in the expanding industrial countries. Unlike the situation with the enormous waves of overseas emigrants in past centuries, the primary target for these people was to return to their homelands after a couple of years of profitable work abroad.

At the end of the sixties, however, a growing tendency to permanent dwelling became noticeable and, in the year of 1972 one fifth of the foreign workers in the FRG had become residents. This is clearly shown by the fact that on January 1st of that year 2.2 million foreign workers, men and women, were living together with 1.4 million dependents in the FRG. *The foreign labourers thus represent a mixture of different forms of migration, reaching from seasonal workers to permanent residents, with the corresponding individually different processes of psychological adaptation to the host-country.*

II. Psychological situation

Many members of the host country with a narrow outlook on life regard the foreign labourers, with their different looks and language, as a disturbing element in society and meet them very often with rejection and sometimes overt hostility. This might even be the case when the foreigner falls ill and has to seek medical help. His position becomes a real awkward one confronted with a complex and completely unfamiliar public health service. He finds himself both unable to formulate his complaints, and to obtain the information necessary. Very often, he does not even know whom he ought to address in the matter, and it is usually not easy to get hold of an interpreter to solve his problem in a jiffy. He might, in addition, be afraid of losing his job or even being repatriated on account of his illness. Back home, his family, badly in need of his financial support, may now have to wait in vain for non-arriving remittances etc. No small wonder that, under these circumstances, he might lose his mental equilibrium and develop a state of anxious agitation.

The lack of understanding is, however, mutual, especially when the foreigner «plays his sick role» as he is used to it from his home-country. Both the medical and auxiliary personal do not understand completely that each ethnic group has its own ways to indicate disease and grief from childhood. Each culture uses a signal system which is easily misinterpreted by outsiders, and might be regarded as exaggerated and even objectionable and bizarre.

This mutual lack of understanding is probably the main reason why illness in foreign labourers is so very often classified, at first sight, as a mental disturbance with diagnoses like «hysterical personality structure», «anxiety psychosis», «maniform agitation» or «suspected schizophrenia». The seemingly odd behaviour demonstrated by the foreigners in the situations where they feel helpless, may remind the doctor of the behaviour, shown by mentally ill persons, a fact, which may, in the sequel, serve as a cover for such a classification.

This assertion takes us right into the middle of the topic: is there perhaps really an increased proneness to mental morbidity linked up with the status of the foreign labourer? Is it, generally, possible to work out specific «guest workers syndromes»? And, if so, which are the underlying mechanisms, and what are the therapeutical consequences?

III. Psychiatric syndromes found in foreign workers

The first psychiatric publications concerning foreign workers consisted of mainly descriptive reports on behaviour patterns in cases posing particular diagnostic and therapeutic problems to and, consequently, high demands on the host-country's doctors. Following the initial perplexity, how to label the so far unfamiliar psychopathology in these foreigners, certain syndromic denominations were introduced in the literature on the subject like «maghrebenean acute situational disturbance», «Southerners' disease», «Mediterranean syndrome», telling nothing, but betraying the hauteur of sublime contempt. Other terms, like «uprooting depression», «nostalgic reaction» etc., pick up the threads of former descriptions of psychopatho-logical reactions in expatriates and bear witness of certain efforts toward classifying of specific «foreign workers syn-dromes». In this connection very ancient pathographies from the 17th century were rediscovered, describing e.g. «pathopatridalgia», the home-sickness of the Swiss merce-naries in European armies. Other transient situational dis-turbances caused mainly by home-sickness were described in juvenile incendiaries by KARL JASPERS in 1909. Such re-discoveries were raised by CH. SWINGMANN to rank as a nostalgic syndrome of mental disturbances typical of for-eign workers [24].

In the following one will find a brief presentation of cer-tain groups of symptoms chosen from the literature on the subject. These symptoms are particularly frequent and, so far, obviously representing the «typical» psychopathologi-cal clinical pictures. The thorny question, whether or not these symptoms may actually be differentiated and defined as specific syndromes linked up exclusively, or mainly to the status of the foreign labourer, will be discussed at the end of this passage.

1. Hypochondriac-depressive syndromes

POECK [21] was one of the first to describe hypochondriac depressive affections in Italian foreign workers differing from such disorders in native patients, because of the bizarre descriptions of body-sensational disturbances. Similar cases have repeatedly been reported on by other investigators like ÖZEK [20], who gives an account of Turkish patients with dymorphophobia, manifesting itself e.g. in the fear of «the penis shrinking up into the belly» or feeling of «the eyeballs contracting». RISSO and BÖKER [22] reported, within the frame of a paranoid syndrome on such uncommon, vital disturbances in their South-Italian pa-tients, expressed in fears like their «limbs were shrivell-ing», «blood stagnating in the vessels» and «face getting black». Such complaints may, possibly, be heard from German patients with severest endogenous melancholias.

The cases cited above, however, were posing the problem of nosologically hard to define, deliveious-confused patterns of behaviour, relating, according to the sick, to undue magic influence.

Many clinical hypochondriac-asthenic pictures with the loss of potency, gastro-intestinal complaints, lack of drive and vegetative symptoms will be found, analogously, among Central Europeans and remind us of masked depressions and hypochondriac forms of neurosis.

2. Many investigators believe that functional disturbances in different organic systems, especially of the gastro-intestinal tract, are particularly frequent in foreign workers [6]. These troubles develop e.g. after controversies or accidents at the place of work, with feelings of stress and crisis in the host-country. Often, depressions like nostalgic melancholias, seem to develop after a couple of months into somatic syndromes [12]. At the bottom of many cases of insomnia, distaste for work and vague neuro-vegetative complaints, e.g. with young Turks, one may find predominant psychogenic disturbances of the sexual potency. Finally, massive conversional neurotic disturbances have also been found and described in less intelligent and rather primitive labourers from developing countries.

Looking more closely one will find three focal points:

1) *Gastric-intestinal disturbances,* often embedded in depression and complained of with hypochondriac vehemence as a feeling of pressure in the epigastric region, loss of appetite and heartburn.

2) *Loss of sexual potency:* As mentioned many cases of insomnia, distaste for work and vague neurovegetative disturbances turn out to be mainly caused by worries about psychogenic impotency. These troubles are disclosed only with strong reluctance [21]. The normal variations of sexual potency are, often, quickly and falsely interpreted by these young men in a depressive-hypochondriac way, and a temporary sexual failure may become chronic. HÄFNER, MOSCHEL and ÖZEK [12] have also found in Turkish foreign workers a decrease of sexual

potency in almost 70% of their cases in the first couple of weeks after entering the FRG.

3) *Hysteriform behaviour:* As mentioned earlier the misinterpreted behaviour of a sick and suffering foreign worker, his often most «peculiar» way of uttering his complaints may lead to the precipitated labeling «hysteric», because to some observers he certainly strikes a demonstrative, theatrical pose. However, numerous authors have actually described symptoms which have to be diagnosed as typical of conversional hysterical disturbances. LAFFRANCHINI [15] made observations in his Zürich clinical records on psychogenic paralysis, logopathia, dysphagia and even real fits of hysteria, following disputes or accidents, with more than one tenth of his Italian patients, mostly women from Southern Italy. BLUM [5] described in 1972 an «epidemia», lasting for several weeks, of hysteric attacks in 15 Yugoslavic female workers in a Berlin rooming-house, triggered probably by the sight of another inmate seized with cerebral convulsions. As early as in 1970, a series of psychogenic fits were observed in Munich in ten Yugoslavic female patients, following an inmate's plunging out of a window and being seriously injured.

3. *Acute paranoid psychoses* of the type «bouffée délirante aigue» resp. «acute paranoid reaction» have often been described in foreign labourers. These denominations refer to states of anxious agitation centered around delusion-like or paranoid ideas. Usually, there is a sudden syndromic outburst reminding us of acute schizophrenic episodes and psychogenic states of confusion. As a rule, there is a speedy remission.

In the pathogenesis the experience of oppressive feelings of insecurity and isolation seems to play an important role, as described by EITINGER [10] as an essential motive for paranoid reactions in refugee immigrants in Norway. Insufficient knowledge, not only of the foreign language, but also of the rules of conduct and behaviour of the host-country, contributes to such feelings of uncertainty among immigrants and seems to form an indistinct field of perception for the projection of fears, exaggerated expectations and needs for personal relationships. Such demands may turn into doubts and distrust and are, eventually, converted into delusions of reference and persecution, as was described as early as in 1920 by ALLERS in foreign soldiers in Vienna with psychogenic delusional ideas in the form of «an alien's delusions of persecution on account of the isolating different language» [1]. A poor capacity of integration of the ego-system, coupled with an unstable personality, might in times of stress abroad increase the «propensity for projection» (BERNER) and trigger off a paranoid reaction. So far, this would concern a pattern of reactions closely associated with the stress of acculturation on the foreign workers. The acute paranoid reaction, however, can hardly be defined as a specific foreign workers syndrome, since it has been observed very frequently also in developing countries undergoing rapid cultural changes and becoming industrial nations [7].

Transcultural psychiatric investigations have shown that, for instance, depressive patients in non-European cultures very often make use of the so-called «organic language» to illustrate such sentiments, e.g. depressive feelings, which are hard to express in words, and that the experience of bizarre body-sensational alterations is quite frequent with such people. Delirium-like delusional syndromes and pronounced conversional symptoms have been described by COLLOMB to be well-known clinical pictures in the psychiatric hospitals of North-West Africa. Psychiatric-ethnological observations on the rural populations in the South of Italy and on Sardinia confirm the vivacity of magic-animistic ideas in the experience of illness [6].

Therefore, for the majority of the symptoms described, one must stress their existence also outside the migrational context. On the other hand the development of paranoid symptoms in foreign workers abroad seems to be closely linked to the impact of the new and unfamiliar surroundings, isolation, foreign language and culture.

IV. Correlations between psychic morbidity and migration

Both EITINGER and STOLLER have discussed the problem of mental illness among migrants (see page 18 and 33 of this volume). In the following research findings from FRG will be discussed:

1. Age and sex ratio

Migrating workers are characterized by certain age-groups and a specific sex ratio. In 1972, however, there was no considerable difference as to the sex ratio of the foreign workers in comparison to the FRG working population. No differences in sex-linked mental disturbances were found in the records studied. On the other hand the preponderance of the age group 20 – 39 years shows the expected effect on the diagnoses. There are almost no senile or presenile dementias to be mentioned. The age of the foreign labourers proves to be a factor reducing the morbidity rate.

2. Super-individual predispositions

Migrants crossing cultural and language-barriers descend from populations with patterns of morbidity which, in all probability, differ from those of the host-countries. According to the transcultural psychiatric research findings, this is to be expected particularly in the field of the so-called minor mental disturbances (neuroses, abnormal reactions, psychosomatic syndromes, addiction etc.) and less with the endogenous psychoses. The data available in FRG do not give any final answer to these questions, since there is no information on the rates of mental morbidity in the respective countries of origin.

3. The theory of selection assumes that mainly such individuals set out for migration, who are mentally unstable, badly adjusted in their homelands, and possibly prepsychotic [19]. According to COCHRANE [8] this is to be assumed particularly in the cases where the emigrant procedures and the process of readjustment and adaptation to be expected in the host-country, do not pose any considerable difficulties that would wreck the endeavours of the mentally unstable.

On the other hand it must be assumed that the immigration from culturally most different, far-away countries, with scanty possibilities of information and bothersome emigration and travelling procedures — such as Turkey — would produce, rather, a positive selection of mentally stable, self-confident and determined men in search for work.

There are many indications that individual predispositions contribute to the manifestation of mental disturbances in FRG. BENKERT and others [2] have investigated and found in the records of more than half of their 130 foreign patients in the University Clinic of Psychiatry, Düsseldorf, mental disturbances prior to emigration, viz. in such patients who were suffering from endogenic psychoses. HÄFNER, MOSCHEL and ÖZEK [12] have examined 200 Turkish men on different occasions. In the first interview about one fifth of these men were willing to admit having suffered from mental troubles prior to entering the FRG. The first check-up however, about three months later, revealed in respect to the early case histories, that almost half of these patients had had premorbid mental problems. Traumatic experiences in childhood and family conflicts seem, occasionally, to increase the susceptibility and may have a bearing on the decision to emigrate. More precise conclusions, however, cannot be drawn from the findings at hand.

4. The theory of stress of acculturation asserts that the strain of migration in itself would imply a process causing disease, and that, accordingly, an increased morbidity rate is to be expected. Such particularly stressful events would be: The change from country to city or town, the separation from the homeland and the relatives, the experience of the language-barrier, the adaptation to new and unfamiliar standards of values and social order («culture shock»).

The German medicostatistics for 1970 – 1975 do not show a higher incidence of sick reports among the foreign employees on the whole. Such statistics reveal merely the rough outlines of the situation.

A cautious evaluation of psychiatric hospital first-admission rates in respect to foreign patients in Stuttgart and Munich [9, 11], would suggest that, at least as far as the more serious clinical pictures (viz. endogenous and exogenous psychoses) are concerned, the foreign workers do not present an increased, but possibly, rather a reduced risk of morbidity, in comparison to the corresponding age-groups of the German population.

With regard to alcoholism and drug abuse FRIESSEM [11] has estimated the corresponding hospital admission rates to be four times lower among foreigners, compared to the Germans in the age-groups in question.

If we turn to the field of the minor mental disturbances (neuroses, functional and psychosomatic syndromes), however, the situation becomes more complex and difficult to survey.

Leaving the level of clinical diagnoses and taking into account, to begin with, the data collected in the research of the subjective perception of health and illness [4], a further most important criterium of morbidity, we certainly gain the impression that more foreigners in the FRG are suffering from feelings of impairment with regard to their somatic and mental health, than revealed by the figures of the medical statistics.

FRIESSEM [11] has found the hospital admission rates in Stuttgart, pertaining to neuroses, to be significantly higher among foreigners than Germans. We cannot simply deduce from this, however, an increased morbidity rate of neuroses among the foreign workers. German patients with neurotic symptoms are rarely admitted to psychiatric hospitals, they are mainly referred to the outpatient clinics or to the domiciled doctors. Furthermore neurotic disorders in foreign labourers are in all probability and to a large extent, falsely diagnosed. The reasons are a.o. the above-mentioned language-difficulties, and the described culture-specific differences in the foreigners way of complaining. They are therefore admitted to psychiatric hospitals under the suspicion of psychosis (e.g., in the case of free-floating anxiety, as a not clearly defined «state of agitation» or, in the case of pronounced conversional symptoms, as a «vitalized depression»). In all likelyhood, a thorough knowledge of the native language enhances a foreigner's prospects, not only of being classified as a «neurotic» (this observation being supported by BENKERT et al. [2]), but also his chances of being treated, accordingly, as an outpatient. Based on the findings in FRG so far, we will have to leave the question open, whether there is a higher or even lower incidence of neurotic reactions among the foreign labourers as a result of the strain of migration.

5. Social activities among immigrants

Research findings from Israel, Singapore, Boston and Canada [18] show that the rate of admissions to hospitals is dependent on the *size of the immigrant subculture* in the new country. There is a higher incidence of hospitalization among immigrants who are living scattered or in very small groups, in comparison to their fellow-countrymen living in bigger communities with good human relations and mutual contacts (see also the chapter by KORANYI, page 220 of this volume).

In regard to the foreign labourers in Germany, this point has not, as yet, been investigated systematically.

6. «Breeder» hypothesis

An assumption modifying the above mentioned hypothesis emanates from the observation that newly arrived immigrants are prone to gather, with other socio-economically less fortunate people, in certain ecological areas with a comparatively high incidence of mental morbidity. The lodging of the foreign labourers in hutted camps and poor ghetto-like quarters reminds of the slums and many authors are of the opinion that this would be the main reason for an increased susceptibility [6].

In one third of the patients in Düsseldorf, the housing conditions were described as «particularly unfavourable» such patients having merely a sleeping-place of their own. Findings in Munich [9], would confirm this correlation. Once more, we have to assume not a simple causal relationship but a combined action of many variables.

7. Personal and social status etc.

There are a number of additional circumstances influencing the morbidity resp. the rate of hospitalization among the migrants. Thus unmarried people are supposed to show a higher incidence than the married [16], a finding, however, that, according to MURPHY, would be of a certain importance only with the people aged over 50 [18]. Low social class and poor education are other features increasing the risk of hospitalization. The discrepancy between the social status striven for and the one actually attained, is assumed to be another causative factor for mental disturbances [3]. This point is of importance for those immigrants who are working in subordinate positions below their qualifications, their ambitions and willingness to work «running partly idle».

The mentioned Munich hospital report shows that 52% of the 179 foreign patients were single, a ratio clearly above that of the total foreign population in the FRG. BENKERT et al. have found an increased ratio of unmarried people only among the schizophrenic patients. The significance of this variable in the epidemiology of the psychoses [19] is well-known. The incidence of hospital admissions of schizophrenics seems to be higher among unmarried and single foreign workers as opposed to married.

The meagre findings on the subject in the FRG, do not allow any conclusions on the social status [6].

V. Therapeutical viewpoints

We are most aware of the fact that the psychiatric public health services in Central Europe present a number of grave imperfections, as described in the report of the German Enquiry Commission 1975. The foreigners are among the first to suffer from the inadequate facilities, handicapped as they are in many directions, but perhaps mainly because of their difficulties with the language. Therefore, most authors stress the necessity of arranging for a *qualified* medical interpreter service in hospitals, outpatient clinics and factory casualty wards. Being able to talk to a foreigner in his mother-tongue, means, in many cases, a first important step towards healing in mental disorders. It is indispensable for the doctor to bear in mind that he is dealing with human beings for whom he, as well as the system he represents, may seem frightening, which hinders the necessary confidence in the doctor. This is specially important if doctor and patient differ much in age or are of different sexes. A clear, simple language should be used when labeling the disease and giving directions for the treatment, in order to avoid anxious reactions. With such patients, *a suggestive piece of good advice* together with an impressive, likewise, *suggestively effective corporal application,* supported by a mild sedative, may prove to be more helpful than interactively neutral «expert» therapeutic procedures, especially in cases of hysteria. It may be very tempting, particularly in cases posing more problems due to difficulties with a foreign language, to try to arrive, at long last, at an «exact diagnosis» with the help of an immense number of appliances, testing methods and laboratory findings, exposing the patient to the danger of iatrogenic chronicity of his anxiety state.

Risso and Böker [22] reported on somatic self-healing endeavours among their Southern-Italian clinical cases: Such patients, haunted by fears of being poisoned, would rub a preparation of, for instance, onions or beeswax into the skin all over the body, gulp down 2 lb. of meat daily, or swallow expensive tonics, to regain their strength, would sleep on amulets, etc. A clever doctor, however, does not in the least think scorn of such magic conceptions, but will make use of them, including same in his plan of treatment. At times, he must in addition counteract regressive tendencies. Some authors are of the opinion that a repatriation would be indicated in certain severe types of psychosis. Such an action, however, could possibly be taken, only too swiftly, by a clinic and/or the aliens police authorities, in order to avoid further difficulties. On the other hand, in certain, e. g. depressive cases, there would be reasons to expect comparatively speedy recovery in the homeland, after the patient's withdrawal from the strain of acculturation abroad.

Finally, *providing for social psychiatric services for foreigners,* in accordance with the suggestions in numerous social-medical publications, would probably, turn out to be an effective preventive measure. In welfare centres for foreign workers, the newly arrived should be given an opportunity to obtain practical, useful information on the living conditions in the host-country. Earlier arrived countrymen can be of great value in this function.

Bibliography

1 ALLERS, R.: Über psychogene Störungen in sprachfremder Umgebung. Zbl. Neurol. *60,* 281, 1920.
2 BENKERT, H., FLORU, L., FREISTEIN, H.: Psychische Störungen bei ausländischen Arbeitnehmern, die zur stationären Behandlung in die Psychiatrische Klinik eingewiesen wurden. Nervenarzt *45,* 76 – 87, 1974.
3 BERNDT, H.: Zur Soziogenese psychiatrischer Erkrankungen. Ein Bericht über ökologische und epidemiologische Forschungsergebnisse. Soziale Welt *19,* 22 – 46, 1968.
4 BINGEMER, K., MEISTERMANN-SEEGER, E., NEUBERT, E. (Hrsg.): Leben als Gastarbeiter – Geglückte und missglückte Integration. 2. Aufl., Westdeutscher Verlag, Opladen, 1972.
5 BLUM, A.: Über eine Anfallsepidemie bei einer Gruppe jugoslawischer Arbeiterinnen. Nervenarzt *43,* 192 – 197, 1972.
6 BÖKER, W.: Psychiatrie der Gastarbeiter. In: Psychiatrie der Gegenwart. Bd. III, 2. Aufl. Springer, Berlin/Heidelberg/New York, 1975.

7 Böker, W., Schwarz, R.: Über Entstehung und Verlauf akuter para-
noider Reaktionen im Zusammenhang mit Kulturwandel und Migration. Nervenarzt *48,* 19 – 24, 1977.

8 Cochrane, R.: Mental Illness in Immigrants to England and Wales:
An Analysis of Mental Hospital Admissions, 1971. Social Psychiatry
12, 25 – 35, 1977.

9 Cranach, M. v.: Psychiatric disorders among foreign workers in the
Federal Republic of Germany. Paper presentedat the WPA-Symposium on Transcultural Psychiatry in Europe. Kiel, April, 5. – 8., 1976.

10 Eitinger, L.: Psychiatric Symptomatology in Refugees. Paper presented at the WPA-Symposium on Transcultural Psychiatry in Europe. Kiel, April, 5. – 8., 1976.

11 Friessem, D.H.: Methodologische Probleme der Migrationspsych-
iatrie in der BRD. Paper presented at the WPA-Symposium on Transcultural Psychiatry in Europe. Kiel, April, 5. – 8., 1976.

12 Häfner, H., Moschél, G., Özek, M.: Psychische Störungen bei tür-
kischen Gastarbeitern. Eine prospektiv-epidemiologische Studie zur
Untersuchung der Reaktion auf Einwanderung und partielle Anpassung. Nervenarzt *48,* 268 – 275, 1977.

13 Institut für Arbeitsmarkt- und Berufsforschung der Bundesanstalt für
Arbeit, Nürnberg; persönliche Mitteilung 23. 8. 1973.

14 Kurz, U.: Partielle Anpassung und Kulturkonflikt – Gruppenstruk-
turen und Anpassungsdispositionen in einem italienischen Gastarbei-
terlager. Kölner Zeitschrift für Soziologie und Sozialpsychologie *17,*
814 – 832, 1965.

15 Laffranchini, Sp.: Psychiatrische und psychotherapeutische Probleme der italienischen Arbeiter in der Schweiz. Praxis *26,* 786 – 795,
1965.

16 Lazarus, J., Locke, B.Z., Thomas, D.S.: Migration differentials in
mental disease. Milbank Mem. Fd. Quart. *41,* 25 – 42, 1963.

17 MARPLAN – Forschungsgesellschaft für Markt und Verbrauch, Of-
fenbach/Main. Zur sozialen Situation der Gastarbeiter in der BRD
1972. Typoskript – Eigendruck.

18 Murphy, H.B.M.: Migration and the major mental disorders: A reappraisal. In: Zwingmann, C., Pfister-Ammende, M. (Eds.): Uprooting
and after . . . Springer, Berlin/Heidelberg/New York, 1973.

19 Ødegaard, O.: Epidemiology of the psychoses. In: Psychiatrie der
Gegenwart, Bd. II/1, 2. Aufl., Klinische Psychiatrie I. Springer, Ber-
lin/Heidelberg/New York, 1972.

20 Özek, M.: Soziale Umstrukturierung als Provokationsfaktor depressiver Psychosen. In: Probleme der Provokation depressiver Psychosen. Internationales Symposion, Graz, 1971, pp. 109 – 115.

21 Poeck, K.: Hypochondrische Entwurzelungsdepressionen bei italienischen Arbeitern in Deutschland. Dtsch. med. Wschr. *87,*
1419 – 1424, 1962.

22 Risso, M., Böker, L.W.: Verhexungswahn – Ein Beitrag zum Ver-
ständnis von Wahnerkrankungen süditalienischer Arbeiter in der
Schweiz. Bibl. Psychiatr. neurol. (Basel/New York), Fasc. 124, 1964.

23 RISSO, M., BÖKER, W.: Delusions of witchcraft: A cross cultural study. Brit. J. Psychiat. *114*, 963, 1968.
24 ZWINGMANN, CH.: Nostalgic behaviour — A study of foreign workers in West Germany. In: Ch.Zwingmann, M. Pfister-Ammende (Eds.): Uprooting and after . . . Springer, Berlin/Heidelberg/New York, 1973.

Chapter 11

After the holocaust:
Migrants who survived massive stress experiences

FREDERICK H. HOCKING

Introduction

Throughout history, nature and man — acting usually on
behalf of the State — have subjected people to the mental
and physical suffering imposed by the extreme stresses of
starvation, natural disasters, torture, prolonged military
combat, solitary confinement and imprisonment in overcrowded conditions. However, it is only in relatively recent times that any serious attempt has been made to study
the immediate and long-term social, behavioural and psychological consequences of these experiences for the individuals who survived them.

The Nazi persecution of Jews

Possibly no other large group of people has ever been subjected to such prolonged physical and mental traumas as
were those incarcerated in the concentration camps of Na-
zi-controlled Europe and it is the relatively few survivors
of this catastrophe who form the specific group of migrants
to be discussed in this chapter. However, in order to understand the special problems of migration faced by these
survivors, it is necessary to know something of the experiences that they had endured in the years preceding their
migration. In other words, one needs to understand what
was involved in what is somewhat euphemistically called
«persecution».

Briefly, racial laws were introduced in the early years of the Nazi government — a regime which, it is salutary to remember, was elected by a democratic vote on two occasions. At the beginning of their persecution, Jews were deprived of their possessions, forced to wear the Star of David, beaten in the streets and made to carry out menial and degrading work. Many German Jews were able to flee the country before the war, but it was the Jewish people in occupied Europe — Poland, Czechoslovakia, Hungary, Rumania, the Baltic countries, parts of the USSR, and so on — who between 1940 and 1943 were confined in ghettos which were actually giant prison camps where grossly over-crowded conditions, starvation and disease decimated the prisoners. In 1942 and 1943, the Nazis set up the giant extermination camps of Auschwitz, Chelmno, Belzec, Treblinka and Maidanek; «these names are endwords», wrote PHILIP TOYNBEE, «they stand for an extremity of human experience that is beyond conception». From all over Europe, Jews were herded into cattle trucks in such numbers that movement was virtually impossible. The doors were locked and the train set off on a journey that could take more than a week. As food and water, if provided at all, were grossly inadequate, many prisoners died of hunger or thirst, or were choked under the weight of the bodies of their fellow captives. Sometimes the greater number in a transport died during the journey, but the dead were not removed until the train reached its destination. On arrival at the concentration camp, there was an initial «selection» for the gas chambers which resulted in about two-thirds of the survivors being killed. Infants and children, pregnant women, the old, the sick, and even those who did not appear particularly robust after the train journey were shot or sent to gas chambers. The remainder had their heads shaved and numbers tattooed on their bodies, were issued with ragged prison garb and wooden clogs, and were then usually put to heavy work until they died of starvation and disease or were killed by gassing, shooting or beating. Their existence was a constant state of humiliation, degradation, hunger, overcrowding, cold, pain, terror, lack of sleep, beatings, infestation with fleas and lice, the threat of death, and the knowledge that family, friends and fellow Jews were being exterminated. Resistance was virtually impossible, because, like all starving people, they were apathetic and passive — something long known to the less scrupulous slave-owning communities. The prolonged horror of concentration camp existence has been described as the most stressful situation which human ingenuity could devise [11]. As it has been estimated that one person survived of every six hundred of those imprisoned in concentration camps, it would seem that chance was the biggest factor in survival, although a strong mental and physical constitution would surely have been a necessary prerequisite.

The survivors

In 1944, the first sick, filthy, emaciated survivors of these camps were liberated by the advancing United States, British and Russian armies, and where possible most of them tried to return to the place where they had lived before their persecution. However, few were able to find any trace of family, relatives or Jewish neighbours, and eventually they had to accept the fact that they were virtually, or even literally, the only survivor of an extended family. For most, once they had recovered from the severe malnutrition that afflicted all, and the tuberculosis, typhus and other diseases that affected many, the next move was to a Displaced Persons' Camp, while waiting as long as several years for the opportunity to migrate to a new country. Over the following ten years, thousands of these survivors migrated to the United States, Canada, Israel, Europe, and to Australia and New Zealand. Although migration and resettlement is difficult for almost all individuals, this group was particularly disadvantaged, as, in addition to the common problems of uprooting, language difficulties and unrecognized skills, they had lost family, friends and home, and had already been subjected to prolonged and severe physical and mental stress. Over the past twenty years, published studies from many countries have reported the presence of chronic psychological disability in the survivors of concentration camps. These reports indicate that the individuals who survived are crushed and apathetic; they are anxious, have difficulty in concentrating, and their memory is impaired. Terrifying nightmares disturb the small amount of sleep they get at night, and almost all of them have illogical feelings of guilt because they survived when their families and friends did not. HERMANN and THYGESEN [6] seem to have been the first of many authors [1, 3, 5, 8, 9, 12, 14, 15] to give these symptoms the name K.Z. (Konzentrationslager) Syndrome, and it should again be stressed that those who suffer from it have in most cases also had to cope with the universal difficulties of migration [2, 13].

Own investigations

Between 1959 and 1967, the writer interviewed and made a psychiatric and social assessment of three hundred and twelve people who had been subjected to some form of severe stress during the Second World War [7]. Some individuals had been incarcerated in ghettos and concentration camps, some had been in hiding in forests, cellars, or the walls or ceilings of houses, some had survived a combination of these experiences, and some had escaped from German-occupied territory and spent part of the war years in Russian labour camps, the Shanghai ghetto set up by the Japanese, or had been fortunate in making their way to Britain or some similar country. All had eventually migrated to Australia.

Virtually all of the individuals who had been incarcerated in ghettos and concentration camps for more than a few months presented an apathetic and depressed appearance that was so characteristic that they could almost invariably be identified among the patients sitting in the waiting-room. On the other hand, people who had been in hiding for more than a few weeks, or who had escaped from the Nazis, whether or not they had also been imprisoned in ghettos or concentration camps, showed a marked degree of tension and anxiety overlaid their depressive symptoms. Further, this latter group all complained that their symptoms began while they were in hiding, and that the fear that they felt at that time had never left them, whereas almost all of the concentration camp survivors stated that their symptoms started after the war, either on the day of their liberation or when they finally discovered the fate of other members of the family. The exceptions were all individuals who had been subjected to some particularly horrifying event, such as seeing their father beaten to death and then being forced to bury his body, or watching an S.S. guard pick up their baby by the heels and smash it against a wall. Like the people in hiding, those subjected to these extra stresses dated the onset of their symptoms from these war-time events.

Clinically, it was found that these survivors complained of a syndrome that comprised depression, anxiety, headache, disturbed sleep with traumatic dreams, tension or irritability, and difficulty in concentrating and/or impairment of memory, all of which were complained of by more than half of the people examined. Between one-third and one-half of the group described symptoms of backache and/or generalised aches and pains, fatigue and lack of energy, and abdominal pain and discomfort. About one-quarter of the subjects complained of palpitations, dizziness and black outs, «startle reactions» to harmless stimuli, the sensation of a lump in the throat, and obsession with thoughts of their war-time experiences. Feelings of guilt because they had survived when most had not were almost universal, as they are in the survivors of all natural and man-made disasters.

Results of psychological testing

Psychological testing was found to cause distress to those few patients examined in this way, so it was carried out on only five individuals, all of whom had been imprisoned in concentration camps. The clinical psychologist who carried out the tests (Dr. R. LEONARD) reported on each patient as follows:

1. Mr. M.

«Considerable variability is shown in his intellectual functioning, but seldom does he attain an above-average standard, although I am confident that his original capacity would have been at least bright-normal, and possibly higher. Many temporary inefficiencies occur, due to his poor concentration, and memory is very weak − in fact well below average. His very low scores on the practical tests are quite striking. His perceptual acuity is poor, he cannot plan ahead in any effective manner, he is slow in learning new material, and has relatively poor visual-motor coordination. This pattern of test scores is suggestive of an organically-caused deterioration of intellect. When the test results are seen in relation to his past professional accomplishments, there is even stronger reason for thinking of him as deteriorated. For example, he is a qualified optometrist (pre-war in Rumania) and a qualified engineer (post-war in Australia). He considers that his reduction in ability was noticeable during his engineering studies, but that he has become worse in recent years.

He is an emotionally inhibited man who can show little healthy affect; in fact, his affect is depressed and he has feelings of self-depreciation and inadequacy. He is an introverted person who has a moderately rich fantasy life, which, however, affords him little comfort or refuge because of unpleasant past experiences which break into his reverie. One particularly vivid Rorschach percept was of a German soldier from the execution squad, such as he often saw and feared during his concentration camp incarceration. He was beaten over the head in the concentration camp on more than one occasion, and from his account, was rendered unconscious − in one instance for as long as one and a half hours».

2. Mr. T.

He obtained an IQ of 102 on the verbal section of the W.A.I.S. I think that this under-estimates his true ability, for despite the facility with which he learned English, he was under some slight language handicap in doing the test. General knowledge and conceptual thinking are above average, but his concentration is poor, and because of this he makes many errors in arithmetical calculations.

His basic personality structure is obsessive-compulsive. He was unusually and unnecessarily thorough and meticulous is his approach to the tests, considered the stimuli from every possible angle, was indecisive, slow and inflexible. Although he was eager to please, I believe that he has many oppositional and negativistic traits which are not immediately apparent. Furthermore, it is likely that he would rely heavily on intellectualization and isolation as defence mechanisms. As one aspect of his tendency to split off affect from ideas, he appears to be afraid to reveal his more private thoughts and feelings. One gets the impression that he has learned to his regret that psychic hurts can follow openness in human relationships, and that it is far better to maintain a facade of disinterested amusement towards people and the world in general, rather than become emotionally involved. In this respect, it is noted that he saw in the Rorschach blots a number of signs and symbols of power (crowns, emblems, etc.) and of aggression (German hand-grenade) which suggests that his war-time traumatic experiences have left an indelible mark. Associated with the fear which he has towards threatening authority figures is an underlying hostility which has found no adequate outlet. I think that there are also some mild paranoid trends in his personality make-up. These, however, are apparently kept in reasonable bounds, and have not caused any ego disintegration; nor do they suggest any imminent psychotic break.»

3. Mrs. C.

«She is emotionally very disturbed in a non-psychotic way. She is an introverted woman who tends to draw into her own world of fantasy and away from object relationships. She perceives her environment as frightening and challenging, and there are recurring things in her test imagery which suggest that she is fearful of physical assault. She has marked feelings of self-depreciation, inferiority and inadequacy, along with vague and poorly expressed or understood guilt. Her affect is depressed and she views the future with anxiety and insecurity. She worries about being deserted and left alone in life, and in her test associations there are recurring images of death, loss of loved ones, etc. This concept of death dominates her thinking. For instance, in response to a picture which ordinarily elicits stories of a couple embracing, she spoke of a frightening dream, and finished her story in a most atypical manner by describing the people as dead. The content of her fantasy indicates that her concentration camp experiences have left a permanent and disabling scar.»

4. Mr. O.

«The impression is of an introverted, introspective, somewhat withdrawn man. On the one hand, he is ambitious and conscientious and aspires to wordly success. Yet he has deep-seated feelings of inferiority and self-depreciation, and is never free of anxiety that he may fail in life, and that all his efforts may prove worthless. There is also a great deal of ambivalence and uncertainty, with the ever-present dread of the future. A mild, but chronic persistent depression is suggested by his test imagery. A great deal of fear is also shown. As in the case of so many concentration camp survivors, there are specific images of frightening experiences. One gets the impression that such people are quite unable to free themselves from their fearful and horrifying past, and that their efforts to repress are never really successful. This patient, like so many others, has been so emotionally scarred that the intensity of his trauma is such that, in certain instances, there is a relative breakdown of rational control, and what begin as ordinary conventional percepts are invested with fear-laden affect. For example, what is frequently seen as a canyon or gully becomes, for him, a grave — and not just any grave, but the clear image of specific types of graves that he was once forced to dig with the knowledge that they could be for him and his friends. Again, a response of a countryside vista becomes the particular view he once had in the concentration camp of rows and rows of prepared graves. Despite this recurring preoccupation with his frightening past, which has assumed a persistent dream-like quality and notwithstanding his fears and insecurity about the future which he feels may suddenly collapse, he has a number of adaptive strengths which carry him forward.»

5. Mr. L.

«His present intellectual status is well below average; in fact, it is at a defective level (performance IQ 52-WAIS). Furthermore, he is functioning consistently at this standard. Perceptual acuity, planning ability, visual-motor co-ordination, and efficiency for acquiring new learning are all extremely poor. On manipulative tests he is slow, retarded, perseverative, and shows a fairly marked rigidity and loss of skill. Memory, as measured by recall of digits, is very poor. Non-verbal testing was quite beyond his present ability, and he passed only the simplest of questions. Throughout the testing, his facial expression was sad, his approach lifeless, and his verbal remarks sparse and often monosyllabic. There is strong evidence that depression is responsible for much of this man's retardation of associative, perceptual and motor processes. In addition to this, however, there is probably some intellectual deterioration of organic type. On the basis of the test results, it is not possible to estimate his innate intellectual capacity, but from his occupational and educational history as known, it would seem that he has deteriorated from at least average mental ability.»

Surveys carried out in a number of countries — particularly Norway and Denmark — indicate that the organic-type intellectual impairment suggested by these psychological tests may be, at least in part, a consequence of prolonged, severe under-nutrition [5, 6, 14, 15].

Case histories

The following case histories give some indication of the problems faced by migrants who had survived concentration camp experiences.

1. An attractive woman aged twenty-seven years when examined, was four years old when sent to a ghetto; she was later transported to Auschwitz. Although the normal procedure was to send all children to the gas chambers on arrival, she had somehow been spared, and had spent the remaining years of the war in the horror of the extermination camp. Her parents, brothers and sisters, and every uncle, aunt and cousin were killed by the Nazis. She was interviewed in hospital after having taken an overdose of sleeping capsules — her third serious attempt to kill herself, in addition to several lesser attempts. On each occasion, she would discharge herself as soon as she felt well enough to do so, and refused treatment, stating that it was her business if she killed herself. She had had many unfortunate relationships with men, and was virtually an alcoholic. Nevertheless, she was able to conduct a dress shop with the help of staff. Although eligible to do so, she refused to claim compensation for her wartime experiences. At first, she was unwilling to talk about herself, but eventually she volunteered the information that she drank to ease her constant feelings of fear and depression.

2. A woman who was aged seventeen at the start of her persecution in ghettos and concentration camps, and forty-three years old at the time of her examination. She was the sole survivor, as every relative was killed by the Nazis. For many years she attended medical, surgical and psychiatric clinics at a large teaching hospital. Since the end of the war, she had suffered from anxiety and apprehension, constant depression, difficulty in concentrating, disturbed sleep, traumatic dreams about her experiences, and impaired memory for recent events. In 1964, she received the minimum compensation available under the German Restitution Laws (anything less than twenty-five per cent being non-compensable) and, although she stated that her symptoms were slowly worsening with increasing age, she refused to make a further claim, as she did not wish to talk about her experiences again.

3. A woman who endured five years in ghettos and concentration camps from the age of sixteen. None of her family or other relatives survived the war, and those killed included her parents and eleven brothers and sisters. She attended various out-patient clinics at a large general hospital for many years, mainly for abdominal complaints, and tended to emphasise these and to insist that she was suffering from a physical illness, while minimising any psychological complaints. She stated that since the end of the war she had suffered from almost constant abdominal pain and discomfort, nausea and vomiting, backache and generalised aches and pains, but, on being pressed about the presence of nervous symptoms, admitted that her sleep was disturbed by nightmares about concentration

camps, and that she was depressed and lethargic and felt anxious and apprehensive. The only abnormal sign found on physical examination was that the liver was enlarged to two or three fingers breadth below the right rib margin — a finding that had been present for many years and was assumed to result from her years of semi-starvation. Intensive investigations revealed no other physical abnormality. All of her symptoms improved when a combination of antidepressant and tranquillizing drugs were prescribed, but as soon as she felt better she stopped taking these drugs, and, as soon as there was a recurrence of her symptoms, asked that further abdominal investigations be performed. She refused to make any claim for restitution, ascribing all of her symptoms to some as yet undiagnosed abdominal condition.

4. A man aged fifty-three at the time of his examination in 1966 was twenty-six years old at the start of his persecution, which involved three years incarcerated in ghettos and concentration camps and three years in hiding in a cellar. Almost all of his relatives had been killed by the Nazis. He had been attending the psychiatric out-patients department of a large teaching hospital for a period of more than ten years, complaining of disturbed sleep, terrifying dreams about his experiences, anxiety and apprehension, irritability, «startle reaction» to harmless stimuli, duodenal ulcer, difficulty in swallowing, obsession with thoughts of the past, impairment of memory for recent events, difficulty in concentrating and constant depression. Despite the distressing nature of his complaints and their seemingly obvious connection with his war-time experiences, he would not make a claim for restitution until their increasing severity prevented him from working. Even after he had decided to make a claim for compensation, he tended to play down most of his symptoms and said that he did not want to talk about them or about what happened to him during the war.

5. A man aged forty-seven who had been attending a large general hospital for many years with a variety of psychosomatic complaints that had been intensively investigated. When interviewed, he displayed the classical apathetic appearance of the concentration camp survivor, but was reluctant to talk of his experiences, stating that he just wanted help with his stomach and back. He eventually revealed that he had spent five years in ghettos and concentration camps and was the sole survivor of a once large family. He had worked as a house painter since just after his liberation until a few weeks before his consultation, and had reluctantly agreed to see a psychiatrist because of the continuing deterioration in his symptoms. He kept repeating that his back and stomach constituted his only complaints, and that if these could be cured he would be able to work again. On being questioned more specifically, he admitted to feeling depressed and anxious, but ascribed these symptoms to his back and stomach trouble. Later, he said that he slept badly because of vivid dreams about his war-time incarceration and the brutalities to which he had been subjected. He admitted that he felt hopeless and suicidal because he was finished and would not be able to work again. He seemed rather hostile about the failure of

doctors to relieve his symptoms, and in particular, about seeing a psychiatrist who had stirred up memories that he wanted to forget. Antidepressant and tranquillizing drugs were prescribed, and after a few weeks he admitted to feeling somewhat better. To the writer's surprise, because he still seemed rather resentful, he suddenly said, «Thank you doctor, you are a good man». Although he has never regained a state of normal psychological health, he was able to return to work.

Four of the patients were psychotic, and these are of particular interest as all of the published work indicates that psychosis is seldom the result of severe stress.

1. A thirty-three year old male who had been sent to a ghetto and then a concentration camp at the age of thirteen. He survived three years of this form of extreme stress and starvation, and discovered after his liberation that all the other members of his immediate family had been killed, although some more distant relatives survived. He claimed to have been well until shortly after his liberation in 1945, when, soon after learning the fate of his family, he developed a paranoid schizophrenic psychosis characterised by delusions of still being in the hands of the Nazis, depression and preoccupation with thoughts of suicide. In 1955, after migrating to Australia, he had a similar breakdown, and on both occasions he was certified to a mental hospital. When examined in 1963, his only complaints were of obsession with thoughts of his persecution by the Nazis and depression.

2. A woman who was aged twenty when sent to a concentration camp from which she was liberated after a year. She was the sole surviving member of her family, as her parents, brothers and sister, and all of her uncles, aunts and cousins had been killed in the camps. After her liberation in 1945, she felt inferior to other people, lacked confidence, was depressed and felt increasingly suspicious of other individuals. Fourteen years later she had a paranoid schizophrenic breakdown with marked depression, anxiety and apprehension, in addition to paranoid delusions that were largely concerned with Nazis. When interviewed twelve months after her discharge from a mental hospital, she complained of continuing anxiety and apprehension, obsession with her war-time experiences, and depression, but was not delusional.

3. A man who had been imprisoned in a pre-war concentration camp in Germany for a few months, had then been forced to leave Germany, and was eventually able to reach England just before the invasion of France in 1940. Being an enemy alien, he was sent to Australia, where he was interned for four years. Most of the other members of his family, including his parents, were killed by the Nazis. Soon after his release from the internment camp, when more than thirty years old, he developed a paranoid schizophrenic breakdown and has had several episodes since that time. Nazis have played a prominent part in his delusions, and each breakdown has necessitated certification to a mental hospital. When ex-

amined, he impressed as a rather withdrawn and suspicious man, but there was no other evidence of psychological disability.

4. A woman aged thirty-seven when she commenced four years incarceration in ghettos and concentration camps. Almost all of her relatives had been killed by the Nazis. Since her liberation, she has had frequent paranoid schizophrenic breakdowns in which Nazis form the basis of her delusions. She was seen during a period of remission, and her only symptoms were that her sleep was disturbed by dreams about her persecution, and that she felt a sense of lassitude and lack of energy.

It is worth noting that despite the psychotic nature of their breakdowns, these patients still complain of symptoms that seem basic to the concentration camp syndrome. Perhaps it is significant that the only exception was the man who had spent only a few months in a pre-war camp, where conditions, although harsh, could not be compared with those in the ghettos and slave labour and extermination camps set up later in German-occupied countries.

Discussion

In assessing the findings of this study of migrants who had survived massive stress experiences, the following factors may have decreased the validity of the results.

First, because (unlike the writer) all of the patients examined were Jewish, their symptoms may have resulted, at least in part, from cultural and/or constitutional factors that are not present in non-Jewish people. That similar findings have been reported in Japanese survivors of nuclear bombing and non-Jewish resistance workers in Norway and Denmark lessens the possibility that race, religious group or cultural factors play more than a very minor part in the production of the symptoms.

Secondly, with the exception of the individuals described earlier, all of the patients were claiming compensation from the Federal Republic of Germany under the restitution laws that enabled the survivors of Nazi persecution to claim for any subsequent impairment of health arising out of their experiences. The prospect of obtaining compensation might suggest that many of the patients were motivated by gain, and it would be ingenuous not to believe that some, and perhaps many, exaggerated their symptoms — not only in order to obtain compensation, but also to make the Federal German Government return some of the money that the Nazis had seized from the Jews. However, there is a great deal of evidence that the desire for compensation is a secondary issue with most people, as apart from the cases discussed earlier, all of whom refused to make a claim for restitution, the writer has seen eleven people who refused to claim compensation, making statements such as, «Money can't buy blood». All of these people complained of the same symptom-complex as those who have claimed compensation. In addition, the writer has interviewed three people who received restitution many years ago; all claim that their symptoms are worsening with increasing age, but refuse to make another claim. Obviously, many factors determine whether or not any individual will claim restitution, but it seems unlikely that the desire for compensation is an important factor in the form of the symptom-complex or in its persistence.

Thirdly, the symptoms may result from an inability to adapt to life in a strange country, rather than from wartime persecution. Migrating to a foreign country is undoubtedly a form of stress requiring an adjustment that becomes more difficult with increasing age. Nevertheless, the degree of stress entailed in such a move can hardly be compared with the prolonged extreme stresses to which these individuals were subjected during the Second World War.

Fourthly, it could be claimed that the people examined were not representative of all survivors. However, this statement can be refuted on two grounds: those individuals who do not claim compensation describe the same symptoms as those who do, and descriptions of the same symptom-complex have come from virtually every country where survivors have settled. Although many survivors seem to have achieved occupational and material success, this is obviously not necessarily synonymous with social and psychological well-being.

Fifthly, the people examined may have been predisposed to the development of neurotic symptoms as a result of constitutional or early environmental factors. It is impossible to refute this claim because any pre-war medical records have been destroyed. However, research workers in Scandinavian countries had access to the medical and social histories of resistance workers up to the time of their imprisonment, and could find no relationship between present disability and any pre-existing factor; furthermore, they found a strong correlation between incapacity and the stresses endured while incarcerated — particularly the degree of starvation. Although luck was the biggest factor in surviving concentration camp existence, it seems unlikely that neurotic predisposition would increase any individual's chances of remaining alive.

However, some psychiatrists still hold the view that psychological symptoms following exposure to stressful situations occur only in predisposed individuals in whom the stress triggers a neurosis that would almost certainly have occurred in its absence. As LEOPOLD and DILLON [10] have pointed out in their long-term follow-up study of the survivors of a marine disaster, this form of reasoning stems from the ignorance induced by an almost total absence of knowledge of the late social, occupational and psychological effects in individuals who have survived situations involving great physical danger and psychological stress. Another psychiatric dogma is that when people do develop symptoms of psychological disability after exposure to stressful situations, the symptoms will resolve within a period of two years. EITINGER [5] has drawn attention to the fact that this pronouncement was laid down by KARL JASPERS before the First World War, and has remained accepted for so long because no satisfactory investigation of the survivors has ever been carried out. In fairness to JASPERS, he was expressing his views about individuals who have been subjected to sudden episodes of severe stress, such as skiing injuries, and a reading of his writings on this subject indicates that his opinions were less rigid and dogmatic than those of some of the psychiatrists who quote his works to support their own opinions. By applying diagnostic labels such as «post-traumatic neurosis» to the behavioural reactions to stress, many psychiatrists and other physicians seem to regard the label as a sufficient explanation of the patient's symptoms, and to disregard the nature of the biological stresses to which the individual has been exposed. Inevitably, although perhaps unwittingly, the reactions are then mistakenly seen as a part of a neurotic pattern of behaviour to which the patient was predisposed.

It should be remembered that current psychological theories of human behaviour are based on the study of individuals leading the comparatively sheltered existence of members of Western civilisation, and subjected only to the stresses that befall most people in a lifetime. However, although clinical experience indicates the importance of previous personality characteristics in the individual reaction to these relatively moderate stresses, it cannot be assumed that the same relationship is valid for all degrees of stress. Further, the common tendency to divide people into the «normal» and the «predisposed» when assessing their capacity to adapt to psychological stress is meaningless unless one has some indication of the type and degree of stress involved. Our knowledge of other aspects of psychological capacity, such as intellectual capability, suggests that there may be a gradation of all personality characteristics that could be expressed in the form of a normal distribution curve. In fact, in his conclusion to *The Origin of the Species,* CHARLES DARWIN wrote, «In the future, I see open fields for far more important researches . . . the necessary acquirement of each mental power and capacity by gradation.» If this is in fact the case, a gradation in the capacity to adapt to stress may have contributed to the evolution of man. Thus, individuals at the lower end of the stress distribution curve may break down under the everyday stresses and strains to which most people adapt, the type of breakdown being determined by inherited personality characteristics and life-time experiences, including those of early childhood. However, as the degree of stress is increased, there is an increase in the percentage of individuals breaking down, so that if the stress is sufficiently severe, virtually all individuals will develop what would be, in an everyday setting, neurotic symptoms. A corollary of this hypothesis is that stress is a cumulative process, so that each stressful experience in a lifetime takes the individual nearer to the limit of his stress tolerance. Although we still know very little of the long-term consequences of most forms of stress, it is only by a consideration of the environment which a person has existed, and its possible relationship to an individual's present physical and psychological condition, that we can increase our knowledge of what may be an important aspect of biological function in its widest sense.

Thus, it is possible that individual reactions to stressful situations at all stages of life are determined by the capacity to adapt to stress, plus the quantitative effect of all of the stresses to which the person has been subjected in the past. It then follows that the greater the stress at any period of life, the closer the individual is brought to the limit of his stress tolerance, and the greater is the possibility of breakdown when exposed to further stress, including the physiological and psychological stresses of aging. It could therefore be expected that individuals who have had a traumatic childhood would be more likely to break down in adult life, particularly since trauma is generally more harmful to growing organisms. If the effects of stress are, in fact, cumulative, and if the type of childhood stress determines the form of neurotic breakdown in later life, the apparent differences between psychoanalytic and stress theories of neurosis disappear, at least in so far as reactions to the stresses and strains of everyday life are concerned. However, when individuals are subjected to a prolonged threat to their survival, the evidence suggests that pre-existing personality characteristics resulting from inherited and earlier environmental experiences are replaced by a universal and basic biological reaction. The symptom-complex that constitutes this reaction, and the social, family, occupational, intellectual and emotional changes that result from it form the burden which migrants who have survived extreme stress experiences take with them to their country of adoption.

Final remarks

The English doctor COLLIS who has described the situation at the liberation of Bergen-Belsen wrote already in 1945: «The problem what to do with these forsaken, almost lost, souls is immense.»

We know to-day that the problem has not diminished (inspite of the high mortality rate of the survivors) since then. Reports from all over the world indicate that traditional psychotherapy (including Feudian psychoanalysis) is insufficient. Neither can these persons be confused with patients suffering from so-called post-traumatic neurosis, hungry for compensation. Experience has shown that they need continuous psychological and practical support and empathy, because they will never be able to compete in the struggle of the fittest.

Bibliography

1 BAEYER, W. V., HÄFNER, H., KISKER, H.P.: Psychiatrie der Verfolgten. Springer, Berlin, 1964.
2 BANCHEVSKA, R.: Migration and Mental Health: The Longer Settled Migrants at risk. Paper delivered at The Fourth International Congress of Social Psychiatry. Jerusalem, 1972.
3 CHODOFF, P.: Effects of Extreme Coercive and Oppressive Forces: Brainwashing and Concentration Camps. In: S. Arieti (Ed.): American Handbook of Psychiatry. Vol. 3, Basic Books, New York, 1966.
4 Editorial: Aftermath. Lancet *1,* 415, 1966.
5 EITINGER, L.: Concentration Camp Survivors in Norway and Israel. Allen & Unwin, London, 1964.
6 HERMANN, K., THYGESEN, P.: K.Z. Syndromet. Ugeskr. Laeg. *116,* 825, 1954.
7 HOCKING, F.: Unpublished M.D. Thesis. Department of Medicine, Monash University, 1968.
8 HOCKING, F.: Psychiatric Aspects of Extreme Environmental Stress. Dis. Nerv. Syst. *31,* 542, 1970.
9 KRYSTAL, H. (Ed.): Massive psychic Trauma. International Univ. Press. New York, 1968.
10 LEOPOLD, R.L., DILLON, H.: Psycho-anatomy of a Disaster; A Long-term Study of Post-traumatic Neurosis in Survivors of a Marine Explosion. Amer. J. Psychiat. *119,* 913, 1963.
11 LIDZ, T.: Chronic Situations evoking Psychological Stress and the

Common Signs of the Resulting Strain. In: Symposium on Stress. Walter Reed Army Medical Centre, Washington, D.C., 1953.

12 MATUSSEK, P.: Die Konzentrationslagerhaft und ihre Folgen. Springer, Berlin, 1971.

13 STOLLER, A. (Ed.): New Faces. Ceshire, Melbourne, 1966.

14 STRØM, A. (Ed.): Norwegian Concentration Camp Survivors. Universitetsforlarget, Oslo, 1968.

15 THYGESEN, P., HERMANN, K., WILLANGER, R.: Concentration Camp Survivors in Denmark. Dan. Med. Bull. *17*, 65, 1970.

Chapter 12

Immigrant's adaptation in aged population

ERWIN K. KORANYI

Introduction

This chapter will deal with the psychiatric aspects of the old immigrants. Migration in old age is fundamentally unnatural and is not known to take place in any species other than humans. The eel, having a complex migration pattern, is known to return to its birthplace when it reaches old age. A similar migratory scheme is claimed anecdotally concerning other animals, but migration to seek out strange and new territory occurs only in the young in all species.

Young men have a need for adventure, even though this urge is much less explored by social scientists than by novelists and poets, a fact testified by the total absence of reference to it in contemporary major textbooks of psychiatry. What starts off as an adolescent effort to seek out distance and independence from the established milieu, to test individual skills and fortune, the craving political freedom and economic fulfillment in a far land are simultaneously at the root of the immigration of the aged. Once established, it is the young immigrant who will bring out the old ones, for the immigration of the aged, almost exclusively, represents a family reunion.

Earlier studies

The concept of «adaptive behavior» clearly refers to an individual's functioning within a specific milieu. Transposition of the same individual to a different environment demands varying degrees of reorganization of his acquired modes of behavior and values, a process causing prolonged, high-level stress. Discernible patterns in new immigrants' adaptation to the host country with potential breaking points, constitute a well-studied area in social psychiatry.

Some recent and sophisticated statistical studies [6, 7] now conclude a lower rate of psychiatric hospitalizations in immigrants versus the native-born population.

The first to report a lower rate of psychiatric admissions among immigrants was MURPHY [7]. MORGAN and ANDRUSHKO [6] in a Canadian survey. He found the rate of psychiatric admissions for psychoses to be 84%, 79% in the immigrant male/female group when parallelled to the native-born population; while the non-psychotic disorders were only 35%, 46% in the male/female immigrants in comparison to non-immigrants. Strikingly, they found that the rate of non-psychotic disorders was lowest in groups which were culturally the most distant to the local society. They concluded a distinct underutilization of these facilities by the mentioned immigrants. COCHRANE and STOPES-ROE [2] found similar data concerning the Pakistani patients in Britain. These data bring into dispute the relationship between immigration and mental disorder, particularly that of the non-psychotic variety.

Dependent upon cultural, motivational, socio-economic and psychological attributes, the attainment of acculturation – a process akin in nature to identification – was found to require an average of five years in the young, new immigrants.

In the younger group of new immigrants, the rate and degree of acquisition of the language spoken in the host country often proved to be a valuable, indirect tool in gauging the grade of achieved acculturation [9]. This, like all generalizations, should be interpreted with caution. MORGAN and ANDRUSHKO [6] reported wide variance in different ethnic populations as to the use of the mother tongue by the immigrants in their homes. The highest rate of adherence to the mother language spoken at home was found among the Southern Europeans, quite particularly among the Portuguese, closely followed by the Asiatic immigrants. A more relevant index of acculturation is, however, the immigrant's ability to communicate in the local tongue.

Inherent vulnerability of personality, and impaired adaptational range determined by the premorbid personality, by previous severe emotional traumatization or by physical illness, represent a potential hazard of breakdown, particularly in the early stages of resettlement. All of these factors might provoke an acute disintegration in a person with a predilection for a transient depressed, suicidal or paranoid clinical manifestation. Latent or compensated psychotic propensities may flare-up with an overwhelming tendency to follow a chronic or an intermittent course. These observed pathologies were especially frequently found in the face of a grossly unrealistic motivation for migration, and with overrated expectations upon the host country on the part of the immigrant. Strict adherence to an ethnic enclave within the new milieu is generally regarded as an adverse factor in the younger age group of immigrants, obstructing acculturation.

During the postwar years there was no shortage of published, valuable, clinical, transcultural and theoretical work on the issue of individual and mass immigration. Unfortunately there was also no shortage of incredible human tragedies of enormous scale, from the holocaust of six million Jews in Europe, to the liquidation of an uncounted number of Biafrans, Ugandans in Africa, to the now occurring horror of the Vietnamese «boat people» in Asia; to supply sad material on enforced mass migration. Nor was there any shortage of theoretical analyses of the perpetrators of these crimes and of those who incited the flames of these tragedies.

The problems of the AGED migrants

If sufficient data has accumulated on the acculturation of the younger immigrants, much less work has been done on the elderly immigrants. To be sure, almost all of the mentioned work embraced fragmentary information on the old aged immigrants, including ØDEGAARD's original work, but few studies dealt systematically with the geriatric immigrant population, thus the remarkable difference between the younger and older immigrant groups has not emerged with clarity. To best illustrate this point: a recent, computerized literature search listed no publications at all on this specific issue. Nor were age-stratified data on psychiatric hospitalizations in the immigrant versus native-born population available by Statistics in Canada.

Similarly, no such information is available in our hospital record room. Thus, no responsible statistical work could be obtained on this subject on the local scene. If geriatrics is a notoriously neglected area, research into the adaptational processes of old-age immigrants is practically non-existent.

Migration for the old immigrants rarely, if ever, represents a primary choice arising from their own need or stemming from their own initiative to move to a new milieu and face its novel scope and challenge, but usually constitutes the fulfillment of a yearning for reunion with children or families. While such a reunion itself might be greatly desired, the stress of migration and the change of environment often stands for an unwanted price to be paid. The exchange of cherished expectations for fulfilled reality might soon bring a letdown and emptiness. In contrast, however, permanent and consuming frustration and an inability to join their loved ones in the new country often proves to be an unbearable stress in its own right.

Sometimes aged immigrants might be catapulted, as it were, from their original home environment due to war, revolution or natural catastrophy with a still higher vulnerability and toll. Such was well observed by the immediate and unhesitant extermination of the elderly in the concentration camps of the past and by the present reluctance of immigration officers to accept the few remaining old aged «boat people» who miraculously survived the ordeal of their journey.

Once in the new country, old immigrants do not acculturate. Far from being identical, the concepts of acculturation and adaptation are to be distinguished as strictly separate processes. Already alluded to is the fact that acculturation requires an identification with the spirit, language, traditions and political ideology of the host country, by the development of a sense of belonging and a degree of unity with it. In aged immigrants such an identification is either minimal or altogether non-existent. Thus, in striking absence of such acculturation, other styles and more modest forms of adaptational modalities are frequently employed by them.

The aged immigrants and ethnic enclaves

Already described as being undesirable in younger newcomers, the close adherence to ethnic enclaves in the aged immigrants represents a compelling and absolute necessity. Frequent emergence of severe psychological and even organic pathologies in old immigrants can be observed in their inability to find or to retain participation with their respective ethnic enclaves.

It is not a simple matter to define what constitutes an ethnic enclave. Such a colony may be a well-established, social-cultural organization or a church group with volunteers, planned programs, meals and regular membership. It might also be a semiformal club or an informal minienclave, arising spontaneously in the waiting rooms of certain clinics or doctors' offices or in small, inexpensive ethnic restaurants. Different as these places may be, they all share a common feature in that senior immigrants find it possible to recreate in those circumstances a fragment of the «old country» which is remote both in geography and in time. There they are able to reassert their waning self-esteem and participate in a cohesiveness which provides them with a relative balance in their emotional state. Even the built-in negative aspects, such as rivalry, jealousy and competition turn to positive features, for they represent the realities of life. Whatever the size, the inner dynamics of these enclaves can best be understood by transposing onto them observed principles of group psychotherapies. This is probably the reason why small, spontaneously engendered groups or enclaves are more successful, more personal, and have a higher sustaining power. On the other hand, they often are short-lived and subject to fast disintegration. There is usually a high and mutually-shared tolerance within these groups for boasting of past achievements and for reminiscences, the psychosocial importance of which is instinctively understood by its members. The ego-reinforcing quality of reminiscence in this age group was recently pointed out by BOYLIN [1]. Larger enclaves on the other hand provide more stability.

All enclaves are comfortably narrow in scope and offer sufficient familiarity to enable its members to feel secure, permitting a fast acclimatization for most. Safely rooted in such groups or organizations, even modest degrees of acculturation to the new country may eventually take place in some of their members.

The attitude of the government towards ethnic cultures, whether in fostering or inhibiting such circles, is of fundamental importance. Certain countries with a continual influx of immigrants such as the United States, Canada, and Israel maintain not only a high tolerance to ethnic cultures, but actively and financially support them. Multi-culturalism is a growing trend in civilized countries.

Old-aged immigrants in Canada — Own investigations

I was able to collect some material on the psychiatric and physical illnesses in 39 (female 24, male 15) old-age recent immigrants. In the absence of matched controls and with no valid comparison as to such events in the total number

Table 1. Clinical features of 39 recently-arrived aged immigrants.

Country of origin, number of patients	Sex, number of patients	Age upon arrival					Marital status				Motivation to re-unite		Physical illnesses					Psychiatric illnesses							Previous psychiatric illness
		60–65	65–70	70–75	75–80	over 80	single	married	widowed	divorced	siblings	children	cardiovascular	diabetes	mild OBS	marked OBS	other	depression	depression with anxiety	transient OBS	permanent OBS	suicide attempt	suicide	confusional state	
Hungary 19	male 7	2	4	—	1	—	1	3	3	—	1	6	4	—	3	1	2	3	1	1	1	—	2	1	1
	female 12	4	4	2	1	1	—	4	7	1	—	12	3	4	4	3	1	6	1	1	3	1	—	1	3
Yugoslavia 2	male 1	1	—	—	—	—	—	1	—	—	—	1	1	—	1	—	—	1	—	—	—	—	—	—	—
	female 1	—	—	1	—	—	—	—	1	—	—	1	1	—	—	—	—	—	—	—	—	—	—	—	—
Austria 2	male —	—	—	—	—	—	—	—	—	—	—	—	—	—	—	—	—	—	—	—	—	—	—	—	—
	female 2	2	—	—	—	—	—	1	1	—	—	2	1	1	1	—	—	2	—	—	—	—	—	—	1
Czechoslovakia 6	male 2	1	1	—	—	—	—	2	—	—	—	2	1	—	1	—	2	—	1	—	—	1	—	—	—
	female 4	2	2	—	—	—	—	2	2	—	—	4	2	2	2	1	2	2	—	1	1	—	—	—	1
Roumania 2	male —	—	—	—	—	—	—	—	—	—	—	—	—	—	—	—	—	—	—	—	—	—	—	—	—
	female 2	2	—	—	—	—	—	2	—	—	—	2	1	—	—	1	—	2	1	—	—	—	—	—	—
Italy 8	male 5	3	1	—	1	—	—	3	1	1	—	5	2	2	2	1	3	2	—	2	1	—	—	1	—
	female 3	1	1	—	1	—	—	2	1	—	—	3	1	1	1	1	2	2	1	—	—	1	1	—	—
Subtotal	male 15	7	6	—	2	—	1	9	4	1	1	14	8	2	7	2	7	6	2	3	2	1	2	2	1
	female 24	11	7	3	2	1	—	11	12	1	—	24	9	8	8	6	5	14	3	2	4	2	1	1	5
Total	39	18	13	3	4	1	1	20	16	2	1	38	17	10	15	8	12	20	5	5	6	3	3	3	6

of immigrants versus native-born population, the trend may not reflect true proportions.

For purposes of this study the «aged, recent immigrant» was arbitrarily defined as a person over age 60 years upon his arrival to the new locale and being a resident there for not longer than five years. Instances of major psychiatric illnesses, both adaptational and organic in nature were studied as to their premorbid personality features, the circumstances of their arrival, their motivation for migration and the nature of their connections with their relatives in Canada. Their physical health and socio-economic status preceding their psychiatric illness were considered and special effort was made to enquire as to their belonging to any ethnic enclave, if such existed. Table I summarizes some of these data.

All patients, with the exception of a single male who subsequently committed suicide, migrated in order to reunite with their children.

The female immigrants in this sample outnumbered the males with a ratio of 1.6 : 1, and they were widowed more than twice as often as the males. Of the entire group almost half were widowed. Approximately a third were between the age of 60 – 65 years upon their arrival.

Psychiatric and somatic ailments

Various degrees of physical ailments were nearly universal in this group of old immigrants — most of these conditions existing, however, under ordinary life situations in a mild and compensated way. Slightly less than half of them suffered from various cardiovascular diseases (more frequently the male) but only in three of them was the condition serious enough to impede their everyday life. Many of these conditions fell into the ambiguous diagnostic category of «senile heart disease» while others had moderate-severe hypertensive heart disease or diffuse pains after a coronary. One-fourth of the immigrants, mainly females, suffered from diabetes with bloodsugar values beyond what could be regarded as age approximate. None of these conditions, however, was severe enough before the commencement of their psychiatric complications to hamper their daily life.

The frequency of organic brain syndrome in this group of patients was present in a striking 85%, if mild to moderate dysfunction of the retention and recall, which KRAL [4, 5] terms as benign senescence, is included. More severe organic illness was found in one out of five patients in the advanced age groups mainly, with a distinct female predominance in this sample. The minimum symptom in this latter group was nocturnal confusion.

Other physical illnesses, ranging from arthritis to emphysema, once again prevailing in a mild to moderate degree, were common findings.

In only one male and five female patients was a history of previous psychiatric treatment admitted. The reliability of this figure is questionable.

Most patients were within the range of a comfortable socio-economic class with the exception of two male patients with stressful finances, including the one already mentioned as having committed suicide. It is noteworthy that the male patients in this group were less frequently widowed than the female patients, thus, one might say that they experienced more support than their female counterparts.

Psychiatric illnesses in this sample of patients became manifest between one to thirty-eight months after their arrival to the host country. There were three instances of suicide, one by hanging and two by overdose. Despite the small sample size, one might venture to state that the suicide rate in this group of patients was excessive compared to that in the general population. There were also three suicide attempts, all of them with small doses of tranquilizers. Apart from the three instances of suicide, knowledge was obtained of four instances of death in this group of patients resulting from natural causes as well as about the death of two spouses.

The outstanding psychiatric diagnosis in more than half of the cases was depression and by adding those with mixed depression, anxiety and all sorts of bodily complaints, the frequency of all depressions would embrace two-thirds of the population. These illnesses frequently showed symptomatology characteristic to the endogenous-type depressions or appeared as a pseudodementia. The remaining one-third of the cases exhibited mainly transient or permanent organic brain syndromes, some with depressive coloring. A small number of patients were diagnosed as nonspecific, confusional psychoses showing acute hallucinatory and delusional states, offering a delirium-like clinical picture. One of them eventually blended into a frank depression, but all three of them cleared up well, within a relatively short period of time. It is of importance to remark that one male and one female patient suffering from this condition lost their respective spouses just prior to their psychotic episode. Although recovered, the female patient died two months later of myocardial infarction, an event which invokes a reference to PARKES' «broken heart syndrome» [8].

Old-aged immigrants without ethnic enclaves

Subsequent to their arrival, seven patients were unable to find an ethnic enclave. All seven patients in this group began to show rapid deterioration within one to thirteen months after their arrival. Also, invariably, there were repeated and sometimes vocal regrets expressed by the patients' relatives for having permitted or encouraged their parents' immigration. After partial recovery two of the female patients returned to their country of origin where they had other children. During their treatment both of these patients expressed a continuous longing for their children at the home country, and in addition to marked organic symptoms they revealed paranoid suspiciousness about food and medication. Both these women were widows. The low grade of social reaction and the heavy loading of medical and organic problems in this group of patients apparently contributed to their rapid decline − a collection of symptoms representing a poor prognosis as pointed out by KLEBAN [3]. Additionally, an adverse family relation was considered to be a significant contributing factor.

A group of eleven patients who maintained only an episodic contact with various ethnic social organizations and tended to withdraw, developed a reactive type of uncomplicated depression, sometimes tinged with many bodily complaints and anxiety. All of these patients improved rapidly with the administration of minor tranquilizers, reassurance and the intervention of their families to encourage active social participation in their preferred organizations.

For the purposes of this particular study two other groups of patients represent a point of major interest. Upon their arrival these individuals found and actively participated in various ethnic organizations and showed a reasonable adaptation to both their children and the new milieu. One group of thirteen patients, however, dropped out of the supportive enclave due to the aggravation of their physical illnesses, and, another group of eight patients were forced to make a second move to another city because of their children's occupational or business opportunity.

A few whose physical health had deteriorated were, for a while, visited by or maintained telephone contact with members of their respective circle or newly-acquired friends, but these contacts eventually faded away.

Most of the patients in this group developed depressions and one of them, a female with a heart disease condition and diabetes, became markedly anxious and depressed. A male patient in this group developed a serious disease of the kidneys and a total intoxication and died four months later. Of course one might argue that in these instances the physical illness per se and the consequentially imposed isolation provided the decisive contributions in bringing about the emotional responses. There is no measurable way to separate the proportionate importance of these factors.

However, the group of aged immigrants who originally made a good adaptation subsequent to their arrival, but were later uprooted a second time as a result of following their children to a new location, demonstrated most prominently the role of the ethnic enclave in their adjustment.

This group of patients, for a variety of reasons, were unable to rejoin an ethnic organization in their new locale and within weeks to months developed a depression, often showing a flat affect and in other instances, anxiety with a hypochondriacal component. In some of these patients, previously existing mild organic symptoms gained a distinct dominance and besides memory disturbances, nocturnal episodes of confusion developed. The coincidence of depression with organic signs seems apparently to be more frequent than heretofore recognized.

The almost ubiquitous depression and the rapid physiological deterioration observed in these old immigrants cannot be distinctly related to anything and it is speculative to invoke the concept of stress in old people in general terms. Biological changes in old people could represent a biological tendency for depression. The event-related timing of the depression in these groups of patients, however, reflects our current inability to translate the psychological and social impact into direct biological data.

Conclusions

What little one could conclude from these observations is merely old knowledge. Containing the quintessence of Gerontology, in «De Senectute» Marcus Tullius Cicero has said it all in 44 B.C.: «The unripe apples must be wrenched from the tree but fall off on their own accord when ripe and mellow». He also stated that «old age has no fixed term and one may fitly live in it, so long as he can observe and discharge the duties of his station». The vulnerability of the old person becomes a real peril in the old immigrant. Consumed by his desire to unite with his children if he stays behind, or his narrowed world crumbling if he migrates, the choice is not his own.

Bibliography

1 BOYLIN, W., GORDON, S.K., NEHRKE, M.F.: Reminiscing and ego integrity in institutionalized elderly male. Gerontologist *16,* 118 – 124, 1976.

2 COCHRANE, R., STOPES-ROE, M.: Psychological and Social Adjustment of Asian Immigrants to Britain: A Community Survey. Social Psychiatry *12,* 195 – 206, 1977.

3 KLEBAN, M.H., LAWTON, P.M., BRODY, E.M., MOSS, M.: Behavioral observations of mentally impaired aged: Those who decline and those who do not. J. of Gerontology *31,* 3, 333 – 339, 1976.

4 KRAL, V.A.: Psychiatric problems in the aged: A reconsideration. Can. Med. Assoc. J. 583 – 590, 1973.

5 KRAL, V.A.: Psychiatric Problems. In: Von Hahan, H.P. (Ed.): Practical Geriatrics. S. Karger Publ., Basel/Paris/New York, 1975.

6 MORGAN, P., ANDRUSHKO, E.: The use of diagnosis-specific rates of mental hospitalization to estimate underutilization by immigrants. Soc. Sci. Med. *11,* 611 – 618, 1977.

7 MURPHY, H.B.M.: Migration and the major mental disorders. In: Kantor, M.B. (Ed.): Mobility and Mental Health. Ch. Thomas Publ., Springfield, Ill., 1965.

8 PARKES, M.C., BENJAMIN, B., FITZGERALD, R.G.: Broken heart: A statistical study of increased mortality among widowers. Brit. Med. J., 740 – 743, 1969.

9 SARWER-FONER, G.J., GELLERT, J., KORANYI, E.K.: The immigrant acculturation scale. Laval Medical *41,* 465 – 477, 1970.

Part III

Transcultural approaches

Chapter 13
By land and sea:
Hispanic press at the southern borders of the United States

Diana Hull

In the short 200 year history of the United States 60 million immigrants have come from abroad either as slaves or as refugees. Before 1921 there was no limitation placed on migration to the U.S., and as a result of the «open door policy», 25 million people entered the country between 1881 and 1921. From 1921 until 1965, the rule was to admit Northern and Western Europeans, and exclude most others from any part of the world except the Western Hemisphere. These regulations represented a national origins quota system that was highly selective. However, there had never been any limitation placed on immigration from any country in the Western Hemisphere because there was little demand for entry by Central and South Americans. In the late 19th century, rather than restricting migration, American farmers, mining companies, and the railroads actively recruited Mexican labor. The United States had in fact developed two policies, one for admitting immigrants from our hemisphere, and another for all others. In 1965, for the first time, a numerical ceiling was placed on entry from Western Hemisphere countries, and visas could only be gotten after the labor department had agreed that the individual was not competing with American workers and that the terms of the employment would not effect prevailing wages and working conditions [20]. This was unlike the conditions of admission for all other nationalities, which depended instead on the individual's high level or unusual skills.

Since this law also provided for the reuniting of families, relatives receive 80% of the available visas, and this provision, although humanitarian in motive, defeated the intent to give preference to professionals, doctors, scientists, and artists. In choosing applicants from the Western Hemisphere, there is no occupational preference system, or any other procedure for choosing between individuals, and the demand for visa's now far exceeds the supply. This has resulted in at least a two and one half year delay in obtaining one of the 120000 available entry permits. Legal Mexican immigrants received 70000 of these visa's, and Cubans received 24000 [1].

The purpose of the 1965 Immigration Act was to upgrade the type of arriving immigrants in terms of occupational skills, but giving this kind of preference has resulted, for example, in there being more foreign educated physicians being admitted into the United States than were graduated from American Medical Schools [1]. Others maintain that what the U.S. needs instead are workers willing to fill the low status, low paying jobs that they believe most Americans will not accept. For opponents of a liberal immigration policy the heart of the issue is whether or not immigrants are in competition with Americans for the same jobs, and if they are not, whether their children will be. Do these foreign workers and professionals, legal and illegal, assist the economy of the host country, or increase unemployment? Are they a help or a burden? Attitudes towards migrants, an important factor in their adaptation, depends upon how these issues are perceived.

Recent migration trends

Tracing the changes in the stream of migration both into and within the United States, it is possible to see a response to political, social and economic developments. Up until the last half of this century the main thrust of migration has been toward the west, bringing both new arrivals from Europe and Easterners to the middle and far west. The movement from south to north began within the U.S., as blacks from the rural south moved to the large cities of the north, east and midwest. In the last fifteen years we see a move of individuals and business to the south and south-east, as an alternative to the high taxes, and the high wages of union labor in the older cities of the northeast. Minor trends are a move to smaller cities and rural places.

The largest recent migrations into the United States are of Cubans to Florida, and the continuing migration of Mexicans, both legal and illegal into urban centers. In the past twenty years 1.5 million Puerto Ricans, half of their population of 3 million, have left the island for mainland cities. Although Mexico contributes about 60% of the His-panic press at our southern borders, Peru, Columbia and Haiti, all of whom have small legal quota's, send a large, but difficult to document, number of illegals to the U.S. Two-thirds of recent immigrants have settled in just six states, New York, California, New Jersey, Illinois, Texas and Massachusetts. Chicago, for example, has a Spanish speaking population of 600000, the nations second largest Mexican population after Los Angeles, the second largest Puerto Rican population after New York, and the third largest Cuban population after Miami and New York [18].

The U.S. has not one, but two virtually open borders. There are about 500 million border crossings each year as visitors come from both Mexico and Canada. Fewer than one percent arrive from overseas, and these people are counted as they enter, but not when they leave. Plane tra-velers are better documented. We know from VINING's [24] examination of U.S. international air travel statistics that the excess of arrivals over departures is very large, perhaps 500 to 700 thousand a year. Thus, about one-half million people a year have simply been overlooked by those who estimate the volume of illegal entry.

This chapter discusses the Mexicans and the Cubans, and describes the change in attitude toward both political and economic migrants as their numbers increase in pro-portion to both the established population, and to other minority groups. Attitudes harden as the resources of the cities become strained and as they struggle to deal with the overcrowding from internal migration as well. The immi-

236

gration and refugee debate is becoming increasingly unpleasant with anti-immigrant and anti-refugee sentiment growing and strident. The most recent national polls show that 91% of the sample supported an all out effort to stop illegal entry of the estimated one and a half million foreigners who do not have entry visas, and 80% were in favor of reducing the quotas for legal entry as well.

This has not always been so. The Mexican has always been recruited and encouraged during periods of economic expansion when labor was in short supply. Although once admitted, working class Mexicans suffer the same prejudice, and are held back by the same language and cultural barriers that made the lives of earlier European immigrants so difficult, and live in «barrios» that resemble the ethnic ghettos of the nineteenth century.

Mexican immigrants, and the first Cuban refugees differed markedly in social class membership, past history of migration, and in the nature of the community of earlier arrivals. Mexicans have traditionally come because of impoverished circumstances at home, and reasons for entry, as well as education and occupation status, are more likely to effect acceptance than ethnicity.

Social scientists have studied the social, emotional, economic, and health problems of immigrants, but what has received less attention is the motivation, and the social and emotional responses of established inhabitants, and the results of the interactive effects on both groups.

Both the primitive and learned responses of host populations need to be acknowledged, like the suspicion and dislike of strangers, and of those different than ourselves, protective feelings about the established culture, and apprehension that it may be altered, the fear of being outnumbered, or simply of population increases because of the higher fertility rate of some immigrant groups, and, the always present uneasiness about the envy of any underclass who might become powerful or aggressive.

When expatriates come in an atmosphere of benevolence or rescue, the receiving country, pleased with its own behavior, may have a more positive attitude. This would be a fair overall statement about the reception of Cubans until the last decade.

The U.S. has a history of less than altruistic motives toward Mexicans and where entry policies have been based primarily upon self-interest, if not exploitation, newcomers have not been treated as well, or as highly regarded.

The Cubans

The modern population of Cuba derives from a migration of Spaniards from Andalusia, and to a lesser extent from the importation of blacks from West Africa. After Spain's occupation was challenged and the country became politically independent, economic ties between Cuba and the United States became close. However, the progress of Cuba as a republic was uneven and disappointing. There was a revolution against a corrupt president in 1933, and the adoption of a new and progressive constitution in 1940. Although Cuba was stable financially, political upheavals have been continuous. General Battista took over the government in 1952, but dissatisfaction was deep and revolutionary counterforces were continuously at work.

The mass immigration from Cuba to the U.S. which has now reached more than one million, did not occur until Fidel Castro seized power with the promise to restore the constitution and free elections. The immediate immigration of Battista's supporters was followed by the exodus of landowners, entrepreneurs, merchants, and professionals as soon as it became clear that they could not identify with the new regime. Thus, the Cuban migration of the 1950's and early 1960's was a direct result of political events.

RUMBAUT and RUMBAUT [19] view the culture of the United States as congruent, even though unlike the culture of pre-exile Cuba, and believe that this accounts for the resilience and success of the early Cuban expatriates. The stress of being uprooted, though not insignificant, may have been somewhat less for them than for earlier Europeans and for contemporary Mexican immigrants. The

238

adaptation of Cuban refugees was helped not only by positive attitudes in the U.S. but by the practical aid that was offered through federal and private agencies.

Despite a history of corrupt governments, there was in pre-Castro Cuba a large professional and middle class. The poor, mostly rural workers who had very low incomes, numbered about one million. It was not, however, this group who contributed to the mass exodus, at least not for the first fifteen years. However, even before the 1980 boatlift, there was an increasing number of workers leaving Cuba whose motivation was as much economic as it was political, but they were usually more skilled workers than a comparable group from Mexico.

The first wave of Cubans were the beneficiaries of a new U.S. policy that provided for the admission of special political refugees. This included 40000 Hungarians following the failure of their anti-Communist revolution, and in 1979 accounted for the admission of one-half million Southeast Asians. In the case of the Vietnamese, the U.S. certainly had responsibility for the chaos and terrible agony in that part of the world.

Despite this, national opinion sampling now shows that there is an increasingly negative attitude toward migration of all kinds. It is likely that some of the change in attitude toward the Cubans was building over a twenty-five year period, and was related to both their concentration in the Miami area and to the very large numbers that continued to come and to bring their families. A crisis resulted in the spring of 1980 when Castro sent about 120000 people to Florida, many of them sick, unemployed or unemployable or admitted criminals. The Cuban-American community sent out boats of all kinds to facilitate their arrival, and at first President Carter stated that he would accept the boatloads with «open arms and hearts». As it became clear that the Cuban government expelled those they considered undesirable, the U.S. Coordinator for Refugee Affairs declared that human beings were being used as a weapon in a new kind of warfare, «population warfare».

Unfortunately, Dade Country, where Miami is located,

was already dealing with high unemployment and racial tensions. It is 40% white, 17% black, and 38% Hispanic. In 1979 the murder rate had climbed 70% and the police commissioner announced that «an absolute war is being fought in our streets at night» [22]. The sale of personal firearms increased dramatically, and many of those able to move away were going further north in response to the press from the south.

Public indignation at the strain on resources and community funds, resulted in the delivery of 12 000 letters to the President of the U.S. and a decisive vote on election day against further bilingual education in Florida.

Thus, acceptance of future refugees, especially in large numbers, will require a much narrower and more precise definition of «political expatriate». Such a category becomes problematic when hundreds of millions of the impoverished, also live under repressive regimes.

The events in Miami warn that changes in the structure and composition of human groups need to evolve and develop, because racism and violence can erupt when populations and human systems are abruptly altered. Makers of immigration policy need to be sensitive to people impact, especially in already crowded urban centers where delicate balances have often been achieved with much effort over time to contain a multitude of dormant tensions and antagonisms.

The Mexicans

The abundant natural resources of Mexico have never been of benefit to the ordinary Mexican. Each of the geologic ages left a wealth of mineral deposits, silver, gold, lead, zinc, copper, iron ore, coal and petroleum. This wealth has enriched the few in every era, as the Mexican people endured the Aztec class system, the Spanish occupation, massive and frequent revolutionary disorders, and a series of corrupt and dictatorial governments.

In pre-Columbian times almost all of the indigenous inhabitants lived in the lower two-fifths of the country. By the sixteenth century at least five different groups had developed distinctive cultural patterns with their own religious and civilian hierarchies. There were skilled craftsmen of all kinds, a complex economic system, instruments for astronomical observation, and calendars more accurate than those of contemporary Europeans. There were beautiful public buildings, ornate attire and beautiful art objects. It is said that when Cortes arrived, the Aztec Montezuma II used his golden dishes just once and then had them destroyed. Like the Spanish rule that followed, these societies were also repressive and barbaric. The rich were rapacious and the lower classes were destitute.

To the Spanish conquerers, Mexicans were non-Christian heathens who deserved extermination if they resisted conversion. What the Spaniards and Aztecs had in common was the establishment of social systems with rigidly enforced class and economic distinctions, a problem that still exists in contemporary Mexico.

The scarcity of Spanish women at the time of the Spanish occupation is largely responsible for the composition of the present Mexican population. Concubinage, casual liaison, and marriage with Indian women produced the Mestizo, and the importation of African slaves introduced a third racial strain. The Castas, people of this tripartite background, outnumbered Europeans two to one by 1800, and the indigenous inhabitants had already diminished in size even more rapidly[1]. Of the original native population of twenty million, about one million were left by 1650. When Europeans invaded formerly isolated societies, the

---

[1] Different ethnic groups who live side by side do meld, whatever their original historic or class positions, and despite strong taboos, and differences in color, race, and religions, but the same time schedule is centuries not generations. In Beyond the Melting Pot: The Negroes, Puerto Ricans, Jews, Italians, and Irish of New York City by NATHAN GLAZER and DANIEL MOYNIHAN (M.I.T. Press Cambridge Mass., 1970), the authors note that the five or more ethnic groups in New York City have remained fairly discrete. However, the large in-migration from Europe only ended after the first World War.

military conquest was often less life threatening to the inhabitants than the unfamiliar pathogens that ravaged the virgin population[2]. The Amerindians of Mexico were decimated by measles, small pox, and an influenza type infection in a series of epidemic cycles.

Mexico was plundered and exploited by Spain for three centuries. Hundreds of thousands labored under debt bondage, and other forms of forced labor. After the establishment of independence in the 19th century there were fifty different governments in fifty years, republics and dictatorships, rebellions, and continuous and violent internal struggles, war with the French, war with the United States, and through it all the Mexican worker remained in essentially the same situation he had been in for centuries. As late as 1910, in a country where the majority of people were agrarians, only two percent owned land, and peonage for debts was still widespread. The huge haciendas contained millions of acres and this unreasonable concentration of land in the hands of a few, and the vicious struggle between the clergy and the government kept Mexico in a constant turmoil, and the population in misery [9].

The Hispanic countries that are the source of most of the migration to the U.S. are becoming industrialized, but the wealthy classes continue the Colonial tradition, and neglect the rural development that would not only help the poor, but stop or slow the rural to urban migration. The drawing power of industrial development, in addition to the high birth rate, accounts for the projected doubling in population in twenty years in at least three Latin-American countries. Unfortunately, industrialization has not created the jobs that were supposed to take the place of lost livelihood in the country. Much of technology is capital intensive, and most standardized products can be made with less problem by expensive machines than by cheap

---

[2] Amerindians were extremely vulnerable to the disease organisms that Spaniards and Africans brought with them. See Plagues and Peoples by WILLIAM H. MCNEILL (Anchor Press, 1976) for a discussion of the effect of disease epidemics on politics.

labor. There is no sign, however, that labor intensive industry is being developed on any scale in Latin America, even though it would seem more appropriate in countries with huge and exponentially growing number of people out of work.

The escalation of the Hispanic press at the southern borders of the United States can be explained by the Mexican unemployment rate, which Mexican officials privately admit is about 50% [4]. Thus, impoverished individuals and families press into the United States, swimming, wading, and walking across a border so long that effective control has never been accomplished.

The extent of Mexican migration into the United States is unknown. From 1930 to 1977 eight times as many Mexicans were apprehended for illegal entry as were admitted legally. There were ten million *known* illegal entries during that time and one million two hundred legal entries. In 1977 almost one million illegal migrants were caught, and the actual number of illegal migrants living in the United States has been estimated at anywhere between two and twelve million. Cornelious, who has done extensive research on this subject for government study groups, believes that 13% of the Mexican labor force works for some period of time in the U.S. each year, and if each of them supports 5.8 dependents (as his data indicates), then about 21% of the population of Mexico is dependent upon money from the U.S. [4]. The Inner City Fund has estimated that about three billion dollars a year is sent home to families in Mexico. Even though most Mexican workers have jobs in the secondary labor market, success to them depends on whether or not they achieve what they came for.

Unlike the Cubans, most of whom were never in the United States before, there have always been Mexican workers, visitors, and «illegals» going back and forth over the 2000 mile border between the United States and their country. This great distance makes it impossible to patrol as a practical matter, and it was, before 1929, open and without restriction in fact, if not as a matter of policy. Therefore, it has always been difficult to determine the extent of Mexican migration, and during certain periods, like the depression of the 1930's, there were far more Mexicans going home, than coming to the U.S.

Both CORNELIUS [7] and BACA and BRYAN [3] content from their survey research that a majority of the illegal Mexican workers are unwilling to relinquish their Mexican citizenship, and would continue to live in both countries; that is, continue to travel back and forth between the U.S. and Mexico, even if they were granted legal alien status. The fact that they do not sever ties or stop living in the homeland, makes the Mexican, and to a lesser extent other Hispanics, different from the European immigrant of the past.

It is likely that Mexicans who work in cities in the southwest and west tend to travel back and forth between Mexico and the United States, while those who come from deeper in the interior of Mexico are the ones most likely to settle in American cities far from the border.

Economic adjustment

Successful adaptation in a group of first generation immigrants might be a satisfactory economic and social adjustment, and a low rate of depression. There is some evidence that such success or lack of it is determined by the immigrants' expectations, the attitude of the host society, the ability to maintain an identity, and the support of a community of earlier arrivals.

No research has been done comparing rates of depression in Mexican and Cuban immigrants. This kind of information would be difficult to obtain, since the condition would have to be severe enough to require hospitalization, or at least outpatient treatment in order to be counted as a case. Studies of immigrants to other receiving countries (Israel and Singapore), indicate that where new arrivals find a large community from the home country, mental hospitalization rates are low, and where immigrants are isolated, mental hospital rates are high [14]. Social adjustment is also difficult to measure, although it is generally conceded that both the immediate and extended family, and community affiliation is a strength in both Mexican and Cuban sub-societies.

Economic adjustment is pivotal to the entire processes of adaptation. It should not be overlooked that economic well-being has clear psychological and symbolic meaning in terms of being cared for and receiving both nourishment and love [15]. Therefore, it is just as well that a measurable factor like economic status is the variable studied in the only research that compares the adjustment of Cubans and Mexicans.

Portes and his associates have contributed two major studies, the first compared the aspirations and attainments of both Mexicans and Cubans in the United States [17]. In a second study PORTES and BACH [16] selected differences in income between Cuban and Mexican immigrants as an objective and fundamentally important indicator of their situation. They established education, occupation, age, and income aspirations upon arrival compared with actual occupation and income as determined by a follow-up interview three years later. This work finds the expectations of both groups realistic, and soundly based on their past occupational and educational status, as well as their knowledge of English. Cubans, however, often worked for Cuban employers and for this reason they had some protection from the vicissitudes of the open labor market.

CORNELIUS [7] reported that Mexicans join the open U.S. labor market and become scattered in many locations in the same way as domestic workers. They are employed mainly in what has been called the secondary labor market, that is in small scale, labor intensive kinds of businesses such as small farms, restaurants, small construction firms, and greenhouses, or in businesses with a low profit margin, or in competition with low priced foreign manufacturers. He believes that both the conditions and the wage scale of these jobs make them unappealing to most American workers. In general, the income of the Mexican worker was more dependent on the segment of the economy in which he worked than upon his education, skills or occupational experience.

The Cubans, on the other hand, are not as dispersed over the country. About 97% live in Miami where at least 10% of business is Cuban owned [17]. Here, Cuban migrants at first enjoyed protection and sponsorship, and used the whole network of formal and informal kinship ties found in this cohesive community.

Although the achievments of first generation Mexicans and Cubans are generally in accordance with their aspiration level, expectations change from one generation to the next, and the social and economic aspirations of the children and grandchildren of immigrants resemble more and more the expectations of the children of established residents. Until recently little attention was paid to the adjustment of second and third generation Hispanics, perhaps because it was believed that they would do as well as the children of earlier European immigrants. Prejudice because of color may be one reason for the slower economic progress of dark-skinned people, but there is little understanding about why both Mexican and Puerto Rican children[3] have so much difficulty with the English language. Mexican children often begin school with no knowledge of English, and this is one of the disadvantages of self-contained subsocieties. There are very large Spanish speaking communities, in urban centers, where it is possible to both live and work without ever needing to know English, or have much contact with Anglo society. Children who speak Spanish as their mother tongue cannot function at age six in a classroom where school is conducted in another language. English must first be learned, and until it is mastered, the curriculum and the teachers need to be bilin-

[3] GLAZER and MOYNIHAN note that this difficulty persists despite the fact that «probably no public school system has ever spent so much money and devoted so much effort to the problems of a group of minority school children as the New York Public school system has to the Puerto Ricans.» These authors speculate that the children who could not master English forty years ago, simply left school before their learning difficulty became too noticeable.

gual. The experience of failure, and the development of a sense of inadequacy in the early school years is undoubtedly a major contributor to a resistance to education, and to the often difficult process of acquiring knowledge and skills. Mexican-Americans have the highest school drop out rate of any ethnic population in the country [2].

The children of legal Mexican immigrants are at least able to attend school, and twenty-four percent, about one quarter of all students in the Houston Texas School system, for example, are Hispanic. In the barrios (Mexican neighborhoods) are thousands of children belonging to illegal aliens, and the tax supported schools until recently were not permitted to admit these students without charging tuition, a regulation which effectively excluded them[4].

The controversey over whether it is appropriate for Americans to be taxed to provide for the education of children of citizens of another country who are here illegally, is an ethical and legal question which will probably be debated for some time.

Cuban refugees have not been here long enough for a study of several generations, but the children and grandchildren of Mexican immigrants, despite their educational limitations, are not satisfied with what they have achieved.

ALVAREZ [2], a Chicano scholar, believes that the children of migrants, whom he calls the Mexican-American generation, took pride in being a part of the United States, and saw that their status compared favorably to that of their parents. The Chicanos (third generation) have returned to an ethnic consciousness and to militancy because despite their acculturation, they do not have any realistic prospect of escaping virtually complete lower and working class status. They believe they have been excluded from the benefits of American society, and blame inferior schools and racism.

Although there are real pockets of poverty in the United States, where people live at well below subsistence levels,

[4] Churches and other private groups have sponsored some alternative schools.

the demand for upward mobility comes in the main from other segments of the population. Poverty is also very relative in this country. There has been a marked improvement in the last 25 years in the standard of living for all socio-economic groups, and although it is true that there are as many people today at the bottom as there were twenty-five years ago, the bottom is much more adequate than it once was. The children of immigrants are sufficiently sophisticated to know that there are other solutions to poverty than low status, arduous work, and they exercise these options in the same way as the native poor white and black underclass. Welfare payments in California, for example, are higher than the earnings of a typical agricultural migrant worker[5], so that these and other jobs with similar pay and status are often disdained by the native born unemployed [23]. Having the necessities of life does not seem to change a feeling of being poor and underprivileged if middle class status has not been achieved. Currently Mexican-Americans join native Whites and Blacks, and almost every one else in lower socio-economic positions in seeking upward mobility, and as rapidly as possible. All groups in the United States seek to wrest from society, by political and other means, more of the material and symbolic rewards to which there seems to be a universal sense of entitlement.

If, as CORNELIUS [7] argues, nonrestrictive migration policies serve the best interests of American and Western European economies because of the need for workers in the secondary labor market (jobs he claims established residents won't take), this solution is for one generation only. It is necessary then to accept the prospect of a continuous stream of new immigrant labor. Receiving nations evidently want the benefits of migration, but balk at the hidden costs in the long term.

---

[5] Welfare payments in Texas are extremely low. Less than 1500 Mexican families received the main form of public assistance (Aid to Families with Dependent Children) in 1978 in Harris County, Texas.

Motives and responses to migration

Attitudes of Americans toward immigrants vary with cultural congruence between host and newcomer and this is frequently more a function of social class than ethnicity. Formerly affluent, educated Cubans from the upper and middle classes, who were English speaking upon arrival, were well accepted. Mexicans and South Americans of similar status in their own country do not usually emigrate, and the Mexican peasant who does press at our southern borders is valued for the contribution of labor rather than for other characteristics.

There were personality as well as class issues that accounted for a more positive attitude toward the early Cubans than toward Mexicans. Cubans tend to be active, open and effusive. They are usually direct, and although the culture and mores are complex, they are fairly transparent about their likes and dislikes. Americans find this easier to relate to than the Mexican personality which is more masked, subtle, and outwardly passive. Perhaps the greatest problem between Mexicans and Anglos has to do with the apparent agreeableness of the Mexican that may have little relationship to actual feelings or intentions.

There is some resistance to the notion of national character because it tends to create stereotypes and foster unwarranted generalizations about individuals, but cognitive processes are derived, at least in part, from the cultural organization of groups. If one is willing to assume that socialization can create a modal personality, then the Mexican Catholic is fatalistic and mystical, and the Protestant American is compulsive, and literal minded. These polar traits can and do create mutual misunderstanding and antagonism.

Most studies of migration emphasize the importance of identifying who the migrants are, examining motives for migration, charting the stages in the adaptation process, and evaluating how the migrant is affected by the move. As might be expected, investigations of motivation find multiple causes, social, political, economic and personal — all that individuals are willing to reveal, or that can be inferred from objective information. At least equal in importance are personal motives that are intentionally hidden, or beyond awareness.

However, the adaptation of migrants is, after all, a result of the interaction between themselves and the receiving society. In much that is written on the subject, it is as if the receiving society provided a stable and consistent structure for the immigrant to accommodate to. Actually the social climate in a receiving society is very variable, and attitudes, both official and unofficial, towards immigrants are in a constant state of flux. The range of responses from accepting to rejecting can depend on the number of immigrants and their visability, as well as the congruence of their behavior and attitudes with the host culture. Social, economic and political issues that are not directly related to the newcomers can also have a part in their reception [14].

It is often overlooked that immigrants can cause conflict and stress in societies they enter. Immigrants are not always political or economic refugees who become minorities both numerically and ethnically in fairly powerful and established cultures. European immigrants have been invaders who destroyed or enslaved indigenous inhabitants on every continent. Americans took over the land, and overpowered the culture of the American Indian and the Hawaiian, and examples of intrusion and imposition of culture are part of the history of almost every group. The fear of «invasion» in the social or psychological sense can also be experienced by sophisticated people in modern nations. There is also no reason to expect the educated or the technologically advanced to be free of tribalism and tribal loyalties.

Systems theory offers some productive ways of thinking about the impact of immigrants upon societies they enter. Migrants in small numbers are like guests who can be treated benevolently when they do not disturb the ongoing processes, and in effect, know whose house it is. Thus, small numbers of newcomers can be absorbed into the «family» so long as the homeostasis is not challenged. At some critical point the number or impact of outsiders can be potent enough to threaten the majority, and certain predictable exclusionary actions follow. These are often met with active or passive resistance and hostility which in turn escalates the conflict.

Interactive effects are always part of the picture, and it is doubtful that immigrant groups are completely naive about the effect of their behavior, and in fact, are simply doing what they have always done in their home country. As the study of acculturation and adaptation indicates, the legal immigrant, especially in a democracy, has many defensive and aggressive weapons at his/her disposal. The difficulty with advanced societies who take in newcomers, especially the impoverished, is that they, like parents except gratitude. This is not possible because those with less power are usually angry, perhaps even more so when apparently submissive.

In order to deal with these issues it is essential that there is a recognition of just how emotionally loaded the subject of territory and boundaries are to established residents, and how critical the matter of acceptance and exclusion is to the immigrant. The group and personal psychodynamics involved, the pain, anger and apparent irrationality results from arousing core issues of identity and belonging on both sides.

As a results of legal and illegal migration from Mexico, the one million refugees from Cuba, and other migration from Central and South America, the United States has become the fifth largest Spanish speaking nation in the world. It is interesting that this has taken place in the last ten to fifteen years and is unrelated to the fact that the U.S. took half of Mexico's territory in the U.S. Mexican War, (some of Texas, all of what is now California, most of New Mexico, Arizona and Utah, and part of Colorado and Wyoming). The present pervasiveness of Hispanic language and culture is recent, paralleling and exponential increase of migration from the south since the early 1970's.

The impact of the Hispanic press at our southern borders can be seen, for example, in the industrial city of Houston, Texas. From 1949 until 1979, Houston has grown from 250000 to 1500000 people. Now Spanish surname residents number about 225000[6] and the illegal Mexican who is, in effect, an underground group whose true size cannot be known, is estimated by the Catholic Diocese to number 300000. Thus, the overall Hispanic population is at least 500000, one-third of the inhabitants, and is twice as large as the population of the entire city thirty years ago.

Thus, the composition and the overall ambiance of the fifth largest city in the United States has changed markedly, especially in the last five to ten years. Rapid growth has probably been as important a contributor to the change as ethnic composition, but faced with accelerating traffic problems, and all the other pressures of high population density that were not well planned for, the immigrant, especially the illegal immigrant accounts for some proportion of the problem, and is a convenient and identifiable target. Even if CORNELIUS is correct, and a large number of Mexican illegals go home, others come to replace them and have at least the same impact as a permanent group. In fact, constant new arrivals may be even more costly to schools and medical care facilities.

In 1980, testimony before the Congressional Select Committee on Migration documented the soaring public school costs associated with bilingual programs. In Denver the number of non-English speaking students rose 700% in nine years.

Yet to be done is a thorough study of the effects of large numbers of non-English speaking students on the public schools country-wide. Immigration, plus busing to achieve racial integration, has resulted in a movement of Anglo's and English language speakers out of the city centers into

[6] In 1976 the U.S. Immigration and Naturalization Service estimated that there were between 250000 and 500000 illegal Mexicans in Houston, and that Mexicans whose status was not in question, either citizens or those with proper papers contributed 12 to 20% of the total population.

the suburbs, and a turning to private schools by the middle, as well as upper classes.

Since a strong and first class system of public education has in the past provided the vehicle for the upward mobility of both immigrants and the American poor, it serves nobody's best interest to foster the creation of a dual system of public and private education.

It is not surprising then that indigenous inhabitants are often angry and resentful, although earlier arrivals from the same country are often the most threatened by newcomers, and Mexican-Americans and legal immigrants may sense correctly that they will be effected by a mounting exclusionary sentiment toward the large numbers entering illegally.

Protests of every kind against migration are as old as the country's beginnings. In the eighteenth century, George Washington and Thomas Jefferson warned about the massive entry of people supposedly less experienced in free government, and in the 1940's there was considerable alarm that Protestants would be outnumbered by the large influx of Catholics, or that a combination of recently naturalized citizens and political bosses would take control of the cities. The objections to free migration were ineffective in the main as long as the new arrivals provided a source of cheap and willing labor.

Unlimited entry into the United States was finally ended during the time organized labor began the long struggle to improve conditions of work and the level of wages. The first successful exclusion act, in addition to an earlier prohibition against admitting paupers and convicts, was directed against the Chinese in 1882. Then, following the increase in immigration after the first World War, the Congress put numerical limits on total migration, and established special quota's for each country. These restrictions were not put into effect easily, since a whole array of opposing forces made this one of the most intensely debated domestic issues in the country's history.

The exploiters of migrant labor have often been on the same side of the conflict as those who, for humanitarian reasons, wanted the United States to continue to be «an asylum for the oppressed of all lands». Factions interested in limiting migration, even at the present time, include both the bigoted, as well as those who believe that it is not in the best interests of the country or its present and future citizens to try and absorb substantial numbers of new-comers.

Currently two groups in the U.S. are in favor of a more restrictive migration policy, representatives of organized labor who claim immigrants compete with Americans for jobs, and those in the environmental movement who view population increase as one of the most important sources of environmental degradation. They point out that the United States took in more people legally in 1979 than all the other developed nations combined, and that immigration is a substantial component of the two million persons per year population increase [8]. This view was advanced as early as 1972 in a comprehensive study by the *Commission on Population and the American Future*[7] authorized by Congress. This report stated that no substantial benefits would result from continued growth of the nation's population . . . and that stabilization of the population would contribute significantly to the nation's ability to solve its problems.

There has been no official governement recognition that the poor air and water quality, the shortage of energy, the recreational overuse of national parks and forests, the traf-

[7] According to the National Center for Health Statistics, in 1978 the birth rate per thousand was 15.3, the death rate 8.8 leaving a natural increase of 6.5. Add net legal migration of 1.8 for a population growth of 8.3. This is known growth of about two million people a year. The U.S. Dept. of Justice estimates that 500000 illegal immigrants of all nationalities enter each year and there are from three to five million illegal immigrants residing in the U.S. at the present time. Probably ⅔ of the illegal migrants are Mexican. See: DAVID S. NORTH, MARION F. HOUSTOUN: The characteristics and role of illegal aliens in the U.S. labor market: An exploratory study. Report prepared for the Employment and Training Administration, U.S. Dept. of Labor, Contract No. 20-11-74-21, Linton and Co., Inc., Washington, D.C., 1976.

fic and other congestion problems in the cities are related in any way to migration policy.

It has been argued that environmental problems may accompany population increase because of the energy intensive way we live rather than because of the weight of sheer numbers. However, it is unlikely that this country will give up the production of increasing amounts of goods and services and the demand for natural resources and land in order to accommodate a higher population density.

In 1979 the population of the United States was about 220 million, with a growth rate of at least one percent a year [8]. This growth is unevenly distributed. Contemporary migrants, with the exception of agricultural workers, move to the cities where the jobs are, and existing ethnic communities continally attract others from the same country. Population problems appear to be mainly urban problems, but as the cities extend into the countryside, farmland is often lost as it is sold to developers of housing and industrial sites.

The social significance of population growth is far more complex than it would appear from simple comparisons of density between regions, the so-called man: land ratio. There has been too little systematic research on social organization and the carrying capacity of various types of regions. ALICE DAY and LINCOLN DAY [10] believe that although government officials and other policy makers recognize the existence of limits to population size and the numbers of immigrants that can be accommodated, inaction results from a fear of the economic consequences of a non-growing society, and the political implications of the steps necessary to slow or halt growth.

The Hispanic press at the southern borders of the United States is a result of the growing population of Mexico (and the other South American countries) which escalates the economic inequality between the regions. Worldwide the yearly increase of new poor is about 60 million[8]. GARRETT

[8] Fertility is apparently less related to culture or ethnicity and more related to the state of technology. The technologically advanced countries have lower birth rates, and the fertility of immigrants tend, over time, to approximate fertility of the adopted country.

HARDIN [13] calculated that if the United States decided to solve this problem by permitting all the poor to immigrate to this country, it would have to accommodate two thousand million poor people, or forty people for every family in the U.S. Obviously this is an absurd suggestion, but even if this were possible, the solution would only be temporary because the high birth rates of underdeveloped countries would soon replace those who had emigrated.

Rather than being helpful to less developed countries, migration appears to encourage population growth. Kingsley Davis cites convincing data that countries which export a large proportion of their excess population postpone inevitable changes in birth rates. There are more landless peasants in Mexico today than before the 1910 Mexican revolution which was fought over the issue of land reform [21].

TANTON [21] points out that the major food-exporting countries are also those that are the major immigrant receiving nations. He worries that the food exporting capability of these nations will be drastically reduced because of the requirements of a larger population at home. He says, «If certain regions of the world are over-populated and food deficient, others must remain relatively less populated and have a surplus of food for export. The massive movement of persons from food deficient regions to food sufficient regions is, therefore, not a solution to third world problems.»

The short-term benefits that developed nations get from the comparatively cheap and willing labor of the imported poor last for one, occasionally two, generations, and the children and grandchildren of these immigrants are handicapped by prejudice and a variety of social and economic barriers.

In lieu of more lasting solutions, better temporary solutions are possible than the present illegal migration. The labor needs of the United States, as well as the need for work on the part of the poor Mexican can be achieved by a «guest worker» program that would eliminate the onus of illegality. The «guest workers» would not be hidden or afraid of deportation, and would not be as susceptible to exploitation. The children would be enrolled in school, and appropriate health care and other programs could be arranged if their numbers were known, and their presence planned for.

EHRLICH [11] suggests that migration from Mexico could be slowed down by importing more goods from there, thereby creating more jobs.

The general problems of adaptation, acculturation, integration and assimilation are dealt with by STOLLER (see this volume p. 27) and are in principle the same for Mexicans and Cubans. It may be added, however, that the Mexicans in the southwest and west are such a large group that they will exist for a long time as a parallel but certainly not equal subsociety. They are also likely to be contained for at least three generations by their unicultural nature, i.e., where religious sanctions are interwoven with birth, death, marriage, food habits and ways of behaving in the family and the community. The future of the Cuban refugees as a subsociety is less certain, and is likely to be shorter for the business and professional classes who came as political refugees.

Toward a rational immigration policy

The Mexican worker, here legally or illegally, certainly contributes to the U.S. economy with his/her energy and productivity. The objection to giving the right of citizenship to the very large number already here, as well as to those who will continue to come, is that a very strong case can be made for restricting population growth. In addition, this country is not now providing the kind of educational and social development necessary to help the children and grandchildren of it's own underprivileged citizens achieve the kind of middle class status they aspire to. What will happen to the children and grandchildren of Mexican migrants? There is some evidence that the Chicanos (3rd generation Mexican) are as dissatisfied with their position in

American life as the rest of those with lower social status. We have not been very successful in helping the less privileged improve their situation, and this is as much a matter of not knowing how, as being unwilling to do so.

If the consensus is that the U.S. wants to restrict population growth, but permit Mexican workers to come here, they should be given «guest worker» status, and should not have to live in fear of being picked up and deported by the immigration service. The temporary worker program administered by the Department of Labor admits 1000 Mexicans a year claiming that there aren't any more jobs than that. This is obviously absurd. This department is the logical one to undertake the legitimizing of Mexican workers.

Unfortunately, many factions are opposed to a rational immigration policy. Some employers benefit from the precarious position of the illegal Mexican, and some segments of organized labor view the availability and productiveness of Mexicans as a threat to their bargaining power.

Migration can indeed rescue temporarily the sending nation from the consequences of its own governance.

A position paper written by Otis L. Graham, Jr. for the Federation for American Immigration Reform makes the following comments about this issue:

«Large scale immigration may be seen as a sort of individually activated and unconscious triage, in which the interests of a few mobile young people are protected at the expense of those less able to move, who stay behind and make what peace they can with oppressive social systems . . . those seeking individual and family solutions come to our attention and gain a natural sympathy, while the losers in sending societies far out number the few gainers who solve individual problems by escaping. Deeper and more candid thought needs to be given to the extent to which migration in the 20th century (at least) has always acted within and among nations, as a conservative force delaying social reconstruction» [12].

Despite the inscription on the Statue of Liberty in New York Harbor, immigration policies have not been a product of altruism in the main, but the result of a decision by influential groups that the rate of entry was to their best interests. In the case of Cuba, we received at first their most talented productive, highly skilled and motivated people. The United States also received good marks for providing refuge to a politically persecuted group. In the case of Mexico, our policy over the years has been aimed more frankly at satisfying this country's need for manual labor. Since this also coincided with the needs of impoverished Mexicans, it is problematic whether they have been exploited by the United States, or whether the relationship has been symbiotic.

Altruism toward those outside of the group or tribe has never been characteristic or even expected behavior, and whether a national policy of deliberate altruism could or even should be carried out is debatable. Some argue that Americans benefit from the ambiguous status of the undocumented foreign worker, but those helped most by illegal migration are employers in the secondary labor market, a relatively small group.

Responses to the Mexican and Cuban immigrant, the formulation of migration policy, the restriction or ease of entry, the way in which the immigrant is helped or rejected, is usually more related to what politicians perceive about the attitudes of their constituents, than to quantifiable or objective data about economics or jobs. But this time it is different. As the popular response to the 1980 Cuban boatlift shows, elected officials now seem to be particularly insensitive to the mounting restrictionist sentiment that is clearly evident in the polls. Official migration policy has never been related to population policy, because the United States has unfortunately not developed a population policy or population goals. Immigration policy and population policy cannot continue to be regarded as separate problems.

Legal immigrants need to be given every opportunity for first class citizenship, and other Mexican migrants in the United States should not be permitted to continue in the never-never land of illegal status. It is incomprehensible that at least five million people live here in that category, and that new illegals increase at an unknown rate, perhaps as many as one million a year now[9]. There are, in fact, en-

[9] In 1978, 350000 Mexicans were apprehended in San Diego alone. Many more migrants are successful in crossing the border than are caught.

tire industries like the garment and shoe industries in Los Angeles that are almost entirely staffed with undocumented aliens [6]. These employers apply pressure not to do anything about the problem, and unions fight to restrict entry. The government responds by doing nothing.

Each country has every right to decide on its rate of population growth through immigration and what category of newcomers they are willing to admit. The United States should expect and be prepared for the press at our southern borders to become more urgent. Both Mexico, and Central and South America are experiencing exponential population increases and their problems in supporting this growth will rival that of India and the Far East. Mexico City, as recently as twenty years ago, was very attractive to tourists, a beautiful city with clean air and fine boulevards, the Paris of the Western Hemisphere. It is now polluted and overcrowded and in twenty more years its present population of eleven million will triple in size to 32 million, making it the world's largest city. The second largest city in the world will be Sao Paulo, Brazil which will grow from eight million to twenty-six million[10]. Neither of these countries have the remotest prospect of being able to provide for this level of population.

What constitutes excess population is much more complicated than the ratio of people to land. It is true that certain parts of the United States, like Alaska, might not be harmed by some additional growth, but Hispanic migrants do not go there, or to the Australian outback. They go to Los Angeles, Chicago and Houston.

For every single person that is added to the population, we consume .987 acres of land for urban development, highways, airports, reservoirs, etc. Such urbanization has been using up one million acres of prime farmland a year, when it is estimated that the U.S. has just two-hundred thirty million acres of such land left.

So, surprisingly there is no conflict of interest between what is good for our Hispanic neighbors to the south, and

[10] Report: International Labor Office, Geneva, July 1979.

what is good for us. Restriction of migration at this time in history is not derived from «lifeboat ethics»; it has a strong moral base and is essential for the preservation of our resources and the ability to help provide for world food needs [12]. All the food exporting countries have special obligations, and the U.S. public, if not it's elected officials, seem to be in favor of a healthy and long delayed concern for our viability. Misguided altruism and pressure from both employers of illegals, and self-serving ethnic blocks threaten the continuing role of the United States as a major food exporter.

The world is getting older, and growth and expansion either as a continuing policy or a policy by default will have to end. The future of all countries lies in limiting population and restricting immigration. For this to take place, all jobs, including the least skilled and most arduous, will have to be undertaken by established populations, and accorded dignity, and adequate financial reward. If the population of poor countries have nowhere to go, perhaps they may begin, belatedly, to deal with their excess fertility.

It may be best for all nations in the long run, for the industrialized west to give up the unrealistic, impossible task of trying to solve their problems, and change the conditions of life for people who live in other places, and whose history, religion, and culture are different from our own. No matter how appealing, there is a certain arrogance and grandiosity in the continuing position of helper and rescuer.

It is hoped that the movement in psychology that emphasizes the taking of responsibility for the conditions of one's life, will move into the political area, a view that is consistent with less intervention in the affairs of other countries.

In matters of immigration policy, it is appropriate to distinguish between acute situations like the first Cuban and Vietnam refugee crisis, where a humanitarian response is mandatory, and long-term chronic problems like the over-population-poverty scenario of Mexico and much of Central and South America. Real solutions for them require less concentration of wealth, land reform, more appropriate industrial development, and population control. The U.S., by refusing to control migration, and thus providing a safety valve (that also benefits the U.S. temporarily) helps delay the needed solutions, and our lack of policy ultimately has a negative outcome for both ourselves and our Hispanic neighbors to the south.

Bibliography

1 ABRAMS, E.,ABRAMS, F.S.: Immigration Policy – who gets in and why? Public Interest *38,* 3 – 29, 1975.

2 ALVAREZ, R.: The Psycho-Historical and Socio-Economic Development of the Chicano Community in the United States. Social Science Quarterly *53* (4), 920 – 940, 1973.

3 BACA, R., BRYAN, D.: Citizenship Aspirations, and Residency Rights Preference: The Mexican Undocumented Worker in the Binational Community. A Sepa-Option Inc. Report, Compton, California 1980.

4 BARNET, R.J.: The World's Resources, Human Energy, Part III. The New Yorker Magazine, April 7, 1980.

5 BIKALES, J.: Immigration Policy, the New Environmental Battlefield. National Parks and Conservation Magazine, December 1979.

6 CASTILLO, L., Jr.: Castillo and The Immigration & Naturalization Service. Los Angeles Times, August 19, 1979.

7 CORNELIUS, W.A.: Mexican Migration to the United States: Causes, Consequences and U.S. Responses. An expanded and revised version of a paper prepared for presentation to The Study Group on Immigration, and U.S. Foreign Relations, Washington, D.C., June 8th, 1978.

8 CORSA, L.: Population Policy in the United States. Sierra, May-June 1979.

9 CUMBERLAND, C.C.: Mexico: Struggle for Modernity. Oxford Univ. Press, New York 1968.

10 DAY, A.T., DAY, L.H.: Cross National Comparison of Population Density. Science *181,* 1016 – 1022, 1973.

11 EHRLICH, P.R., BILDERBACK, L., EHRLICH, A.H.: The Golden Door. Ballantine Books, New York 1979.

12 GRAHAM, O.L., Jr.: Illegal Immigration and the New Reform Movement. Immigration Paper II, Federation for American Immigration Reform, 1980.

13 HARDIN, G.: The Limits of Altruism: An Ecologists View of Survival. Indiana University Press, Bloomington/London 1977.

14 HULL, D.: Migration, Adaptation & Illness. Soc. Sci. & Med. *13A,* 25 – 36, 1979.

15 KENT, D.D.: The Refugee Intellectual. Columbia University Press, New York 1953.

16 PORTES, A., BACH, L.: Dual Labor Markets and Immigration: A Test of Competing, Theories of Income Inequality. Paper prepared for delivery at the session on «Immigrants Old and New», meetings of the American Association for the Advancement of Science, Houston, Jan. 1978.

17 PORTES, A., McLEOD, S.A., Jr., PARKER, N.: Immigrant Aspirations. Socio of Educ. October 1978, 241 – 260.

18 REINOW, R.: The Great Unwanteds Want Us. Viewpoint Books, 1980.

19 RUMBAUT, R.D., RUMBAUT, R.G.: The Family in Exile: Cuban Expatriates in the United States. Am. J. Psychiatry 4, 133, 1976.

20 TAEUBER, C.: American Immigration and Population Growth. International Migration Review 10, 7 – 17, 1972.

21 TANTON, J.: Rethinking American Immigration Policy. Immigration Paper I Federation for American Immigration Reform, 1979.

22 Time Magazine: November 24, 1980.

23 VILLAPANDO, M. et al.: A Study of the Socioeconomic Impact of Illegal Aliens on the County of Santiago. San Diego, Calif. Human Resources Agency, Country of San Diego 1977.

24 VINING, D.R., Jr.: University of Pennsylvania, Private Communication reported in the Houston Post, January 9, 1980.

Chapter 14

At home but alien:
Internal migration and mental problems

Kivuto Ndeti

Part A

I. Introduction

The material forming the subject of this paper comes from the Nakuru area, one of the most important agricultural districts in the Rift Valley Province. It is one of the most rapidly growing districts both in natural and human resources. Because of its high agriculture potential, it has witnessed intensification of new settlement schemes in the last ten years. The formerly European owned large scale farms were bought by the Independent Government, subdivided into smaller land units and distributed to the landless people from other parts of the country, especially from Central Province. Thoughts in this chapter reflect the observation of these new settlers in coping with their situation.

These new settlement schemes have provided new opportunities to many individuals and families who otherwise would have been stranded in the former «native reserves». Most of these are unproductive and have deteriorated ecologically. However, like everthing else, the new opportunities have brought some side effects which were not unanticipated but whose seriousness could not be determined initially. They include such factors as demand for high productivity; regular loan repayments; different modes and patterns of work; acquiring new values and discarding the old ones; severe competition in unequittable situations; self-propelled reliance, etc. All these new challenges affect the present state of community mental health.

All these forces and others to be mentioned later, have contributed to the growth of «wear and tear» among the uprooted. The general state of affairs in the communities reflects confusion; value conflicts; mental breakdown; violent crimes; murdering opponents; fundamentalist ideas, messianic cults; etc. All the evidence at our disposal seems to suggest that uprootedness is a major part of these syndromes. Undoubtedly there are environmental and genetic factors that have contributed to the predisposition and the emergence of some of these problems. Nevertheless, uprootedness from traditional «tribal reserves» coupled with rapid social change make a fair share of the problem. In analysing uprootedness and failure to adapt or adjust to a rapidly changing environment consideration will be given to the basic ecological, cultural and demographic factors accelerating the process in the district.

II. The setting of the problem

Rift Valley Province of which Nakuru District is a part has an area of 173 878 sq. kilometres, approximately 30 percent of the total land area of Kenya. The province stretches all the way from the borders of Sudan to those of Tanzania. The altitude varies considerably with basins dropping between 4000 – 6000 ft. below the level of the land blocks on either side.

Nakuru District is in the Central section of the province. The soil is volcanic and it is one of the richest in the world. Practically all types of cereals, fruits, tubers and animal feeds can be grown. Wheat, barley are most suited for large scale farming. Dairy industry is very important in this area.

III. Ethnic distribution

Generally Rift Valley has always been a zone of low density compared to Western, Central or Eastern Provinces. Traditionally this region has been settled by the Nilo-hamitic ethnic groups namely the Kalenjin and the Maasai, and the majority of these tribes were pastoral, cattle herders and hunters. Some of them continue this pattern of life, but a large number has settled for agriculture or mixed economy.

In recent years the ethnic character of the Nakuru region has changed drastically. The majority of the ethnic groups are the new migrants who have come to settle from other provinces for farming. The Kikuyu now form the majority of the land-owning class both for large and small scale farming. Political, economic, security, administrative, civil and leadership structures are now de facto manned by them.

During the colonial administration, the Rift Valley Province was divided into two land tenure systems. After independence the land tenure system changed. All the lands have been de jure reverted to the government and it was left to its leadership to define who should be given land under which circumstances.

This land has been a serious bone of contention between various political power factions wanting to settle their followers. It has also been the main source of intratribal and intertribal divisions, and consequent conflicts in the post-independence period.

IV. Demographic factors

Kenya's population has been growing beyond the capacity of its resource development and unless measures are taken to reduce it in time the whole country may face a grim future. With an annual growth rate of 3.4 percent the country's population is estimated to double in approximately 21 years which is before the end of this century. The pressure exerted by rapid population growth would require highly capitalized development. The present level of the country's resources cannot meet the basic needs of its growing population. External assistance in manpower, resources and technology will be needed.

The population problem is very clearly demonstrated in the Rift Valley Province and in the Nakuru district in particular. In 1962 the population in the province was 1.74 million with a gross density of 10.2 persons per square kilometer. According to the 1969 census, the Nakuru district density was 40 persons per square kilometer.

The urban population has also grown considerably. According to the last census enumeration, the urban population was 47151 out of the district's total population of 290853. 57.4 percent of the municipal population was born elsewhere in Kenya. The Central Province has been the major supplier of the migrants but this does not mean that other provinces have not been sending migrants.

Part B

I. Uprootedness and new settlements

The uprootedness covers three sets of problems. Problems which result from the breakdown of cultures in the former «native lands» and which, when transferred to the new settlements, result in «polarization of meaningless identity», i.e. individuals living on the values of original culture that are inapplicable in the new situation. The second class of problems include those identified with specific historical events, which at one time played important role in uniting people ideologically for a cause once considered noble in spite of alienating its followers from the main stream of society. Those who fail to comply are meted out the same style of justice, in accordance with original rules of the group, usually death or bodily mutilation. In the new environment this approach to human affairs runs against the principles of constitutional society and is totally unacceptable to the government organs responsible for administering human justice. The government puts a lot of pressure on a group of this kind to force it to change its ways.

It would be unfair to imply that uprootedness and the new settlement environment are solely responsible for the emergence of the stresses which eventually lead to disease. The general social transformation which is taking place in the Kenyan society is part of the global process taking place in the areas of modernization, industrialization, urbanization and technological changes. These forces have their own share in the problem of uprootedness. Undoubtly the problem of transition from tribal society to national-state within a very short time has contributed to the emergence of various stresses even in a non-uprooted environment. However, uprootedness and new settlement environment seem to intensify the gravity of stress. More psychological and cultural resources are needed to sustain an individual but this situation does not pertain to the new environment. Thus uprootedness adds more fuel to the stress process.

II. Case studies

a) Akorino: Akorino is a fundamentalist sect which is very common in the Nakuru district. This religious movement is found in all the rural and urban centres of the district and some people claim it started here. Others say Akorino is a splinter sect which has very close links with the Mau Mau rebellion. The Akorino followers have no ecclesiastical monuments. They do not even have clerical leadership. Trees are the only places where they congregate. The followers believe in Christianity, but in a transformed context. They violently oppose the institutionalized church. What they mean by this is that Christianity presented in non-Akorino situation is extremely formalized and does not allow people to communicate meaningfully with God. Other religious sects emphasize hymns, followed by reading the Holy scriptures and depend on an ordained person to interpret the scripture for the congregation. This formalized and institutionalized way of worship alienates most of the members of the congregation according to Akorino interpretation. Individual participation in worship is limited to those holding special office in church hierarchy. Thus the distinction between the laity and the clergy becomes a source of stress.

The Akorinos have resolved this problem by incorporating liberalism in their style of worship which encourages free thinking, participation by everyone, personal interpretation of holy scripture for congregation, singing, dancing and participation in preaching by members of the congregation. No church building is necessary which means very little ecclesiastic stratification. Akorino identify themselves by wearing Kanzu (White frock) with stripes sometimes for both male and female. They wear white turbans and beards like sikhs. The music of the congregation is based on traditional music of a particular ethnic group. The drum is always the key instrument. The Akorinos worship is their own tribal way of harmonizing the teaching of Holy scriptures with traditional usually evoked by music. The physical shaking accompanying this music interprets the spiritual symbolism. Unity with God is perceived as a function of both musical intensity and personal emotional involvement in dancing. This state of spirituality is mainly attained by evoking spiritual music found in the traditional cultures, accompanied by repetitive chants. That is why Akorinos emphasize tribal congregation as the best medium through which their religious philosophy and practices are achieved.

Music as a therapy for escaping from the stress or constraints of institutionalized worship is the distinctive feature of Akorinos. Otherwise variation in cults and language of worship in traditional societies which are tribally specific is the excluding factor in Akorinos sects. Recruitment of the member is either by birth or congregational assimilation. Hedonistic spirituality in traditional dances serve as the medium of incorporating the new philosophy embraced by the Akorinos in their new situation. The practical expression is rigidly enforced on individual Akorinos through very strict discipline based on traditional oaths.

b) X-Freedom Fighter Group

This group of people come from those who fought during colonial times under the eagis of the Mau Mau. They form an extremely powerful group in the district. The origin of this group is closely linked with colonial affairs. Appropriation of land from some ethnic groups forced people to emigrate to urban centres or other parts of the country to seek opportunities. Those who did not succeed became Majangiri (outlaws) especially in the urban areas. They became politically conscious but only for regaining the appropriated lands. Others went to the jungle to be «forest guerillas» and actively became involved in guerilla warfare. The underlying motive was to regain the land appropriated and drive away the invaders in order to gain political and economic independence. The binding force for the freedom fighters (actually freedom «flighters») was tribal loyality established through blood-brotherhood. Once one had taken the oath he must live by it and must execute all duties assigned even if it is commiting the most inhuman act.

Part C

Synthesis and Interpretation

In studies carried out on the traditional perceptions of mental disorders (NDETI, 1973) the forces identified reflect correlation of these syndromes with dual existence of the uprooted. Among the Luhya who are Western Bantu forming an important component in Nakuru district, mental disorders were characterized by three syndromes *Kamalalu* − viz. wild running, characterized by violence; *Kumu-*

sebe — viz. possession of madening spirit; *Mukalo* — viz. addicted to certain ways of doing things e.g. reading the Holy Scripture; *Wayononokha Murwi* — viz. talks to himself, smiles, split mind. Among the Kikuyu who form the most important segment of the Central Bantu, their perceptions were as follows: *Mupuruki:* viz. one who runs mad, dresses strangely, eats anything, collects rubbish, is very violent, talks widly, shouts; *Mundo wa ngoma* — viz. possessed by spirit; talks to spirit by himself; a person of spirit or demon. Among the Akamba who also are part of the Central Bantu the perceptions are as follows: *Nduuka* — viz. extreme madness, violent person; strips in public, speaks loudly; does not fear; eats and does anything. *Mbo-su* — viz. scaring, behavioural disturbance, talks strangely, glides over things; negative quickness in mind and action. *Ena Kathambi* — viz. possessed by spirit, witchcraft belonging to demon, sorcerer. Finally among the Luos — the Nilotes from the Lake region who are an important component in the district the perceptions are as follows: *Jane-ko* — viz. spoiled brain, can eat anything, can sleep in water; complete mental distruction; no shame; beats people. *Ng'ama Orundore* — viz. says wrong things at the wrong time; talks and laughs to himself; does not fight, quiet, begs, mild insanity. *Jajuogi* — viz. madness of sterility, talks to himself, unconventional, jerks at night, sorcerer, witchcraft.

The existence of these syndromes in the traditional cultures reflect the causes of the mental diseases and implict cures. For example, if it was a aspiritual demonic possession then the cure was administered by those who had power over spirits and demons. Traditional witchdoctors, medicine-men, exorcists and soothsayers had some control over these forces within a given cultural setting. This traditional spiritual and mental disorientation trails the uprooted wherever they go. It is a part of dual existence they cannot escape.

In the new environment these perceptions on mental disorders are complicated by the new factors originating from the demands of changing environment. These in-

271

clude social, economic, cultural and political arrangements that must be evolved by individuals, family, or interest groups in order to cope with problems of rapid social and technological changes in the contemporary community. Complications arise when there is uncritical mixture between the traditional and modern sources of mental disorders especially involving cures and treatment perceptions. The uprooted tends to assume that the solutions for one set of mental disorders can be readily transferred to another in different cultural and environmental contexts. This is one of the problems encountered in persuading a husband to take a mentally disturbed wife or a member of the family into a modern mental hospital for treatment and rehabilitation. The mental disorders were always handled very effectively by the traditional healers and not by professional psychiatrists who often are not familiar with the client's culture. Thus incapacity to make technoligical transition is one factor increasing incidences of mental disorders of the uprooted. One cannot do much to an uprooted if he believes the sources of mental disorders is due to evil spirits, demons, sorcery or witchcraft. Cures for these syndromes are deeply embedded in traditional cultures.

The other source of stress is inability to assimilate complex transformations from traditional to modern situations. Demand for high productivity is one of the conditions imposed on the uprooted. This demand concerns both quantity and quality. This means changing the pattern and style of work. For someone who has been used to subsistence agriculture, simple pastoralism, or casual labour, the new challenge must be beyond his/her capability − both mentally and physically. The uprooted in this case is exposed to extraneous stimuli which have both physical and psychosocial consequences.

The impact of overstimulation by the vast and complex changes is another area that seems to affect the mental health of the uprooted. Overstimulation takes all forms among the uprooted. It is a convergence of many demands that must be met within specified time. The uprooted settlers who have been settled are expected to meet their commitment regularly. If they default continuously their only means of survival can be repossessed and sold to someone else. The inability to meet these demands becomes a source of anxiety for them. The most powerful source of stress is the demand for the changing of values. Nakuru district has become a melting pot for all types of cultures and people. The preferred medium of communication is *Swahili* and not other local languages. Change of language implies assimilation of new values and ideas and often discarding the previous ones. The two processes going on at the same time cause confusion and conflicts. Listening to an *Akorino* sermon, for example one hears the preacher trying to translate the local dialect into *Swahili* for a wide group of consumers. In the majority of cases the preacher and the translator perceive the issues in different cultural, historical and environmental contexts. The outcome of this is a total confusion to the audience. The bystanders who are very eager to hear the word of *papa* (heavenly father) find themselves completely in the dark. The contexts in which the information is flowing are incompatible. Those who cannot discard the old values because of language, historical, cultural barriers resulting from the new environment become misfits and are likely to be avoided for being either tribalistic or narrow-minded. For those who follow may be branded outsiders or «English». The language is commonly used in this district. The English values are emulated especially by those supplying the uprooted with necessary items and ideas on farming activities. Those who do not speak English and cannot follow instruction lag behind in many things as far as farming and development are concerned. This to them becomes a source of anxiety.

Capitalist development strategy is very well embraced by the values of new settlement schemes. The general orientation of the system in this situation is that the transplanted individual is responsible for his own failures and successes. The traditional society emphasized communal approach to the challenges of life and provided a better social support for the individual. The communal and individual responsibilities were fairly well articulated in the system of extended family.

The capitalistic mode of production and consumption have tended to create more need for the individual. The more one gets the more one wants and there seems to be no end to this artificially created attitude of mind. Communication media — radio and TV — have created needs that are not there and which cannot be gratified under the normal circumstances. For the uprooted in the district the perceptions of his position is that the needs of a capitalist are unlimited and their fulfilment is a source of anxiety.

One of the strong motives for the Mau Mau rebellion was to repossess the lost lands. Those who fought and won independence feel that the land belongs to a certain class or section of the people. The politicians have gone out of their way to reward their supporters with new land in the settlement schemes. How long this will continue remains a source of anxiety for political leaders and their followers.

For those who cannot get into a co-operative or a settlement scheme, land-hunger has been a source of stress. For those who cannot get even an inch of it and yet see big people from other areas owning hundreds of acres which they do not use effectively, this is a source of stress. The call for equitable redistribution of land is one of the biggest sources of anxiety, not only for the uprooted but for the majority of people in the country. Land is a very sensitive and major source of intertribal and intratribal political conflict and rivalry. Land is the base for social and economic development in this district. Some tribes would like to take the entire region for themselves and keep out everyone else. This point is even clearly marked in the district when peole uprooted from different sections or regions of the same community are violently opposed to each other when the matter relates to acquisition of land — the economic and political power base of this area.

The recent trend of events in mental health in the province supports the claim that uprootedness has contributed to the increase of mental disorders. Even if one considers the hospital statistics alone, the figure represents a growth of 56,7% of psychiatric cases in ten years. The increased flow of information from health education, increased health services and special attention given to mental health may have pushed the figures upward without reflecting the reality of the situation. This is perhaps one side of the problem but there is no question of increased mental health problems.

Nevertheless, the general transition that is taking place in the country cannot help but trigger all types of stresses. Abnormal behaviour is that which deviates from the norm or is the unstable expression of the normal behaviour. Thus mental disorders are the reaction of human beings to particular conditions of stress in their environment. Stress is a «wear and tear» mechanism which would apply to all systems — biological, mechanical and human, under particular conditions of work of stimulation. The reaction to stimuli causes distress in the system.

In the context of Kenya and Africa in general there is hardly one single year that passes without changes in the social conditions of individuals and family-life styles. The structure of the family has been altered and will continue to be so in the foreseable future. Instability in the family results in cultural uprootedness through migration — rural to rural and rural-urban render all kinds of emotional disturbances. The rural people moving to urban areas find themselves pitted against the environment that abrogates the values of the extended family which emphasize the communal approach to life. In order to survive in the urban areas they must develop all the types of defensive and aggressive behaviour demanded by urban life. Rural to rural migration forces the individual to acquire new values and to adapt to the new situation. This adaptation requires time, but before one gets used to the new environment other changes in other areas of human life are occuring. The process of adapting to a continually changing situation aggravate the wear and tear process on the adaptor. The demands of work situation, education for children and family, disorganisation of traditional welfare institutions, large families and necessary supporting resources, competition for promotion, etc. — all these become a continuous source of anxiety. The individuals are expected to adapt to this ever-changing environment. The consequence of this drama is that the majority of the uprooted cannot cope. They succumb to mental disorders already mentioned and other health problems related to multi-stimuli anxieties.

For the uprooted in the developing and continually changing environment there is fear of being poor and hungry, fear of lack of old age security, fear of political, cultural and economic oppression, fear of intertribal conflicts, fear of inability to influence decisions on individual and national levels, fear of denial of the basic human rights, fear of elites, fear of tribal social disorganisation and subsequent destruction of the group, fear of political upheavals, fear of breakdown of traditional ethnical values, fear of being powerless and dependent, fear of loan repayment, fear of unfair competition, etc. All converge into a very generalized stress which attacks and distresses from every angle imaginable in the human system. There is no time for the human system to accommodate all these stimuli. What kind of social policies must a country follow to minimize this tragic and unhealthy situation? It is worthy, under the aegis of development, to create a society that is mentally disordered?

These are questions that policy-makers in developing countries must face. The model that has been copied for development in underdeveloped countries is the overwhelming emphasis on the value of growth. This indicator of development, especially in the area of economics, does not consider the limits of growth and its serious side-effects especially in the field of mental health. The anxiety resulting from the «big is better» syndrome needs to be replaced by other social indicators that take critical assessment of human welfare value — physical, mental, spiritual and social. The best mechanism to ensure general welfare value of society is not only to create more institutions for primary and secondary mental health care, but to prevent the problem before it arises. Our policy-makers lack ability to weigh the benefits and disadvantages of a particular development effort. There is need to consider «man-centred» development in our planning activites. «Efficiency» and «quick pay-offs» are a priority in the planning thought in many countries but very little effort is given to the human condition. It is only fair to conclude this paper with a reflection on humanism in social and technological development as traditionally perceived in some African societies. The quote is from thoughts of one of Africa's greatest humanists:

«This high valuation of man and respect for human dignity which is a legacy of our traditions shall not be lost in the new Africa. However, «modern» and «advanced» in western sense this young nation of Zambia may become, we are fiercly determined that this humanism will not be obsecured. African society has always been man-centred. Indeed this is as it should be, otherwise, why is a house built? Not to give man shelter and security? Why make a chair at all? Why build a factory? Why do you want a state ranch? For what else would there be reason to grow food? Why is the fishing industry there? We can go on asking these questions. The simple and yet difficult answer is «man». Simple in the sense that it is clear all human activities centre around man. Difficult, too, because man has not yet understood his own importance. And yet we can say with justification without a sense of false pride that the African way of life with its many problems has less setbacks towards the achievement of an ideal society. We in Zambia intend to keep our society man-centred. For it is this that what might be described as African civilization is embodied and indeed if modern Africa has anything to contribute to this troubled world, it is in this direction that it should» (President Kaunda, 1967).

What is the benefit for man if he gained the whole world and mastered it technologically if the price of this were total dislocation of his physical, mental, social and spiritual well-being?

Chapter 15

The psychological problems of Black African immigrants in Western societies

Jacques Barou

Introduction

This chapter does not deal with the whole black population in western societies but only with Black African immigrants in western countries today, coming from nations which have become politically independent.

Contrary to the «migration» of slaves, forced upon the Black Africans towards the American continent in the 17th and 18th centuries, African emigration of today towards the western world is far from being a massive phenomenon from a demographic point of view. The sociologist's attention has thus not been very much held by it. Indeed, the sociologists are much keener on studying the numerous older African communities of the United States or States of Central and South America without mentioning the great number of research works about the important phenomenon of migration inside the African continent itself.

Yet the African migration of today towards western countries being a phenomenon of small importance does not mean for all that, that it is a simple phenomenon to deal with from the social and psychological point of view. As far as the black populations of America (North and South America) are concerned, we may note a relative social and cultural homogeneity being the fruit of a same way of life for several centuries, while in the case of the recent African migration we notice a very large heterogeneity both in the social and cultural fields: This shows the different motives for migration, the different economic circumstances in which migration takes place and the relations to the African cultures which are still very much full of life and varied [2].

Before dealing with the psychological problems of Black African immigrants in western societies it is necessary to define the general conditions in which they take place.

I. General data

a) Statistical data

Statistical data about immigrants from Black Africa in Western Societies, are quite poor and not very precise. Nevertheless, all of them prove that the phenomenon was not very important from a numerical point of view although at the same time they prove that both the countries where these foreign people come from and their social conditions are quite different. There are very few western countries where we don't find nationals of a very large number of Black African countries. There are, however, only three countries with a substantial African immigration.

The United States, where we find more than hundred thousand nationals of Black African countries, remains above all an immigration country for students, intellectuals and scientists, though the number of foreign unskilled workers, most of the time in an irregular administrative situation, tended to develop in the last few years [9]. The problems of the Black immigrant coming from an African state tend to look less serious than those of the black communities in the United States, which explains that this recent population is not yet well known by the social observers.

In Great Britain the African immigrants frequently live close to the West Indians who are not very different from them as far as their jobs or their social positions are concerned, since they belong to the commonwealth countries as well. Very often the nationals of Black Africa are put in the same category as West Indians who are more than 300 000 in Great Britain and they are considered belonging to the same districts, strongly segregated [7]. British sociology concerning racial relationships so far kept to a study of antogonisms between White and Black people and difficulties the Blacks have to assimilate to the total society without going too deep in the question of the original points of the African communities compared with the West Indians.

In France, where an African community lives, counting more than 100 000 people, there are more conditions grouped together to enable an identification of the originality charcteristic of the Black African immigrants. Indeed here the other coloured population originating from the West Indies and from the Island of Reunion are people of French nationality as they belong to French «departements d'Outre Mer». On that account they can get jobs in public offices whereas Africans, as they are foreigners, can't aspire to that. Therefore in France African nationals can be very clearly distinguished from other coloured populations: on the legal and administrative levels, on the social and trade levels as well as on the cultural level. What's more, whereas the immigration of the people from the West Indies and the Reunion is largely familial, that of the African nationals remains almost exclusively masculine [8].

b) Short historical survey

African immigration to European countries is in fact a contemporary phenomenon which follows the European colonisation of Africa. As a matter of fact, Great Britain and France, the two main colonizing powers in Africa, are today the European countries where the greatest number of African communities live. Most of these African immigrants originate from countries which were formerly ruled by France and Great Britain, countries with which the old parent states still keep up particular relations and in which English or French, if not the official languages, are still the main languages of communication in the administrative fields.

First of all this accounts for the immigration of students and managerial staff who come to follow training courses of shorter or longer duration. The main reason is that it is easier to study in a language you learnt in the country you come from rather than to have to begin learning a new language. But we noticed other reasons as well. O. KLINEBERG and J. BEN BRIKA [4] stress the part played by the image of the old colonizer for the students of the countries ruled by France as to the motives leading them to come to study in France. We can see a very clear urge among the students to identify themselves with a cultural and social pattern forced upon them by the dominating power [3, 4].

The relations issuing from the colonial domination also played a fundamental part in the immigration of the African workers to European countries. British employers used the relations they had with their countrymen settled in some African countries (especially in Kenya) to carry out direct recruiting of labour, meant to guarantee the development of some industries which did not appeal to the European workers [7].

France employing a lot of people from Senegal and Mali in the army and in the merchant services at the time of the colonial domination created the conditions which led the workers to migrate when the majority of them were demobilized shortly after independence.

There were other reasons, too, that influenced African immigration to Europe. After the independence of its colonies, Portugal had to take in many Africans coming from Angola and Mozambique. Recent events on the African continent precipitated a certain migratory movement of refugees from Ethiopia, Guinea and Angola towards different European countries. Nevertheless, we may note that this phenomenon remains extremely small compared with the movement of the refugees inside the African continent. In Africa there are four million refugees belonging to other African states. The easiness to get through the borders as well as the presence of the same ethny in different countries and the different ideologic trends promoted alternatives other than exodus to Europe.

Sociologically speaking we can discern two main groups of African immigrants in western countries: on the one hand the students, on the other hand the unskilled manual workers. Although we find the second group almost only in Great Britain and in France, students are spread all over the western countries in varied proportions. The motives urging them to choose other countries than the old colonial powers for their studies are often the grants they are offered by these countries, political choices (especially as far as the socialist countries are concerned) and the urge to reject the ex-colonizing country's culture. This explains in a way why African students are so much attracted to a country like West Germany.

In his book *Farbige unter Weissen* PRODISH AICH [1] notices the fact that this image of Germany as a non-colonizing country combined with its image of a very advanced country, technically and economically speaking, urges the students to go there to get a technical education. However, Africans who study in Germany experience serious adaptation problems and feel very deeply some kind of discrimination, especially as to housing and their relationships with German girls. Unlike France and Great Britain where we may often note that the students seldom go back to their native countries [6], they almost always return to their native countries after coming to Germany. This is due to the fact that the German market of skilled jobs is inaccessible to them. There is also the difference the foreign student feels between himself and the «reception society» with which he does not have any cultural interchange. Marriages between races very seldom lead to the foreign person settling down in Germany, but usually implies that the couple goes back to the husband's native country.

Therefore it seems that research concerning African communities is the richest and the most interesting in the ex-colonizing countries, because of the importance of their numbers, the ethnical complexity they show, the different social positions of immigrants and because of the peculiar aspect of the cultural relations taking place between the individual immigrant and the immigration society.

II. The particularity of the approach of the psychological problems the Black African immigrants encounter: some theoretical difficulties

a) Psychological or anthropological approach?

The psychological difficulties of the African immigrant, as they are seen by the institutions of the French society, can often be summed up as difficulties in «adapting to the milieu». This concept of adaptation especially reveals a kind of «ethnocentrism». The necessity of assimilating to his new milieu is in fact forced upon the immigrant by the receiving society and it is taken for granted that the immigrant desires to adapt. Before we question the reality of this adaptation desire and before we wonder about the plan the immigrant may have as regards the society he comes to, we shall consider the situation making the assimilation to the new milieu easier for the immigrant. This shows very well the socio-economic relations between the foreigner and the society which takes him in. French society needs the immigrant to assimilate to it more than the latter needs this assimilation. The immigrants will have to face institutions planning to assure their adaptation according to rules which are not theirs, which do not echo the values of their native societies, which ignore the originality and the diversity of their migratory plans and demonstrate the determination of the reception society to assimilate these foreigners. This leads to a lot of mistakes and to inevitable failures caused by the efforts trying to adapt the immigrant to his new milieu.

These mistakes appear particularly in the psychiatric treatment of the African immigrants. The treatment often ignores such important facts as the way the patient interprets his disorders according to the model of his native culture. This is generally completely left aside and very often depressions are considered as manifestations of a failure to adapt. The distance between the native culture wrongly considered archaic and out of date, and the demands of contemporary western societies is considered as the main causal factor [8].

It seems to us, on the contrary, that the connection of the immigrant with his native culture very clearly plays a positive part, especially in the serious circumstance of violent stress [5]. We could notice in France that the most effective way of curing the immigrant affected by psychological disorders was his going back to his original milieu. The communities of African workers know this very well since, as soon as one of their fellows is mentally affected, they try to gather enough money to pay for his journey back to the native country.

Facts like these show the limits of the psychological and psychiatric approach of the immigrants' difficulties and demonstrate the necessity to make anthropological studies, producing knowledge of the immigrants' culture.

b) The individual and his community

The anthropological approach cannot keep to the individual as classical psychological and psychiatric approach does. The native culture has been lived and handed down collectively and we have therefore to examine the relation of the African individual to his community.

In Europe we rarely come across immigrants, and especially African immigrants living by themselves. Many families keep in touch with one another and big families flock together, very close to each other. This applies to family immigration and especially for people from Kenya in Great Brtain. In France, where one sees an immigration of men only, one can observe that people coming from the same village or region live together, either in hostels of unmarried men or in collective blocks of flats which they convert for this purpose, gathering often from 300 to 500 people belonging to the same ethny. This communal life does not only appear in their ways of living together but also in some kind of active unity in the economic field. The sick and the unemployed ones are taken care of by the other members of the group. Collective funds exist in the village and all the people coming from this particular village must give a certain sum of money regularly. The whole system creates the conditions of a deep relation between the individual and his group. On that account the community becomes above all the place where the immigrant can shelter from the «dictatorial» attempts the immigration society promoted to prompt them to assimilate [3]. The African individual strongly identifies himself with it. It is also the place of parties and celebrations of the native culture. It is in the heart of this community that the individual feels most completely African. Here we have more of an ethnicity feeling, an identity through a group you consider your own and in which you recognize yourself rather than an identity feeling in the way psychology usually understands it.

c) Identity and ethnicity

For the Africans, psychological disorders often interpreted as a crisis or a loss of identity, are often connected with a breaking off from the group. The disorders often originate from a loss of collective references and the attempt to find an individualistic way of life or an attempt to identify oneself to a new group. We must rather talk of an ethnicity crisis or a loss of ethnicity in this case.

As a matter of fact, however necessary the returning to the community life may be, it may present a few deficiencies and does not resist effectively enough acculturation forced by the reception society. This implies that the acculturation does not affect the whole African community but only a certain number of people, the ones who feel most strongly the attempts and pressures of the western society.

But even this communal system, where one finds mainly workers (many illiterate) who did not experience the problems of acculturation during studies, provokes a certain stress. These communities carry on a social and hierarchical system which already existed in the native country, a system according to which the power is mostly held by the old ones. This situation is sometimes difficult to accept by the other members of the group, who get the feeling of being kept behind times compared with the society they are living in. All the economic investments are devoted to the native society and the members of the community realize that they are deprived of any possibility of getting the advantages the immigration society offers them. This results in some people splitting from their communities. The youngest elements and the most «modern» are against the ones who cling to the traditional values. In both cases this does not go without complications both for the individuals and the community.

These complications may lead to deep crises of identity and ethnicity. The result of these crises may be a positive one and allow the community to join again around values which have been sensibly modified, this giving birth to a new communal behaviour which is often more demanding. The crises may also result in a different solution. The members of the community try to find a new identity, by joining a group of another kind like a trade union, a company or a political party [8].

But most of the time the breaking off from the community results in a confusion of the individual. The psychological evolution of the African individual is therefore closely linked with the evolution of the community he belongs to and with the strength of the values which the community depends on. This leads us again to stress the necessity of knowing anthropologically the whole phenomenon, which is the only way of making the evolution of the different ethnical African communities understood.

Three examples show the possible future of the different communities: strongly keeping the traditional values, the meaning of the communal life progressively changing, and splitting completely. In each case, we try to show the effect the different evolutions of these communities may have on the people's psychology [2].

These three examples are about African workers living in France and coming from the countries which had formerly been ruled by France. They cannot be applied completely to African communities having a different past, being of a different social position and living in different western societies. Anyhow, the study of the relations connecting the individual with his community has some bearing the greatest number of African immigrants in western Europe.

III. Three different examples of the African workers' reactions in France in relation to their immigration milieu and cultural backgrounds

a) A Hausa immigrant community presenting a strong feeling of ethnicity

The community in question consists of 60 members of a Hausa ethny and natives of Niger, who live on their own . It is a very homogeneous community living in Lyon, most of them work in the same firm and come from the same village. The community gradually settled down around the old ones, who came to France about 10 years ago and they managed to get stable jobs and thanks to the money they saved they could get their younger brothers and their younger relatives to come over [2].

Domination by the old ones, a system typical of the African civilizations is thus strengthened. Indeed the young ones owe everything to their elders. They are indebted to them for the journey to France, for the job and the accommodation. Therefore all of them closely follow their elders' example of living with the intention of working and saving, which imposes the sacrifice of any expence assigned to spare time activities.

So the old ones in this system allways supervise the young ones, and also organize the spare time in the community. They spend it in the same way they would do in their country, that means by endless talking in which the problems of the native village are dealt with. As investments for their spare time activities they mainly buy radio sets, enabling them to get the different programmes broadcast in the Hausa language by the BBC or Radio Moscow. The community can thus be kept well informed in African current events and on events from the whole world without ever going out of its shelter. Any leisure activity that would do something else than encourage the group life is excluded. Going out with European women and especially with prostitutes is not accepted. The sexual abstinence results in different kinds of frustration behaviours. Yet the active unity of the group creates an atmosphere where friendship is a very strong feeling, which very effictively helps the individuals to some kind of sublimation. Moreover the relationships with their wives and their girlfriends who stayed in the native country are often talked of, they correspond with each other a lot and they exchange not only letters but symbolic presents. When they talk about their erotic dreams, the wife who stayed at home comes into view and they never see a woman they would have met in the immigration country.

During the two years we spent studying this community, we only came across one case of deep depression associated with a split between the individual and the community. It was a young man who, being unable to cope with the hard working conditions he had to face and with the ascetic strain forced upon him by the communal life, decided to leave his job and to «enjoy himself». He quickly saw the end of his savings visiting prostitutes and then found himself penniless, while the community whose way of life he had thrown away refused to help him. The result was a deep psychosomatic crisis which got him into a hospital. Then his group took care of him again, paying for the medical treatment he needed and they helped him to find a new job. In this way he owed even more than before to his community and was bound to get back to it and to the ascetic life they imposed.

In this case the psychic strength of the individual depends on the strength of the community, while the communal strength directly depends on the ethny it belongs to in Africa. The Hausa are developing quickly for the time being. The Hausa merchants play a very active part and are present all over West Africa. Most of the immigrants in France were also planning to invest savings in commercial business and these prospects for the future helped them to stand the ascetic strain forced upon them by the communal life.

b) The Soninke communities: A slow and progressive transformation of the ethnic feeling

The Soninke people are an ethny of about 500000 members living in the valley of the river Senegal, populating Mali, Senegal and Mauretania. Since the end of the Second World War they have been migrating to France and there are now about 70000 of them gathered mainly around Paris. From the 11th century, the time of their conversion to Islam, they have formed a society which the influences of the outside world could not reach at all. In their society there is a very strict family hierarchy: the children must obey the head of the family and help him, and every younger brother has got the same duties to his elders. Therefore, the power is only in the hands of the oldest whereas the youngest have got most of the duties. This family hierarchy is reinforced by a social one based on the existence of three classes: the nobility owning the land, the free men mainly consisting of craftsmen and finally the slaves. Though slavery was officially abolished at the time of the French colonization the descendants of the old slaves still have the same relations to the noble class as in former times [2].

Emigration gradually became the main source of income for the Soninke country, so it is very well organized. It is an emigration of men only. The village communities are often very numerous in France, and they easily gather 300 people in blocks of flats they convert to dormitories. This kind of accommodation is generally very unstable but quite cheap. The jobs these workers have are, most of the time, hard and badly paid. An active unity between the members of the group is made necessary by these conditions. This way of living together also encourages the social hierarchy of the native country. The seniors do really rule over the communities. Whatever the differences in their trade life may be, the relations in their traditional life remain unchanged. The young member must give all his earnings to the elders who decide how much they will send to the family and how much will be left for the young one. Even if the trade position of the slave is higher than that of the noble, he must still obey him. So there is a very clear difference between the working world which these African immigrants take part in (around Paris in the working world the trade unions and the political activities are quite strong), and the traditional world built in its social stiffness swallowing all the spare time of these immigrants. This contradiction is sometimes difficult to live with for some individuals and causes serious depressions. We came across the case of a young Soninke originating from a slave family who committed suicide because the old members of his community refused him the possibility of studying. Many are tempted to split from community in order to try to individually join the French society. They are, however, often rejected by it and when no longer helped by the feeling of belonging to a group which is coercive but reassuring, many suffer from serious depressions which get them to psychiatric hospitals. Their cases are, however, often misunderstood by doctors who do not know their background and the real causes of their depressions and these become more and more incapacitating.

The individuals who succeed in joining the French society after leaving their community, are the ones who join an organized group. Some manage to leave their community without any psychological problems thanks to their joining a trade union where they again find some kind of collective unity and help.

Year after year we notice another kind of evolution of the ethnicity feeling. The individuals who earlier were inclined to leave their own group (that is mainly the young ones) are now trying to force their powers inside their community. This reversing of the power mostly occurs in the form of actions or protests against the reception society. Claiming better accommodation enables the young ones who often speak better French than their elders, to act as spokesmen for the community in front of the public authorities and thus to increase their power in relation to the old ones.

So gradually the meaning of the community life is taking a new form. It is no longer a recreated African world which cannot be reached by outside influence, but it becomes a part of the immigration society which asserts its originality and claims its rights.

This evolution is deeply connected with the future of the ethny from the African point of view. Economically speaking, emigration is absolutely necessary to enable the Soninke country to survive, and the emigrants going back to Africa seem to become an ever-increasing problem. This leads them to turn their eyes more towards the western society and without trying, however, to identify themselves with it, they want to claim at least a better place.

c) Acculturation and attempts to climb the social ladder

The two groups we have just described are examples of positive reactions to their immigration milieu. Their cultural background is present as insurance for the group's unity and for the individuals' psychic integrity. These reactions are made possible by the fact that the cultural background, is in itself, solid enough to be efficiently mobilized. They are sahelian and muslim ethnies, and their cultures have not been too affected by the French colonization.

The French colonization created, on the other hand, a deep trauma by forcing a culture, a religion, an educational system, a social order, all completely different, upon the peoples of the forest and the coast who had an animist religion. The hierarchy of these peoples was very difficult for the Europeans to understand. The Africans tend to identify themselves with the socio-cultural pattern left by colonization. Intellectuals and high civil servants are therefore the ones who «set the fashion». A great number of people who could not study for a long time are unlucky when they try to identify themselves to the ruling socio-cultural model. Emigration to France is often a way of filling up a gap for the natives of these countries [2, 8].

Among the nationals from the Ivory Coast, Cameroon and Togo living in France we find, together with the migratory movement of students and intellectuals, a lot of people who are neither manual workers nor students, but who came to complete the secondary education they hardly started in Africa and they are often obliged to take a manual job to make their living.

Beside their ambiguous position from a cultural point of view, there is an obvious sociological ambiguity. Their main problem is that of identity. Away from their ethnic communities, they try to live in a western way, but what they have in common is only their desire to join the French model. They generally spend their spare time playing a round game in which they try to send back to themselves a self portrait corresponding to the model they want to emulate.

This takes place when they meet in smart cafes where these workers wear tidy suits which make them look like managerial members of staff, speak sophisticated French and try to get close to young French girls. One thing most of them aim to achieve by assimilation is to get in touch with or even marry a French woman.

In fact they very seldom succeed in joining the French culture because the reception society rejects them and these immigrants often have to live with the image of the model they aim at rather than its reality. The difference between the real social condition and the social condition they feign or dream of grows bigger and bigger. This creates psychological difficulties because of an unclear identity and sometimes brings about serious problems. These manifest themselves either in the form of mental confusion leading to hospitalisation or a deviating behaviour leading to jail. We came across several immigrants of this group who had been «forced» to steal and to become crooks because they wanted to keep the picture of a «high social position» which was obviously the only thing they longed for, as they could not «admit» their present low social status.

In this last example the breaking up of the original societies, and the explosion of the ethnical communities under the pressure of the acculturation system engendered an individual behaviour that was trying an integration which in reality proved impossible, and thus resulted in deep identity crises.

Conclusion

These three examples stress the importance of the cultural background and of the community life for the future of the African immigrants in the western societies.

Without generalizing too much, we may say that the first two examples we dealt with will be typical also in the future for African immigrants originating from civilizations characterized by keeping the traditional social patterns and traditions. The third example will be frequently found again among the Africans educated by the western culture. This is probably true in whatever western society these immigrants live.

Bibliography

1 AïCH, P.: Farbige unter Weissen. Kiepenheur und Kitsch, Berlin/ Köln 1963.
2 BAROU, J.: Travailleurs Africains en France: Rôle des cultures. P.O.F. P.U.G. Paris/Grenoble 1978.
3 BROOM, L., KITSUSE, J.: The validation of acculturation: a condition to ethnic assimilation. American Anthropology, LVII/1, February 1955.
4 KLINEBERG, O., BEN BRIKA, JEANNE: Etudiants du Tiers Monde en Europe. Mouton, Paris/La Haye 1972.
5 KLINEBERG, O., ZAVALLONI, MARIA: Nationalism and Tribalism among African students: a study of social identity. Mouton, Paris/La Haye 1959.

6 N'DIAYE, J. – P.: Enquête sur les étudiants noirs en France. Réalités Africaines, Paris, *2*, 35 – 60, 1970.
7 PEACH, C., WINCHESTER, S., WOODS, R.: The distribution of coloured immigrants in Britain. In: The social economy of cities. Oxford University Press, London 1975.
8 RAVEAU, F., FALIK, ESTHER, LECOUTRE, J. – P.: Migration et acculturation différentielle. International Review of Applied Psychology *25*, 145 – 165, 1976.
9 SCOTT, A. H.: Census U.S.A.: Facts Findings for the American People 1790 – 1970. The Seabury Press, New York 1968.

Chapter 16

Aftermath of empire: Pakistanis in Britain
Mental health problems of some Asian immigrants

Philip H. Rack

Immigration in Britain

In the period 1950 – 1970 Britain, like other European industrial countries, needed to import labour. The same process of economic expansion which brought Yugoslavs,
Turks, Greeks, Italians, Spaniards and Portuguese into
Sweden, Germany, Belgium, Luxembourg, France and
Switzerland, was experienced in Britain: but with two important differences. There are migrant workers in Britain,
from the countries of southern Europe and from as far as
the Phillipines, and their position is similar to that of
«guest workers» elsewhere: but Britain had two other
sources of labour on which to draw. One was (and is) the
Republic of Ireland – a traditional source of cheap labour
since the eighteenth century. Although Ireland is a separate State from Britain the frontier is open and migrant
workers come and go without formality, and their numbers
are correspondingly difficult to assess. The other important source was the British Commonwealth, notably the
Indian subcontinent and the Caribbean Islands.

Immigrants to Britain from its former colonies are not
quite the same as «guest workers», because, already being
Commonwealth citizens, they have a different legal status.
Migrant workers admitted to Britain from Europe and
elsewhere in recent years are subject to a quota and
work-permit system [13]. Commonwealth citizens, by

contrast, were admitted «*for settlement*» and acquired full legal rights. Those who have settled cannot be repatriated to their country of origin. Nonetheless they have many important similarities with migrant workers in other countries.

In Britain from 1968 the economic outlook deteriorated, and fears began to be expressed about the numbers of immigrants. At the same time some of the Commonwealth immigrants had begun to bring wives and children to join them, recognising some benefits of life in Britain, including education and (relative) social security. The presence of fairly large numbers of dark-skinned people in the population, living in a style which the British found strange, and competing for a diminishing number of jobs, attracted the attention of certain politicians (notably Enoch Powell), and the phenomena of racism and racial discrimination come to the surface. This change of official mood led to a series of increasingly restrictive immigration acts. From 1973 it has been almost impossible for any «new» immigrant to enter Britain, entry being restricted to the wives, children, elderly dependents, and fiancées and fiancés of those already settled here.

This legislation had a paradoxical effect. The immigrant, seeing that it would become more difficult to bring his family into Britain in future, was inclined to safeguard his position by making application for them before it was too late. Sensing that the door was closing, people tried to get in before it slammed. This led to an increase in applications, which itself increased the anxieties of those British who feared that they would be «swamped by an alien horde».

Despite strenuous educational efforts and publicity, many English people believe that there are many millions of coloured immigrants in their midst, whereas the real figure (1978) is 1.8 million or 3.3% of the population [8].

Asians

It would be a mistake to generalise about «Asians» in Britain. There are great differences between the groups of Indians, Pakistanis, Bangla Deshis, Chinese, Mauritians, Filipinos, Vietnamese, and others. Even among those from the Indian subcontinent there are important differences between Muslims, Hindus and Sikhs, those from cities and those from villages, and from different geographical areas. Apart from their pre-existing religious and cultural differences, they differ in demographic profile, length of stay in Britain, and ability to speak English. Different groups have tended to settle in certain cities: for example the midland city of Leicester has 18 000 Indians, amounting to 6% of the population, and they are mainly Gujuratis; Bradford, which is an industrial city in the north of England, has a large group from Mirpur which is situated on the northern frontier of Pakistan. The differences between Gujuratis and Mirpuris (and, therefore, between the problems to be faced in Leicester and Bradford) are instructive.

The Gujuratis − especially the ones who came from Uganda − tend to be relatively sophisticated and well-educated people, accustomed to urban living, frequently having been prosperous business men or shopkeepers before they were expelled. They formed much of Uganda's trading community, and their position had been likened to that of the Jews in mediaeval Europe. On arriving in Britain, either as refugees in 1973 or before that from choice, they endeavoured to re-establish themselves in small business enterprises, often with quite remarkably rapid success. The older members of families may not speak English and are emotionally dependent on the support of extended family networks − hence the tendency to settle in particular cities where this support can be felt − but the younger generation have a self-confidence and a willingness to come to terms with English society which is different from some other commonwealth migrants.

The Mirpuris in Bradford, on the other hand, have different attitudes and they provide one of the clearest examples of the stresses of migration and the obstacles to assimilation. For this reason the rest of this paper will concentrate on them.

Mirpuris

Mirpur District of Pakistan is a relatively underdeveloped region in which traditional village culture has survived longer than in most other parts of Pakistan. The culture and language are variants of Punjabi, with devout Muslim religious observance, and traditional patriarchal authority [17, 19]. The kin network in the village *(biraderi)* expects the primary loyalty of all its members, and this is reinforced by marriages within the network (e.g. between cousins). Marriages are arranged by the elders of the family, and until recently young people did not expect to have any choice of partner. On marriage, a girl would go to live in the household of her husband's parents, and come under the tutelage and authority of her mother-in-law. Thus under the one roof there might be the head of the household with his wife, and two or three sons each with his wife and small children − an extended family of ten or fifteen persons. The social roles, and hierarchy of authority within the family unit were clearly understood. For the young bride, her relationship with her mother-in-law and elder sisters-in-law was probably more important than her relationship with her husband − at least initially. This system of extended families and arranged marriages has stood the test of time as a viable social structure in that particular rural, agricultural setting. It comes under strain following migration.

Mirpur has a tradition of emigration. It is not a fertile region, and has a history of harsh government and social backwardness. Being a disputed territory following the partition of India and Pakistan in 1947 it retarded further progress, and the building of the Mangla Dam in the 1960s flooded the old city of Mirpur and displaced some 100000 people. An obvious way for a family to better itself was to collect sufficient money to send one of its young energetic males to seek work elsewhere – either to an industrial city in Pakistan, or abroad. Since Britain had used Mirpur as a recruiting ground for the British/Indian army in the days of the Raj, and Mirpuri men had also been employed traditionally on British ships, Britain was a favourite choice [9].

«Guest worker» or settler?

The young man who came from Mirpur to Britain in the 1960s had many of the characteristics of a «guest worker». He did not envisage remaining permanently in Britain: he had left his family at home, and was prepared to put up with poor conditions and long hours in order to save money to send home. His aim was to accumulate wealth in order to improve the standing, and prospects, of his extended family at home. He took jobs which the English worker did not want (for example in the textile mills on permanent night shifts), and he found cheap accommodation in a house belonging to a relative or fellow-villager who had preceded him. He was not motivated to learn to speak English or understand English culture, or to modify his own behaviour any more than was necessary to avoid conflict. His emotional roots remained in Pakistan and he lived on news from home. Apart from the important difference in his legal rights, his position was similar to that of the Turks in other European countries which (among others) BERGER and MOHR [6] have so graphically described.

Over the years the position has altered. The migrant worker who is on his own can adopt an isolationist attitude if he wishes, but when he is joined by his wife and family other influences begin to be felt. Many of the older generation still hanker after the possibility of returning ‹home› to Pakistan, and cherish the emotional family ties to their *biraderi.* They view much of British culture with misgivings and are determined to hold on to their own traditions. Indeed, their nostalgia for the culture which they left frequently blinds them to the changes which have occurred in Pakistan in their absence; the culture they remember no longer exists. This creates the paradox that some aspects of Pakistani culture live on in Britain but not in Pakistan. This nostalgic tendency is, no doubt, reinforced by the defensive attitude to which all minority groups are prone, especially if they sense hostility from the majority community. At the same time, however, they are inevitably influenced by the surrounding culture and begin to make compromises: and this process naturally affects most the younger generation and the children educated in Britain. This slow adaptation is part of the process of becoming a settler. Few do it as a rational and conscious exercise: the majority make the transition by a series of reluctant adjustments and part-resolved conflicts. This is the stage at which many Mirpuri immigrants currently find themselves and it is at the root of many of the stresses which they experience (other Pakistani and Indian groups in Britain, which have been here longer or came from less backward areas, may be regarded as a few years ahead of the Mirpuris in this respect).

In the literature on migrants and refugees, attention has been paid to the adaptation problems experienced on, or soon after, taking up residence in the new country. It might be instructive to investigate this other transition from self-image of «guest-workers» to self-image of settler, which can occur insidiously and without recognition, perhaps many years later.

Peasants

The Mirpuris exhibit many attitudes characteristic of peasants and they are experiencing the problems of rapid urbanisation [18].

It is sometimes suggested that those who migrate are the more innovative and less conservative members, and this may be so: but an inherent peasant conservatism can be detected from time to time. In an interesting analysis of this conservatism, FOSTER [10] has pointed out that since, in a village, the amount of cultivable land is not expandable, the peasant takes this to be the model for all resources and perceives everything as existing in finite, or limited, quantity. This applies even to abstracts such as «health» or «fortune». It follows that if one member of a community is seen to be prospering, he is suspected of doing so at the expense of his neighbours, and this leads to the mentality of mutual distrust which is characteristic of peasant societies. The exception is when resources are brought into the village from outside, for example remittances sent home by a migrant worker. These can be used to advance the status of a family without provoking so much suspicion.

Peasant attitudes to authority are derived from their experience of exploitation. In general, they believe that external authorities wish to extract from them as much as possible and give little return. The best strategy is to avoid contact with authorities, and give them as little information as possible. Peasants do not confront authority: they circumvent it. They do not shout their grievances or demand their rights: they discover ways of succeeding in spite of the rules. These characteristics affect their relationship with doctors and social workers. The doctor who tries conscientiously to record a full family history, with the names and ages of every child, may meet a defensive reflex reaction. It is unlikely to be expressed overtly: the preferred peasant strategy is to appear stupid and forgetful, or fail to understand the question.

The traditional strategies for coping with disaster may be inappropriate or impracticable in an alien urban environment: and then the urbanised peasant is more distressed and vulnerable than he would have been at home. There are permitted degrees of emotional expression under various circumstances, and rituals which alleviate the pain of (for example) bereavement. The migrant who receives news of a death in the family suffers not only a sense of personal loss, but an additional sense of deprivation amounting almost to outrage, that he is not able to attend the funeral and participate in the mourning process of the family.

Particular causes of stress

Anxiety is most engendered in those areas of life in which success is most highly prized: the greater the ambition, the greater the disappointment. For most migrants, material and financial advancement are the main reason for migration, and rapid success is necessary to justify the decision to move (and satisfy the family who have paid money in fares). A Pakistani immigrant in Britain may have to live in considerable poverty in order to send regular payments home. He cannot afford to tell his relatives that things are not working out as hoped: pride obliges him to send eulogistic accounts which may be far from the truth. On returning home for a visit, he is expected to take expensive presents to a large circle of relatives and friends. Constant pretence imposes its own strains.

Other sorts of ambition are culture-based. For example, in village Pakistan fertility is very important, and a wife who does not become pregnant is looked at askance. For men, sexual impotence is a grave threat to self-esteem.

Some particularly threatening conflicts afflict the orthodox Muslim in western society. Islam provides directive and prescriptive rules for behaviour, and they are intertwined in the mores and detailed behaviour patterns of Muslim society. In England not only are the religious rules more flexible, but they no longer seem to have much influence in everyday life. Thus the Muslim comes from a situation in which the canons of behaviour are clear, specific, and widely accepted, to one in which individuality, self-determination and the right to ‹do your own thing› are highly prized and there are few imposed sanctions. Muslims regard English society as licentious and decadent, a moral quicksand.

The extended family structure in Mirpur already outlined is recreated in Britain as immigrants are joined by their families, but the attempt is not always successful. Patriarchal authority may be absent or may be assumed by an elder brother or uncle and challenged by other members. Hierarchical roles become confused if some members of the family speak English better than others. Two or three sisters-in-law in one household may quarrel bitterly among themselves. The arranged marriage may be unacceptable.

A young man who comes to England unmarried is expected to make a return visit after a few years for an arranged marriage. If he has spent a significant time in English schools, he may not accept this. Perhaps he is already friendly with a girl in England, or wishes to make his own choice at a later stage. If he makes the trip home, he may reject the chosen girl. To a boy who was born in England the whole idea of an arranged marriage may be repugnant: but even if his parents have some sympathy with his views, they find it difficult to support him against the pressures exerted from the home country. A great deal of coming and going is usually involved before a compromise is reached. The psychiatric out-patient clinic contains a number of young men who are contemplating a return trip to get married, and their conflicts frequently appear in the form of sexual anxieties.

Since sexual prowess is an issue of great importance, it is not surprising to find that sexual dysfunction (real or imagined) features largely among the complaints of Indian and Pakistani men, both in Britain and in Pakistan. This provides a major source of income for the Hakims and other traditional healers who flourish in both places [1, 2]. A Pakistani teenager who listens to his English friends and workmates boasting about their sexual adventures may make the mistake of believing them, and assume that indiscriminate promiscuity is an English cultural norm. If he acts on this assumption he is likely to be disappointed; not many Indian and Pakistani girls are permitted to mix freely with boys, and if English girls reject his advances he may attribute this to colour prejudice. It is not surprising that young men in this situation develop anxiety symptoms and worry about their supposed unattractiveness. It is difficult to give categorical reassurance about impotence to a man who has not yet seen his prospective bride. We have found, however, that in many cases there is considerable ignorance of normal sexual function and simple sex education given in the clinic is reassuring and therapeutic. There is a particular complaint common among Asian men, to which the name given is *Jiryan* in Pakistan and the *Dhat* syndrome in India. This consists of the conviction that he is leaking sperm in the urine, and thereby becoming weak. The cultural belief is that one hundred drops of blood are required to produce one drop of semen. In accordance with the concept of «limited good», persistent leakage of semen is thought to be debiliating and a cause of mental illness.

Problems which affect teenage girls also tend to hinge around the arranged marriage system. A girl in a Pakistani village is not expected to make decisions or show any initiative. The same girl, brought to England at an early age, attends school and develops personal ambitions. The aim of the English educational system is that children should learn to think for themselves and form opinions. Although this ideal is diluted in practice, teachers look with favour on the ‹bright child› who works things out for herself and challenges the conventional wisdom. But to be a ‹bright child› in this sense is almost diametrically opposed to being a ‹good child› in the eyes of Pakistani parents. While she has been developing, her parents may have learned little or no English and all they know about English culture is gleaned from the distorted images of the television screen and the rumours and gossip which circulate in their community. They are anxious to protect their daughters, and often send them to Pakistan before they reach the age of puberty. If not, when she is in her teens they may produce photographs of the boy they have arranged that she shall marry, and be impatient to get this settled. A girl who has her own ambitions may be horrified at this idea; but if she raises objections this confirms the parents fears that she has been ‹infected› by Western permissiveness, and they in turn are horrified. Perhaps surprisingly, most families seem to reach a satisfactory compromise eventually [4], but quite a number of girls leave home, and they turn up from time to time on the doorsteps of social service agencies, police stations or at hospitals after taking overdoses of drugs. The parents will often make any promise to get the girl back indoors and avoid public scandal. Admission to a psychiatric unit makes matters worse because now the girl is not only stigmatised ‹bad› but is also by definition ‹mad›. What is needed is an experienced case worker who understands the cultural conflict and can speak to the parents in their own language to bring about some reconciliation. Even if such a person can be found the task is tremendous and often fruitless. For the helpers the moral dilemma of aiding the girl's rebellion is intensified by the knowledge that a brown-skinned girl who cuts herself off from her own community is not by any means assured of a welcome in white society and is vulnerable to exploitation which she is ill equipped to resist. However, the parents' solution may be simply to get the girl married as fast as possible before she «causes any further trouble» − and this seems unsatisfactory.

The tradition of cousin marriage is maintained as far as possible: parents take the view that the family background of a prospective bride or bridegroom is the best guarantee of compatibility. They do not seem to realise that if one partner has been in Britain for many years, perhaps since birth, and the other partner has come direct from the village for the wedding, there may be differences of outlook which can lead to unhappiness. The problem seems worst when it is the girl who is «westernised». Her new husband expects her to behave in the traditional way and allow him to make all decisions: but if he speaks little English and she is fluent, and she has been accustomed to going out unveiled and unaccompanied, the conflicts are immediate and severe.

In 1979 the British government decided to alter the immigration rules to restrict the entry of male fiances. Previously, if any woman who was permanently settled in Britain chose to marry a man from another country, her husband automatically acquired the right to settle permanently in Britain with her. Thus marriage provided a means where a number of men were entering Britain who would not otherwise have been eligible to do so. The government felt that the arrangement was being abused by some Asian families, and decided that in future the right should only apply to women who were themselves *born* in Britain. This decision was bitterly opposed by the Asian community, who saw it as a denial of their cultural tradition of arranged marriage, and also by many other British who condemned it as a piece of petty racist and sexist discrimination and an erosion of civil liberties. There were, however, some young Asian women who secretly welcomed the restriction because marital incompatibility had been a problem.

A different set of problems may affect the girl who is brought to England to be married; if she has no other relatives in England and the marriage turns out badly or she is maltreated by her in-laws, she may have no-one to whom she can turn for help, and no way of escape.

Even when there is mutual affection and kindness, if the couple are without the support of the extended family and are living together in a ‹nuclear family› situation, the intensity of emotional interdependence may be very difficult to cope with: husbands do not always realise that in this situation their wives require more from them, by way of companionship, affection and shared understanding, than when they were in a larger group.

Mental illness

The apparent incidence of mental illness among ethnic minorities has been studied by several authors (see chapter 1 and 2); some migrant groups seem to have more illness than the rest of the population and some less [12]. For Asians in Britain the most recent figures are provided by COCHRANE [7] and they seem to show that Pakistanis suffer less illness than the British, and less than some other immigrant groups. Experience of Pakistanis in Bradford supports this: they are 10% of the population but produce only 4% of the psychiatric patients. It is important to realise, however, that these are not reliable indicators of the incidence of *illness,* but only of the *take-up of psychiatric services,* which is a very different matter, for the following reasons:

1) It is part of the traditional culture, and a matter of family honour, that personal problems should be solved within the family or *biraderi,* seeking advice from family elders but not from outsiders.

2) Concepts of ‹illness›, for which it is appropriate to seek medical help, are more narrowly defined by Pakistanis. Depression or anxiety are not regarded as medical matters unless accompanied by other symptoms or physical complaints such as pain or weakness. On enquiry it may be easy to elict the *somatic* complaints but the *emotional* symptoms may be concealed or even denied. This is a cultural difference which may be related to language [15]. It leads to unnecessary medical investigations, and eventually the patient is dismissed as a hypochondriac.

   It is difficult for the British psychiatrist to diagnose «depression» in a patient who denies feeling depressed; but if antidepressant treatment is prescibed, the symptoms often disappear.

   As with depression, anxiety is usually manifested by somatic complaints, which include pain, weakness, «gas in the stomach», sexual dysfunction, and general malaise.

3) There is a stigma to ‹madness› or ‹insanity›; treatment at a mental hospital is a matter of great shame, not only for the patient but for the whole family.

4) Alternative sources of help are available, including Hakims and Vaids who are practitioners of traditional medicine (*Ayurvedic* and *Unani* systems), and religious healers.

5) An immigrant who is distressed may attribute this (rightly or wrongly) to being in a foreign country, and decide to go back home instead of seeking treatment.

6) The psychiatric services in Britain, although available free to everyone under the National Health Service, are not always sensitive to cultural differences. A person seeking treatment may well feel that his problems were not understood, and would therefore be unlikely to recommend the service to his friends.

Such factors bedevil, and in the author's view invalidate, any estimates of illness which are based on hospital or clinic statistics. In addition we may note that most Pakistanis came to Britain within the last twenty years as fit young adults, and they have not yet reached the age of maximum psychiatric morbidity. There are relatively few post-menopausal, and hardly any geriatric patients among them. It is unwise to generalize about the incidence of mental illness in such a group, and even more risky to estimate particular syndromes such as schizophrenia or depression, as there are diagnostic pitfalls to these.

The experience of uprooting, cultural deprivation, social isolation and misunderstanding may favour a cautious and suspicious attitude which easily develops into paranoid misinterpretation. Studies of various minority groups have demonstrated this tendency, and it is present among Asians in Britain though to a lesser extent than one might expect.

Belief in the «evil eye», and the use of charms, are widespread in rural Pakistan. Bewitchment and demon possession are a fairly common manifestation of hysteria, especially among young women. A peasant who becomes ill, especially if the illness is unfamiliar and recovery is delayed, finds it quite natural to seek an explanation in terms of *bad kismat* (fate) or *nasr* (evil eye or envy) and to look around for the source which may be human or supernatural. This is also a popular explanation for infertility. Such superstitions are not confined to the uneducated. The intelligent and sophisticated Pakistani patient may have such explanations at the back of her mind. She will probably not state them outright but refer obliquely and with apparent irrelevance to a member of the family whom she thinks dislikes her. It should be assumed that any patient who has ideas of this kind will have already consulted a local healer at the same time as seeking psychiatric treatment; and will be receiving concurrent treatment of a religious or magical nature. It is arguable that in cases of neurosis or situational anxiety the lay healers who command faith may be just as effective as the trained psychiatrist but they are unlikely to cure schizophrenia. Such patients may be noticed on examination to be wearing charms (commonly a piece of thread tied around a limb or digit). For the European practitioner, the important thing to remember is that ideas of persecution, whether generalized or specific, do not necessarily point in the direction of schizophrenia but may be consequences of the fact of being ill and worried about it . Among Asians a severe stress reaction may include delusions, hallucinations, confusion, thought disorder and other schizophreniform features. The syndrome may be regarded as a psychogenic psychosis or a form of hysteria. These *acute schizophreniform stress reactions* tend to recover in a few days with minimal drug treatment provided something is done about the cause of stress.

Problems of providing psychiatric treatment

Language

It has to be accepted that if the patient speaks little English, a reliable psychiatric diagnosis cannot be made unless he is interviewed in his own language by someone who knows what to look for [14]. Linguistic incoherence, hesitancy, and poverty of expression cannot easily be distinguished from psychotic thought disorder, depressive retardation or cognitive impairment. In making allowances for linguistic defects important diagnostic points can be missed. The best arrangement we know is to have a clinical team which is not only multidisciplinary but also multilingual, so that there is always one member who can *communicate on behalf of the team* [11, 16]. An unskilful interpreter can be a hindrance. Some find it difficult to report exactly what the patient says, especially if it does not make sense, and say instead what they think it means. An interpreter must accept a code of confidentiality no less strict than a doctor. In medico-legal matters, the interpreter who is a friend of the patient is not accpeptable and an impartial one must be found, preferably from a distance.

It is a mistake to assume that a doctor, nurse, or social worker who is himself (or herself) from India or Pakistan, is necessarily the best person to undertake the treatment of immigrants from that country. Migrants who come from remote rural areas speak a multiplicity of dialects, and their culture is in some ways very different from that of the cities. The educated doctor from Bombay or Delhi may have very little in common with them. Even if he could communicate more easily than the British doctor he would have a different set of problems to overcome. If he were a Muslim, doubtless he would identify more easily with his Muslim patients: but this would not help him with Hindus or Sikhs. He might be more acceptable to first-generation immigrants but less so to their children. Instead of religious and linguistic obstacles he might have some social class obstacles to overcome. British society is far from egalitarian, but the gulfs which still exist between rich and poor, educated and uneducated, are a good deal less wide than they are in India and Pakistan. There is also a question of motivation. Of the Asian doctors working in European countries, how many really want to work with Asian patients or clients? The immigrant who is a professional often prefers to emphasise that he is a professional rather than an immigrant. Bearing in mind the insults to which coloured people are exposed, and the struggle which the intelligent and educated «brown» man has to establish himself in middle-class «white» society, it is understandable if (with honourable exceptions) he does not choose to identify with the peasant in the ghetto, with whom he has not a great deal in common except skin colour.

One important language problem is that treatment which is prescribed is not always taken is intended, especially by out-patients. In one study twenty Asian patients were assigned randomly to two groups. Half received their medication with only the usual prescription label (in English). The other half received extra written instructions in English and also verbal counselling *in their own language.* When they were visited later at home seven of the ten counselled patients were taking the medication whereas only three of the other ten had presisted beyond the first few days [3].

Problems in hospitals

All sort of problems arise when the non-English speaking patient is admitted to an English mental hospital. With the best of intentions one can hardly prevent such a patient being alarmed by unfamiliar and incomprehensible routines or bored to distraction by social and linguistic isolation. As anyone who has travelled abroad will recall, one's strategy is to watch what others are doing and copy them. This does not work too well in a psychiatric ward!

Both Muslims and Hindus in hospital worry about food. Not only is it not to their taste, but they cannot be sure what it contains. A catering officer negotiating the minefields of non-beef-eating Hindus and non-pork-eating Muslims is tempted to play safe by treating them all as vegetarians. The menu is usually built round eggs and cheese, and Asians often reject the cheese because they think it contains prohibited fats and in any case they do not like the taste.

Other problems include facilities for prayers and fasting especially during Ramadan or other religious occasions. It is essential that hospital staff develop a sensitivity to cultural differences, and the need for training in these matters is now being recognized in Britain [11, 16].

In all psychiatric illness, but especially the neuroses, successful treatment depends on having mutually agreed goals and expectations. The Western-trained psychiatrist may see himself in the role of *enabler.* By helping a patient to face up to the internal conflicts which were repressed or malcompensated, he will *enable* the patient to make his own conscious choices and resolutions.

This view of therapy may seem quite strange to a Pakistani, who expects his doctor to know what is wrong with him, and put him right while he (the patient) remains relatively passive. Such a patient expects his therapist to give detailed and precise instructions, and the confident assurance that if you do this, and this, a cure is guaranteed. It is tempting to collude with the patient by prescribing pills, E.C.T. or injections (particularly injections) and of course this works reasonably well for endogenous depression and schizophrenia. Even when physical methods of treatment do not work, the patient at least feels he is in the hands of a proper doctor. But even if treatment is mainly by physical methods, success depends to some extent on the establishment of personal rapport between the patient and the therapist, and rapport depends upon empathy — the ability of the therapist to enter imaginatively and compassionately into the experiences of the patient. Where the cultural difference is great and empathy correspondingly difficult to achieve, we have to work harder at it. It is helpful to acquire and demonstrate some knowledge of the other person's culture. Even a smattering of the language is a token of goodwill. It may sometimes be possible to bridge the gap by using intermediaries. An intermediary may be an Asian doctor, nurse, or unqualified assistant, and may also function as an interpreter. With training and experience, the intermediary becomes an important member of the therapeutic team, perhaps the most important member in the eyes of the patient. If individuals who can function in this way cannot be found among the existing hospital staff, they might be introduced in the guise of social work aides or occupation therapy assistants. Even the once-a-week volunteer visitor can be incorporated into the team.

We must realise, however, that when we ask someone to fill this intermediary role we are giving them a difficult task which might cause them some personal problems. The person we seek is one who straddles two cultures and can identify with each. We should remember that such a person is himself «marginal» and is quite likely to have his own identity problems, which may come to the surface in this work.

The provision of special services for ethnic minorities

Just as the immigrant seldom manages his transition from *migrant worker* to *settler* on the basis of clear-thinking and logical decisions, but rather tends to muddle his way through with reluctant compromises and gnawing self-doubt punctuated by inappropriate emotional outbursts: so receiving societies have tended to react irrationally to their problem of *assimilation versus cultural pluralism.*

The social and political dimensions of this question are beyond the scope of this chapter, but they do demand careful consideration by all who are involved in the provision of health care and social welfare, since the type of provision made for minority groups, and willingness to make it, must depend on the basic attitudes and political stance which is adopted. One thing is certain: ethnic minorities do have certain particular needs, and there is a professional obligation to meet them. This has been well expressed by an English anthropologist working in this field:

«For the practitioner the question of whether the minorities ought, or ought not, to remain ethnically distinct should be irrelevant. The fact is that they are. Insofar as his speciality, whatever it is, demands that he should take into account the social and cultural worlds in which his clients live, he needs to make a response to ethnic diversity. If he does not, his practice is inadequate in purely professional terms» [5].

The kind of provision which is appropriate must depend on the particular needs of the ethnic minorities in any particular country or city. It is incumbent on practitioners and administrators to identify the needs of their own locality.

313

Transcultural psychiatry unit

In Bradford, psychiatric services provided under the National Health Service are based on a 180-bedded psychiatric unit at Lynifield Mount which is adjacent to the general hospital. In 1972 the Consultant Psychiatrists at the unit agreed that the service provided for immigrants (about 10% of the population served) was unsatisfactory, which has led to the establishment of a Transcultural Psychiatry Unit. One day in the week has been set aside on which a team assembles for an «Asian Clinic», ward rounds and staff meetings. Between them the team can provide fairly wide coverage of different Indo-Pakistani cultures and languages. When necessary, additional expertise can be called upon through local and national contacts. There is no separate ward for Asian patients, nor is this envisaged as it would easily be misunderstood as a form of *apartheid*. The Unit office provides a focal point for members of the team, and others working in similar fields, and contains a reference library on transcultural psychiatry and related subjects.

The primary task of the Unit is to provide a psychiatric service in its area: but requests for information and advice from further afield are becoming increasingly frequent. Once a month the staff meeting is attended by a wider group of interested people from the hospital and outside, including relevant University Departments. There is a constant exchange of correspondence with other centres, and frequent visitors from other parts of Britain and overseas. Members of the staff have been on study tours in Pakistan and elsewhere. The Unit is involved in continuous research and education in the sense that new clinical observations and ideas are constantly collected, discussed and disseminated. Since 1976 a card-index register has been kept to enable retrospective analysis of case notes for particular projects. In addition certain specific research studies are undertaken. Interest in the psychiatric problems of a minority group inevitably leads to an awareness of other problems. In the medical field, the rates of still-

314

birth and infant mortality among Asians in Bradford are about double those of the host population, and the incidence of mental handicap and deafness are high in children of Asian parents.

Future problems

Asian immigration into Britain has now virtually ceased apart from the reuniting of families, but we do not believe that adjustment problems will cease in the near future. In a few years we shall start to face the problems of an ageing population. Equally important are the problems of the second generation, who are at present growing up in two cultures [4, 20]. The kind of problems mentioned in this paper are likely to get worse and more frequent before they improve. There are signs that a generation of rebellious and unhappy Asian youngsters is emerging, and even if only a few of them seek psychiatric assistance, they present us with some of our most difficult problems, which will be with us a long time into the future.

Bibliography

1 Aslam, M.: The practice of Asian Medicine in the United Kingdom. University of Nottingham, Ph.D. Thesis (Unpublished, 1979).
2 Aslam, M., Davis, S.S., Farrar, N., Rack, P.H.: Health Care needs of Asians in the United Kingdom. Paper read at Symp. on Migrant Workers, Orrebro, Sweden. In press (1978).
3 Aslam, M., Davie, S.S., Fletcher, R.F.: Compliance in medication by Asian immigrants. In press (1979).
4 Ballard, C.: Conflict, Continuity and Change: Second Generation South Asians. In: Saifullah Kahn, V. (Ed.): Minority Families in Britain: Support and Stress. Macmillans, London 1979.
5 Ballard, R.: Ethnic Minorities and the Social Services. In: Saifullah Kahn, V. (Ed.): Minority Families in Britain: Support and Stress. Macmillans, London 1979.
6 Berger, J., Mohr, J.: Seventh Man. The Penguin Press, Harmondsworth 1975.
7 Cochrane, R.: Mental Illness in Immigrants to England and Wales. An analysis of Mental Hospital Admissions. Soc. Psychiat. *12,* 25 – 25, 1971 (1977).

8 CROSS, C.: Ethnic Minorities in Britain: statistical background. Commission for Racial Equality, 10 – 12 Allington Street, SW1E 5EH, London 1978.

9 DAHYA, BADR.: Pakistanis in Britain: Transients or Settlers? Race. *XIV,* 3, London 1973.

10 FOSTER, G. M.: Peasant Society and the image of limited good. Amer. Anthropol. *67,* 2, 1965. Reprinted in Potter, J. M., Diaz, M. N., Foster, G. M. (Eds.): Peasant Society: a Reader. Little Brown & Co, Boston 1967.

11 HENLEY, ALIX: Asian Patients in Hospital and at Home. King's Fund/Pitman Medical, London 1979.

12 MURPHY, H. B. M.: Migration, Culture and Mental Health. Psychol. Medecine *7,* 677 – 684, 1977.

13 POWER, J., HARDMAN, A.: Western Europe's Migrant Workers. Minority Rights Group. Report No. 28, 1976, revisted 1978.

14 RACK, P. H.: Some practical problems in providing a psychiatric service for immigrants. Mental Health & Society *12,* 25 – 25, 1977.

15 RACK, P. H.: Diagnosing Mental Ilness: Asians and the psychiatric services. In: Saifullah Kahn, V. (Ed.): Minority Families in Britain: Support and Stress. Macmillans, London 1979.

16 ROWELL, V. R., RACK, P. H.: Health Education Needs of a Minority Ethnic Group. J. Inst. of Health Education. In press (1980).

17 SAIFULLAH KAHN, V.: The Pakistanis: Mirpuri villagers at home and in the city of Bradford. In: Watson, J. L. (Ed.): Between two cultures. Blackwell, Oxford 1977.

18 THOMAS, W. I., ZNANIECKI, F.: The Polish Peasant in Europe and America. Dover Publications, New York 1918, reprinted 1958.

19 WAKIL, P. A.: Explorations of the kin networks of the Punjabi Society. J. of Marriage & Family *70,* 700 – 707, 1970.

20 Various authors in WATSON, J. L. (Ed.): Between two cultures: migrants and minorities in Britain. Basil Blackwell, Oxford 1977.

Chapter 17

Getting an identity:
Transracial, inter-country adoption

Marianne Cederblad

Background

In early Western civilization and Greek and Roman Law, a childless couple adopted a child to provide a direct heir or to perpetuate domestic ancestral worship. Beginning in the nineteenth century in Europe adoption was used to solve the problem of illegitimacy. Although the child often benefitted from adoption, it was used primarily as a means of giving a child to a family in the interest of the adults involved.

World War II dramatically changed Western society's attitude toward adoption. It seemed to be the best way that Europe could cope with the vast number of orphaned and displaced children.

Of primary importance was the fact that the child, so long ignored by society, came on centre stage – his welfare was most important: Research dissolved old myths on the ill-effects of poor birth circumstances and early experiences and confirmed that adoptive success depends chiefly on the personal qualities, right attitudes and harmonious relationship of the adoptive couple. Social workers were trained in case-work techniques in order to find suitable parents to meet a child's needs. New legislation secured the place of the adoptee by giving him the same rights as the child born into the family. Adoption had become a way of giving a family to a child rather than a child to a family.

In post-war Europe adoption was credited with being the best substitute for care by the child's own parents or close relatives provided that practices were based on the child's welfare.

During the 1960s and 1970s in Europe and North-America the number of children given for adoption steadily decreased. The reasons were better contraceptive measures, more liberal abortion laws and improved social and economic support for unmarried mothers as well as diminishing social stigma attached to illegitimate births, which made it possible for more women to take care of their own children. The demand for children to adopt was no longer met by a large enough number of children, who needed adoptive parents in the same country. Towards the end of the 1960s childless couples started to look for orphans in the developing countries. Through the massmedia and widespread tourist travels there was an increased awareness of the appalling situation of many children in these countries. Although the majority of the adoptive parents were still childless couples in search of a child, which could not any longer be found within their own country, there was also a new group of couples, who adopted children from orphanages in developing countries. They were people who were concerned with the depressing prospects of these children, who wanted to help an individual child rather than bearing another biological child. Inter-country adoption became a way to show solidarity with children all over the world. This was the view from the receiving end of the adoption line.

Since World War II the developing countries have undergone a rapid social change. In these predominantly rural countries the extended families have constituted society and cared for the child without parents. The social turmoil which accompanies industrialization, urbanization, and political change now strain these ties to the breaking point. These factors tend to increase the number of children needing care outside their biological extended families. Wars with invading military forces have left biracial children, who are often discriminated against.

The feelings about intercountry adoption at the donating end of the line are often mixed. People who work with these children in institutions or in the streets of the slums of big cities see the poor chances for the individual child to get a decent upbringing. Many welcome the opportunity of adoption for the child regardless of the hazards that might be connected with an intercountry adoption. The alternative for the child would be to remain in his present condition of poverty and psychological neglect.

Politically there have been feelings against this «act of aggression» especially since in some countries there has developed a black market of infants. Middle-men have made a large profit on western couples longing for a child and the methods to «buy» or even steal children from their poor mothers are difficult to control. Governments have also been worried about the future risks of discrimination against the children, since in many cases these are also interracial adoptions. Some countries like Colombia, Korea and India have reported that 75% of their adoptees receive overseas parents.

Many developing countries now try to increase incountry adoption although there are often religious and cultural reasons against placing children among non-relatives. At present 83 countries have some type of formal adoption procedures. The discussions and criticism of inter-country adoption have sometimes speeded up the decision to solve the problems about what to do with the children without families. Still, for many years, many developing countries will not be able to solve the problem of taking care of all the thousands of homeless children. Their only chance to get a family of their own will be through inter-country adoption. However it is very important that the investigation of the adoptive family and the preparation of the adoptive child and, if possible its parents, is done very conscienciously, taking the fundamental principles in inter-country adoption (annex I) into consideration.

International regulations

Whenever two countries are involved in an adoptive placement, complex problems stemming from differing, often conflicting, legal requirements, attitudes, languages, adoption procedures and available social services arise and require specialized attention to safeguard children.

Beginning in 1953 the United Nations sponsored a study series concerning adoption followed by international meetings: i.e. 1957 — Group of Experts of Inter-Country Adoption, Geneva, UN Office; 1960 — European Seminar on Inter-Country Adoption, Leysin, (UN European Office) and 1965 — The Hague Convention on Jurisdiction, Applicable Law and Recognition of Decrees Relating to Adoption.

These were convened under the auspices of the United Nations with the objective of developing a consensus on adoption laws and practices which could facilitate inter-country adoption placements and raise the standards of national adoptive practices. As a result of this work, undertaken by representatives from primarily European and American countries, the United Nations published a set of twelve principles based on the welfare of the child to be found in annex I. These have been reaffirmed at more recent international meetings and with revisions, continue to influence adoption laws and practices, nationally and internationally.

Some statistics

The number of inter-country adoptions has increased very rapidly during the last ten years. USA for example had 1600 entries by «immigrant orphans» for adoption in 1968 while in 1975 there were 5600, most of whom came from Asia (i.e. Korea 2900). In Sweden 2000 children were adopted from other countries between 1950 and 1970. Most of them came from Europe. From the middle of the 1960s children from other parts of the world have dominated. During the latter half of the 1970s nearly 2000 children arrived each year, about half of them came from Korea. Many children have also come from India, Thailand and some South American countries. Few children have come from Africa except from Ethiopia. Altogether approximately 20000 children have been adopted into Sweden from other countries, most of them also belong to non-caucasian races.

Situations leading to inter-country adoptions

The biological mother may be a young unmarried woman. Her pregnancy is a disgrace to the family and she couldn't stay in it with her baby. It is impossible for her to support both herself and the baby alone. The only solution is to leave the infant for adoption.

One or both parents die or disappear. The child lives for some years with a grandmother. When she gets ill she can no longer take care of the child and she has to leave it at an orphanage where she signs a paper freeing the child for adoption.

A woman becomes a widow. She cannot support all her children. The youngest one is left for adoption.

Often the separation has been quite traumatic; a pre-school child is abandoned with a toy at a marketplace or on a train. There the police take care of the child and deliver it at an institution. In other cases a baby was left on the doorsteps of an orphanage or the mother ran away from the hospital after the delivery leaving the child behind.

Often older children who are adopted have experienced several separations before the final adoption. They might have lived with different relatives, moved between institutions and been to more than one fosterhome. Sometimes these moves have also meant changing languages (i.e. in India).

All of these milieus have been poor. The children have often not got enough food, they have had various infections and parasites. The adults have been depressed and despairing before taking the final decision of giving up the child. The institutions have often been overcrowded and understaffed. But there may also have been a caring, loving relationship between the child and its mother or grand-mother.

Strong bonds might exist between the child and one particular nurse at an orphanage or within the group of children sharing the same room at the institution. The child brings these experiences into the new family of adoption. In that way the adoption situation − at least when the child is not an infant − is more complex than the ordinary situation when a family receives a baby. What kind of help do the families get to manage the situation? How well does the child adapt to the new family in a foreign culture, perhaps with a new language?

Aid to adopting parents

In addition to new controls set up by sending nations (Sri Lanka, Korea), Sweden, the Netherlands, the United Kingdom and other receiving countries are establishing official bodies responsible for monitoring the entrance of children into their countries which aim at curbing illegal transfer. A Model Adoption Law adaptable to all states in the USA was in 1979 considered in order to unify the existing complexity of adoption laws and procedures and to tighten control.

Funded rehabilitation programmes which have provided tools and services for self-help have proven effective in reducing the need for permanent substitute care and should be continued and broadened in scope. In Nigeria, Bangladesh and the Sudan where such projects were introduced following national tragedies, thousands of children were successfully reunited with their families who were again able to provide for them.

Adoption allowance or subsidies

Based on the fact that there are heavy ongoing financial obligations involved in parenting a handicapped child or a group of siblings, adoptions are being subsidized under a variety of plans in 41 States in the USA. Two states have enacted legislation. A Model State Subsidized Adoption Act and Regulations instigated by the Children's Bureau, Washington D.C. holds promise for parents otherwise unable or unwilling to shoulder an extra heavy financial load. It may constitute a break-through in finding more adoptive black parents for black children. The British Children Act, 1975 restricts payments to adopters but approved adoption allowances are under discussion there and elsewhere.

Post-placement services

Of significant importance is the widespread movement to extend social agency counselling and other services beyond the time when adoptions are finalized. This practice, while increasing adjustment success in all adoptions, provides essential support required by parents and children creating new families under atypical circumstances.

Parent training

The United Kingdom has been a leader in offering special training in regular scheduled seminars. This increases the security of parents and children and raises parental skills to a more effective level.

Somatic development after adoption

Almost all adoptive children regardless of age have a suboptimal length and weight for their age when they arrive in their new country. Most of them also suffer from different infections and parasites. In an investigation by HOFVANDER [5] of 74 adopted children in Upsala, Sweden most of whom were below one year of age on arrival 39% were more or less malnourished, 9% had severe malnutrition. One third of the children had diarrhoea and the same number had intestinal worms. Only 16% were in full health. Most children were below Swedish standard for length and weight which indicate poor nutritional status since earlier studies in developing countries have shown that well-nourished children don't deviate from Swedish standards during the first 5 years of life. It has also been found by the present author that the children grow 10 – 15 cm during the first year in Sweden and gain considerable weight. The catch-up in length is another indicator of previous nutritional deficit. WINICK [10] in a study of Korean adopted children (see below) found that the previously malnourished children were significally shorter than the previously well nourished children. The whole group was taller and heavier than would be expected if they had remained in Korea but smaller and lighter than a comparable group of American children. BENGTSSON [1] found in stool tests of 2000 children that 49% had pathological intestinal parasites. The most common were Giardia, Trichuris and Ascaris. The children with these infestations often had diarrhoea and anaemia. Various Swedish investigations have also found that about 50% of stool tests contain pathological viruses, 5 – 6% of those are polio and the same amount viruses causing inflammation of the liver. Some cases of pulmonal tuberculosis are discovered each year and single cases of congenital lues have also been discovered. Most infections and other diseases that the children have when they arrive are easily cured. It is very important that the children get a thorough tropical medical examination when they arrive and the receiving families are encouraged to renew their polio-inoculations and to have a dosis of gamma-globulin against possible infections of the liver. The future somatic health of these children seems to be excellent. One Swedish study shows that a group of Korean adopted children had less sickness absence than a group of Swedish children in the same classes.

Intelligence and malnutrition

Many investigations in developing countries have shown that children who suffer malnutrition during their early years function less well on intelligence tests than well-nourished children from the same cultural setting. As mentioned above the adoptive children are often malnourished when they arrive in their new country. How do they develop mentally after adoption? WINICK [10] has studied Korean children adopted by American couples. The 229 girls were all placed in the adoptive family before 3 years of age. At the time of the follow-up they were in elementary school. They had been in the adoptive homes for at least six years. The children were divided into three groups according to their state of nutrition at the placement: «malnourished», «moderately nourished» and «well-nourished». At the follow-up the previously well nourished group had much better results on the intelligence tests as well as on tests of school-achievements than the malnourished group and there was also a significant difference in achievement between the well-nourished and moderately nourished group. However *all* the groups had reached or exceeded the mean values on both tests for American children! Early malnutrition can be compensated by a permanent change to a better environment with adequate nutrition and stimulation. HULTERSTRÖM [6] found that ⅔ of 47 adopted children, most of them between 3 and 5 years old, who were investigated with various intelligence-tests were achieving above average scores. There was no difference in achievement between those who arrived before or after 18 months of age. The children's nutritional state on arrival was not checked. But the investigation still confirms the results of WINICK [10] that the group of adopted children functions intellectually well in their new families in spite of a history of poor nutrition.

Psychological adjustment − initial period

The children who arrive before they are 1 year old are often sick and may show some initial problems of adjustment like difficulty to sleep, anxiety and extreme dependency. Both the somatic and emotional problems disappear within a couple of months [4].

Children who arrive at an older age have more problems during the first 6 months − 1 year in the new family. GAR-DELL [3] found a linear increase of adjustment difficulties with age at placement (i.e. 32% disturbed among those placed at 3, 64% disturbed among those placed at 6 and over). The present author [2] made a prospective study of 27 children above 3 years old at placement during their first year in the adoptive family. About 60% showed various adjustment problems. The most common symptoms were sleep disturbances, overeating and separation anxiety. The overeating is probably due both to earlier experiences of lack of food, to oral fixation due to deprivation and to the fact that the children grow very fast and therefore need large quantities of food. Most children select one parent during the first weeks to whom they attach themselves. While they monopolize that parent they may reject the other members of the household. They often regress for some time showing extreme dependency, wanting to be carried, fed, dressed and helped at the toilet even if they could function adequately in all those areas when they first came to the family.

Children who lose their language when they are adopted tend to be very aggressive during the first months before they are able to make themselves understood.

Only ⅓ of the children still show emotional symptoms after one year in the family. Lack of self-confidence, rebelliousness, outbursts of anger and hyperactivity are the most common deviances.

More striking is a rather large group of children (30%) who *never* show any signs of emotional crisis although they live through such a drastic life-change. They seem happy and well-balanced from the moment they walk into their

326

new families. There are no backlashes later either, as far as we know.

Psychological adjustment — age on arrival

The psychological hazards are different when children are adopted as infants or at an older age. The older children have often suffered from parental deprivation and lack of opportunity to form lasting bonds with one or few adult caretakers. Others have suffered one or more early separations. Both conditions have earlier been described as important risk-factors for impaired capacity to form selective relationships and the latter is also said to increase the risk for deep depressive states.

Investigations in Sweden [3] and Denmark [8] have shown surprisingly small long-term differences between children adopted before 1½ – 2 years of age and those who were older when they arrived. GARDELL made her investigation when most children had spent 9 years in the families (minimum 5 years). The 207 children were between 10 and 18. She found that the 46 children who were below 1½ at placement had suffered less emotional disturbances during the first months in the family. At the time of the investigation this difference had disappeared. Only the 33 children older than 6 years at placement seem to have a little more problems at the follow-up (33% compared with about 23% for the rest of the group).

PRUZAN [8] made her investigation when the 168 children had spent at least 2 years in their adoptive families and were 8 – 12 years old. She didn't find any relationship between emotional problems and age at arrival.

Various investigations made on transracial adoptions in the USA and also in-country adoptions of older and younger children all estimate that between 70 and 80% are «successful», that is the children develop well and adjust to family and society. There are no striking differences between the studies [9].

A recent study on transracial adoption from Britain [7]

including West Indian and African children concluded that 92% were well adjusted.

So far, research has not confirmed the fear that the older children should have developed permanent emotional impairments due to their early experiences. PRUZAN points to the fact that only few children show such behaviour deviations which are said to be typical of children who have suffered from maternal deprivation in the first years (lack of impulse control, aggressiveness and antisocial behaviour). GARDELL [3] didn't find any covariation of psychological or social adjustment and malnutrition at the time of adoption (language difficulties, relationship to peers, anxiety).

Language

Those children who are placed through inter-country adoption after they have started to develop a language face special difficulties. Most children learn to speak the language of the adoptive family very quickly. Two thirds of the children have a basic language ability after 3 months in the new country [2]. To be able to express and understand more subtle nuances takes a longer time. Within a couple of years the children speak so well that neither parents nor teachers note any accent or faulty grammar in the spoken language.

In school, however, GARDELL [3] found that language problems are noticable for nearly half of the children who arrived later than 1½ years of age. These problems are more pronounced when the children reach the secondary school level. They show sudden lack of comprehension of common Swedish words. The children have difficulty to express themselves in writing where they show grammatical weakness. They have difficulties to understand oral lectures. These language problems also influence their capacity to understand mathematical problems and to learn foreign languages. Among those children who arrived in Sweden before the age of 18 months 33% showed late language-problems, 42% of the group between 18 months and 6 years and finally 64% of those who came to Sweden after the age of 6 years showed such problems. PRUZAN [8] didn't find more language problems among the adopted children than among Danish children of the same age. The children in her investigation, however, were still in the intermediate level.

In Sweden adoptive children have the same right to receive tuition in their «home-language» as children of immigrant families. The language-problems of these two groups of children are however different. The adopted child loses his language since most families don't know the language of the child at all. The immigrant child speaks his native language at home and Swedish outside the home. At present the adoptive children often refuse to speak their own language even when the family tries to speak it and if they get immediate «home-language» training. The transition to a new culture may be so traumatic that the child must repress all memories of the old «world» including the language in order to be able to adapt to the new situation.

Identity

In the USA in the 1960s adoptions by white parents of Indian and Black children became popular but then decreased. Research supported it by reporting successful adjustments. Nevertheless fear of the child losing its racial identity by assimilation or suffering from a mixed racial identity led minority group leaders to discourage mixed race adoptions. SIMON and ALTSTEIN [9] found in their study of 204 non-white (mostly black) children in white families that the adoptees kept their racial identity but that they didn't show the preference for fair complexion and hair which has been shown in black children raised in black families in other American investigations. This was measured by projective tests given to the non-white adopted children and their 167 white siblings. They conclude that the mixed racial adoptions seem to decrease the racial prejudices in the children raised in such families.

In Sweden GARDELL [3] found that the adopted children often felt embarrassed by too much discussion about their ethnic background. They wanted to seek information about their biological background and their country of origin at their own pace. Only 30% have actual memories from their home-countries and those are faded and fragmented. The parents are of little help to fill in the gaps since they seldom know much about the factual history of their children either. Frequent thoughts about the time before the adoption seem to be more common the older the child is at the age of placement. These thoughts are also more frequent when the child is in prepuberty (12 – 13 years old) and after 16 years of age (50% of the groups). 11% of the children had requested to change the Swedish name that they had been given when they arrived in Sweden. Most of the time they had chosen a name from their country of origin.

In the summer of 1979 the first group of adopted children and their parents made a tourist tour to Korea to «seek their roots». Some children met their relatives or visited the orphanage that they had stayed in.

The reality of the adoptees' double identity; Korean *and* Swedish, was reinforced in a good way.

To conclude

Transracial, inter-country adoption is still a very new phenomenon. It is a natural social experiment which has shown that children suffering from early malnutrition and emotionally depriving rearing situations can develop into healthy, intelligent and harmonious young people when they are placed permanently in the greenhouse of a loving, engaged family, willing to stimulate and take care of the child in an optimal way. We still don't know however what will happen when these children as adults have to function independently. Will they meet discrimination at work? Will they be able to form intimate relationships with a spouse? Will they have difficulties as parents? Only the future can tell.

Annex I

Fundamental principles in inter-country adoption

Principle 1. That adoption is the best substitute for care by the child's own parents or close relatives, provided that adoption practices are based fundamentally on the welfare of the child.

Principle 2. That sufficient consideration should be given to possible alternative plans for the child within his own country before inter-country adoption is decided upon, since there are various hazards inherent in transplanting a child from one culture to another.

Principle 3. That increased efforts should be made in each country to examine, at as early a stage as possible, whether certain children should be adopted within the country rather than remaining indefinitely in institutions because of rather slight family ties; that careful examination should be made of the value to the child of such ties which act as an obstacle to adoptive placement for him.

Principle 4. That increased efforts should be made in each country to find adoptive homes within the country for children with mental or physical defects and for children whose family background presents an obstacle to adoption.

Principle 5. That extremely careful consideration should be given to all possible alternatives before a child is removed from his own relatives for adoption; that a parent, regardless of social and legal status, should have the oppor-

331

tunity for full consideration of what is involved, including legal and psychological consequences, before a decision is made that adoption is the best plan for the child; that concepts of modern child and family welfare should prevail over economic and social factors.

Principle 6. That those who have ties, legal or emotional, to the child should be helped to understand thoroughly the meaning of adoption in the culture of the new country; that the child, if old enough, should also be prepared for the implications of adoption and life in the new country; that unless this can be done, and the consequences accepted by all concerned, the child should not be considered suitable for inter-country adoption.

Principle 7. That an adequate home study of the prospective adopters should be completed before a child is suggested to, or placed with a couple with a view to inter-country adoption, as well as an adequate study of the child's background, physical condition, and personality development; that it is recognized that a home study of the adoptive parents may have limited value when the parents are living in a temporary setting, so that there are often valid reasons for not considering such couples as prospective adoptive parents unless they live in one setting for a sufficient length of time where they can be studied by a social worker who is sufficiently familiar with their culture, and an appraisal of them in their own home community can be obtained before a child is suggested to, or placed with them.

Principle 8. That the process of matching together child and adoptive parents in inter-country adoption should be a shared responsibility between the child welfare agency which makes the home study of the prospective adopters and the child welfare agency responsible for the child, with the participation of a specialized international social agency acting as intermediary between the two. All relevant factors which are accepted as valid in matching child and adoptive parents in local adoptions shall be taken into consideration, with special attention to the factor of religion.

Principle 9. That before legal adoption is completed, there must be a trial period of not less than six months under the supervision of a social worker attached to a qualified agency, able to understand the cultural patterns of the prospective adopters and of the child; in the case of older children, this period should be longer.

That there is opposition to proxy adoptions except under certain exceptional circumstances where prospective adopters and child have lived together for a reasonable time and established a satisfactory parent-child relationship.

Principle 10. That care must be given, before the adoption plan is finalized, that pertinent documents necessary to complete the adoption are available, particulary that all necessary consents are in order in a form which is legally valid in both countries; that it must be definitely established that the child will be able to immigrate to the country of the prospective adopters and can subsequently obtain their nationality.

Principle 11. That care must be given to assuring adequate protection of the child in his new country; that in view of the difficulty of exercising guardianship functions across national boundaries, the value of the former legal guardianship needs to be examined; that legal responsibility for the child in the new country should be established promptly.

Principle 12. That steps must be taken to assure that the adoption is legally valid in both countries.

Bibliography

1 BENGTSSON, E.: In: Hofvander, Y. (Ed.): U-landsadoptivbarn – hälsa och anpassning. Läkartidningen 3, 1978.

2 CEDERBLAD, M.: In: Hofvander, Y. (Ed.): U-landsadoptivbarn – hälsa och anpassning. Läkartidningen 3, 1978.

3 GARDELL, I.: Internationella adoptioner – en uppföljningsstudie. Allm. barnhuset, Mimeographed, Stockholm 1979.

4 GUNNARBY, A.: In: Hofvander, Y. (Ed.): U-landsadoptivbarn – hälsa och anpassning. Läkartidningen 3, 1978.

5 HOFVANDER, Y.: U-landsadoptivbarn – hälsa och anpassning. Läkartidningen 73, 4673–4680, 1978.

6 HULTERSTRÖM, A.: Psykologbedömning – föräldrasamtal. Personal Communication, Mimeographed, Linköping 1978.

7 JACKSON, B.: Family experiences of inter-racial adoption. ABAFA, London 1976.

8 PRUZAN, V.: Födt i udlandet – adopteret i Danmark. Socialforskningsinstitutet nr. 77, København 1977.

9 SIMON, R.J., ALTSTEIN, H.: Transracial adoption. J. Wiley & Sons, New York 1977.

10 WINICK, M. et al.: Malnutrition and environmental enrichment by early adoption. Science 190, 1173–1175, 1975.

Chapter 18

A migrating world:
Migrants and refugees: Some facts, patterns and figures

ALAN STOLLER

I. Introduction

It is well-nigh impossible to provide other than a very approximate estimate of migrants and refugees at any given
time. The phenomena which displace persons from their
countries of origin are complex and dynamic in nature and
the status of displaced persons tend to change over time —
through political upheavals, through changes in definitions, and through such process as the degree of absorption
within host communities.

An international assessment as to who is actually a refugee has been a relatively modern innovation, though still
not universally acceptable. The UNHCR definition dates
from the 1950 Statute, which was modified through the
1967 protocol. It specified help for persons who «owing to
to a well-founded fear of being persecuted for reasons of
race, religion, nationality or political opinion, is outside
the country of his nationality and is unable or, owing to
such fear or for reasons other than personal inconve-
nience, is unwilling to avail himself of the protection of
that country; or, who not having a nationality and being
outside the country of his former habitual residence, is unable or, owing to such fear or for reasons other than personal convenience, is unwilling to return to it».

Within the process of displacement of peoples, such as
occurred after World War II for instance, or in the process
of decolonization of the African continent, a number of

people find themselves ‹in limbo›, with their nationality undetermined. Some may be subsequently able to reacquire their old nationality; some may acquire a new nationality and enjoy the protection of their host society; some, where the circumstances of their refugee status has ceased to exist, may not wish to return to their original habitat for personal or economic reasons; and finally, there are some who have no wish to acquire the new nationality of their country which has ceased to exist, and so remain stateless. UNHCR does not provide aid for those who wish to remain for purely economic reasons, and is not concerned with asylum seekers.

In national statistics, migrants and refugees are lumped together and, if one merely records ‹place of birth›, the figures will include semi-permanents, temporary sojourners, seasonal workers, students, members of national delegations and international agencies, and so on. In many countries of immigration, there are not insignificant numbers of illegal workers, some of whom have been brought into the country through organized smuggling, besides those who enter on tourist visas and go into limbo. The recent acceptance of movement of labour between E.E.C. countries has introduced a new factor in the migration situation in Europe.

The situation is most easy to record where there are agreements between countries. There is an overall need to use acceptable and uniform definitions of types of migrants so as to avoid generalizing from the characteristics of particular sub-groups. Methods of recording vary from country to country, and within the one country from time to time. Many countries have inadequate census collections and those who have resources to organize reasonable data collection have been handicapped by the long period between censuses − 10 years in general − though a few countries have not moved towards a 5 year interval. This has meant that until the new census data has emerged, which usually takes some years, an efflux of returnees can distort the picture considerably, as can changing differential rates of intake from the various countries of emigration. Economic recession in Europe, for instance, has affected the intake of migrant workers through the 1970s, but the picture will not become apparent until well into the 1980s.

It must be expected that both political upheavals and economic factors will constitute forces for the displacement of peoples. There have already been five major military invasions in the past decade which have resulted in considerable human displacement. Furthermore, the World Bank has projected an increase in the world population to seven billion people in the next 25 years and expects the numbers in urban areas to double. Whilst there are currently 90 cities in the developing world with populations of more than one million, the number will increase to 150 by the year 2000, and there will be a similar number in developed countries. This development will occur in a context of rapid social change; and the massive migration inherent in the process will tax the coping power of individuals caught up therein. This is already well under way, as may be seen from the massive internal as well as international migrations occuring throughout the world today.

II. Historical aspects

A useful historical review of displaced persons and populations is embodied in the book *The Anatomy of Exile* (TABOR, 1972). The author cites the earliest recorded exile as that of Sinuhe, found in an Egyptian papyrus dated 2000 B.C. The Jewish diasporas through the ages have received considerable attention, as have such events as the expulsion of the Huguenots from France in the 16th century and the voluntary transplantation of the Pilgrim Fathers to North America in the 17th century as an escape from religious intolerance. One can only pick on examples to illustrate the constant movement of peoples throughout the history of mankind, resulting from natural disasters, religious persecutions, political upheavals, wars and economic necessity. Prior to the last century, reasonably accurate figures of the numbers of persons exiled from their home-lands have not been available; to obtain adequate perspective, such figures would need to be related anyway to the smaller populations then existing and the lesser degree of urbanization; it would therefore be appropriate to focus on the 19th century and subsequently.

II.1. To America

As examples of the latter, mention may be made of the considerable intake of immigrants into USA arising out of such events as the pogroms in Russia, the potato blight in Ireland (almost 2 million between 1845 – 1880), political repression within the Austro-Hungarian Empire, famine in Sweden (almost 1 million intake from a very small population), rural poverty in Poland, and an influx of Chinese labourers after the Second Opium War had ended in 1858. The series of 1848 revolutions in Europe resulted in a considerable movement of Germans, Hungarians and Italians to other countries. As late as 1879, when an amnesty had been declared after the 1870 deposition of Napoleon III, France had lost over 100000 Communards to Belgium and Britain alone. The liberation of South American countries, from the mid-19th century on, led to the attraction of large numbers of Europeans – 6 million from 1857 to 1930, with over 3 million emigrating to Southern Brazil. Argentina encouraged immigration in the 1880s and, in 1889, 220000 immigrants were accepted.

II.2. The Armenians

The persecution of the Armenians received world-wide attention also in the latter part of the 19th and early part of the 20th century, through to post-World War I. The original Armenian Empire had been divided between Turks, Russians and Persians; and following the Russo-Turkish War of 1877 – 1878, Armenians were subject to atrocities by the Turks and oppression by the Russians. In 1914, Turkish Armenia was taken over by the Russians. Following the 1917 Russian military collapse, the Turks massacred 1 million Armenians and 1.5 million fled to other countries, predominantly to the USSR where the Armenian Soviet Republic was established; though sizeable numbers also moved to other European countries and the Middle East. At the end of World War I, 115000 were officially classified as refugees by IRO and even after World War II, UNRRA recorded 4000 Armenians among the ‹Displaced Persons› in Western Europe. The number of refugees diminished considerably through deaths and through acceptance by other countries; for instance, the recorded numbers in France dropped by 20000 between 1936 – 1946.

II.3. From Russia

Attention may also be drawn to the pre-World War I efflux of left-wing exiles from Russia and the coincidental emigration of large numbers of Jews to escape pogroms and military call-up. The latter transferred mainly to Britain and USA, resulting in New York becoming the largest Jewish urban conurbation in the world with a population greater than Israel itself. The next Russian saga, that of the White Russians, bears recounting, as demonstrating the way in which exiled populations continue to evolve and devolute over time. With the formation of the USSR in 1917, supplemented by the brief Russo-Polish war of 1920, the formation of the independent republics of Finland, Esthonia, Latvia and Lithuania, and the secondary effect of famine, over 860000 refugees were to be found in Europe and the Middle East by 1922, and a sizeable colony was formed in Shanghai. Between 1922 and 1937 this number declined to about 450000, through deaths and naturalizations. The outbreak of World War II and the German assault against the USSR led to a number being recruited by the Nazis from occupied areas and elsewhere; but, as Germany occupied eastern and central Europe, a repeat exodus of White Russians occurred from areas such as Poland, the Baltic, Eastern Germany and the Balkans, and their numbers were supplemented by deserters. Soon after World War II, there were 15 – 20 000 White Russians living in camps under the care of IRO. By the early 1950s these were resettled predominantly in USA, Australia, South America, France, Canada and Belgium. In 1948, when Yugoslavia asserted its independence from the Cominterm, a massive expulsion of Russian nationals occurred and, furthermore, a number who had changed from a position of ‹statelessness› back to Russian nationality, became refugees again and sought international aid. At that time, Russian exiles in France totalled 40 000 (predominantly old vintage), Great Britain 35 000 (50% pre-World War I), some 14 000 resided in Belgium, 2000 in Greece, 1800 in Egypt, 1400 in Trieste, 1000 in Switzerland and a few hundred in Syria and Lebanon. By this time, the impetus of political activity had faded and, of those who had not died, their main effort was directed towards integration within their host communities.

II.4. The divided Europe

Following World War I, the various treaties which altered the map of Europe, especially the break-up of Hungary to form Czechoslovakia and Yugoslavia, also led to a mass exodus from the separated territories. Greece and Turkey continued hostilities through 1919, and an exchange of nationals was arranged. By 1922, Greece had accepted 1.5 million refugees and Turkey had accepted 350 000 returning Turks. Greece also received 50 000 persons of Greek origin from USSR.

II.5. The victims of Fascism and Nazism

Italy lost a large number of anti-Fascists after the advent to power of Mussolini. In August 1930, 11 000 passports for other European countries were issued and, in the next two months, 90 000 were granted but meanwhile, the door of acceptance by other countries had closed, and only some 50 000 managed to get abroad.

The initial rise to power of the Nazis in Germany led to the emigration of over 10000 Communists, Social Democrats and Liberals. By May 1937, 283000 Jews had left Germany, and the attacks in Sudetenland and Austria led to the expulsion of another 120000. Many of these refugees were subsequently trapped as the German juggernaut rolled over Europe. Another group of Jews was caught in Shanghai and they were subsequently interned by the Japanese in a ghetto and were largely resettled by IRO from 1947 to 1952. Between 1938 – 1942, some 215000 Jews were able to leave Europe for resettlement elsewhere, the rest either facing extermination or living underground. Hitler's policy also led to large-scale displacement of those of German ethnic origin who were encouraged to return from Czechoslovakia (Sudetenland), Austria, Italy (40000), Baltic countries (127000), eastern Poland (128000), Bessarabia and Northern Bukovina (13000), Southern Bukovina and Dobruja (69000) and Ljulbjana and Croatia (33 500).

As a result of the Spanish Civil War, 400000 refugees fled to France between 1937 – 1939 and a substantial number moved to Mexico. At the end of World War II, there were still 200000 Spanish refugees in Europe, predominantly in France.

III. After World War II

All in all, it is estimated that, as a result of World War II, at least 100 million persons were temporarily or permanently displaced, not counting persons from military or auxiliary establishments. Within Asia, it was considered a further 50 million suffered such a fate.

III.1. New organizations

UNRRA (United Nations Relief and Rehabilitation Organisation) was established in November, 1943, by forty-four governments to provide relief for the victims of war. It was not a refugee organization but was concerned with ‹Displaced Persons› of which there were 14 million Central Europeans alone. Between May and October 1945, six million people were helped with their repatriation. At the beginning of 1946, there were 1 675 000 people for whom new homes had to be found. Arising out of UNRRA came the IRO (Internation Refugee Organisation) which was ratified in 1948 and, as already stated, dealt with the residuum of refugees from World War II. By the end of 1951, it had repatriated and resettled over a million persons. The IRO ended its work in 1952, being replaced by the UNHCR (Office of the United Nations' High Commission for Refugees). ICEM (Inter-governmental Committee for European Migration) was established at the end of 1951 to take over the resettlement functions of IRO, which was soon to disappear. It was set up to cover not only refugees but other migrants from Europe who felt under threat in their own domiciles. It was mainly concerned though with refugee resettlement, moving over 500 000 persons to final reception countries – mainly United States, Canada, Australia and Brazil – between 1952 and 1960.

UNKRA (United Nations Korean Reconstruction Agency) was established in December 1950 to deal with the hundreds of thousands of Korean people who had lost their homes during World War II and operated subsequently for those displaced by the North Korean invasion and civil war, finally ending its operations in August 1960.

A year earlier, in December 1949, UNRWA (United Nations Relief and Works Agency for Palestine Refugees in the Near East) was established and is still operating. It was originally set up to deal with 750 000 Arabs who had fled the newly established state of Israel. Their number had increased to 1 395 000 by 1969.

The continuing involvement of UNHCR in the ever-present problems of refugees will be discussed in relation to post-World War II developments. Meanwhile, since 1945, there appears to have been an increasing tempo of human mobility. This has been noted in Western countries where, in USA for example, over 20% of the population changes residence annually and, with the development of urban industrialization and agricultural technology, the rural population percentage had declined steadily since the turn of the century. This process has commenced in developing countries, but the absence of an adequate industrial base is tending to the development of shanty towns and a mass of health and social problems. In the two decades following the cessation of hostilities, booming industrial development had led to large migratory intakes into Europe, besides the continuing movement into traditional countries of immigration such as USA, Canada, Australia and Brazil; though the international recession over the past quinquennium has led to a diminution of this process. Many countries have become involved in hostilities, the latest victims being the ‹boat people› from Vietnam, the Kampucheans in Thailand and the Afghans in Pakistan. This period has also experienced the effects of decolonization, mainly in Africa and Asia.

III.2. Recent migration patterns

III.2.1. Europe

III.2.1.1. The displaced persons

The final solution of the World War II refugees and stateless persons took place in 1969, when camps were finally cleared of the residual hard-core through the activities of UNHCR and the co-operation of many governments throughout the world. Two further upheavals, the Hungarian revolt of 1956 and the Czechoslovakian disturbance of 1968, resulted in refugee numbers of 250000 and 60000 respectively; both of these were dealt with rapidly through the efforts of UNHCR.

III.2.1.2. Guest workers

The story of the ‹guest workers› («Gastarbeiter») in Europe is a lengthy one. The term is somewhat euphemistic as the majority migrated through necessity and were recruited to fill specific needs. A joint ILO/WHO Committee on Occupational Health in 1975 estimated some 13.5 million migrant workers and their families, comprising 1.4 million from North Africa, 1.2 million from Turkey, 5.2 million from intra-European sources and 5.1 million from extra-European locations. It was estimated that there were perhaps 10% additional clandestine immigrant workers. Both France and the Federal German Republic had over 4 million foreign workers each; UK had 2.5 million; and Switzerland accommodated 1.1 million (20% of the total work force). Early after the war, guest workers came from nearby countries but, as needs increased, further sources were exploited. Thus, the initial intake of workers from neighbouring European countries was subsequently supplemented by immigrants from North Africa, Spain and Turkey and, later, from Africa South of the Sahara. In the early 1960s, 66% of Italians came from North Italy and 33% from the south; but, by 1971, the situation was completely reversed. The intake into European countries presented a variegated picture. Females represented some 30 – 40% of initial intakes but this proportion steadily increased as the result of policies of family reunion; whilst, in some countries, policies were geared towards female intakes based on needs for female labour. Thus, the Federal German Republic more latterly encouraged Greek and Yugoslav females, whilst France acted similarly with regard to Protugese and Spanish; in fact, married females had begun to precede their husbands to some degree in initiating the process of immigration. Although there has been a not insignificant number of returning immigrants due to the economic recession of the past few years, the number of foreign workers had remained constant as the children of the original immigrants have grown up and entered the work force themselves.

The following brief comments gives some indication of the picture with regard to individual countries in Europe.

As already stated *Switzerland* has 20% foreigners in its labour force; and, in addition, 200000 seasonal workers enter annually.

France imported workers from North Africa, Portugal, Italy and Spain, and later from Africa south of the Sahara. It also coped with considerable numbers of French citizens from its ex-colonial territories. At the close of the African War in 1962, over 600000 citizens came to France and, by 1966, the number was almost a million, this being counterbalanced to some degree by the return of considerable numbers of Algerian citizens to their home country. Over 226000 French citizens had returned from Morocco by 1966, 170000 from Tunisia, 45000 from Indo-China, and smaller numbers from Black Africa and Egypt; all in all, 1.4 million during the 1960 – 1970 decade!

The *Federal German Republic* in 1950 contained 8 million expellees and refugees and, in the next three years, accepted a further 2 million immigrants from East Germany. In 1953, some 30% were regarded as marginal, but these were absorbed, as were further intakes prior to the Berlin Wall being established in 1961. As industry thrived, Turks, Yugoslavs and Italians were admitted as guest workers, with Greeks and Spaniards to lesser degree.

The *United Kingdom* has traditionally absorbed a high proportion of Irish immigrants but this has been relatively diminished through the additional intake of immigrants from the new Commonwealth (from India and Pakistan especially) and from the Caribbean (Jamaica predominantly). This was augmented by the intake of expulsees from Uganda and British citizens from its other ex-colonial territories. The overseas-born increased by 33% between the 1961 and 1971 census and foreign workers increased from 4.9% to 7.2% of the total work force.

Sweden's immigrants have come predominantly from Finland (over 50%), but a high proportion of later immigrants were from Yugoslavia and Greece. In 1980 there were 1 million immigrants, 300000 already naturalized Swedes.

Other European countries have been concerned with human displacement since 1945, but space precludes detailed consideration of these. Attention may be drawn to the return of the many Indonesian-born and Dutch expatriates to Holland after the attainment of Indonesian independence in 1949. Many Greeks returned from Turkey and Yugoslavia and subsequently from the turmoil in Cyprus, whilst exoduses occurred with the establishment of the Junta in 1967 and the following political changes. The intake of refugees from Africa and Asia and the continuing efflux of Europeans to other continents such as America and Oceania in particular will become clearer as the situation in regard to these is outlined.

III.2.2. The Americas

III.2.2.1. USA

The traditional influx into the USA was originally predominantly European in origin. More latterly, immigrants have been accepted to greater degree from South American, Central American and Caribbean countries (especially from Puerto Rico, Mexico, Haiti, the Dominican Republic, Cuba and Jamaica); and, in recent times, there has been a shift towards Asian immigrants, who constituted 55% of the entire foreign population intake in 1975. USA is currently accepting a high proportion of refugees from Indo-China. Legislation has changed from a system based on national quotas to a multicultural one, with preference for family reunion, special skills, and refugees. There is also a continuing influx of illegal immigrant workers from Mexico and South America (Chicanos) which is estimated at around 5 – 7 million, and could be up to 10 million including dependents. In 1972, permanent resident first generation immigrants were recorded as Mexicans (769000), Cubans (600000), Canadians (160000), United Kingdom immigrants (300000), Italians (745000), South Americans (184000), Germans (190000) and smaller groupings of Poles, Greeks, Portugese, Dominicans, Puerto Ricans,

Chinese, Japanese and others. The numbers are swollen by second-generation immigrants.

III.2.2.2. Canada

Canada has followed much the same pattern as USA. It established a high intake of European immigrants following World War II, but with a greater proportion of professionals than USA and relatively smaller proportions of refugees and non-Europeans. Its immigrant intake has been tied to economic factors. In 1945, 40000 immigrants were accepted, the number rising to 200000 in 1958, declining to 62000 with the 1962 recession and building up again to 120000 in 1978.

III.2.2.3. Latin America

This region acted largely as a continent of immigration from Europe following 1945, but the situation has changed considerably in more recent times. There is additionally a high clandestine immigration between countries in the region as well as the aforementioned large illegal immigration into USA. Statistics are difficult to record because of the latter and the large movements of seasonal workers. However, in 1975, it was estimated that there were 5 million immigrants in the region, of whom 3 million were workers, 1.5 million were dependents and 0.5 million were frontier seasonal workers.

West Indians have emigrated to Europe, especially UK (around 200000), and sizeable groups have settled in USA and Canada. Main countries of immigration within Latin America have been *Argentina, Venezuela* and *Brazil.* The latter has acepted regular waves of European exiles from many European countries. The foreign population of Argentina was estimated to be over 3 million in 1975, with large contingents from Paraguay, Bolivia and Chile. Venezuela had over 600000 Columbians at that time. Many of the immigrant workers are illegally in the countries to which they had emigrated, having entered originally on tourist visas and liable accordingly to exploitation. Many live in shanty towns with little prospects of advancement, a situation which is manifest also with the large rural-urban immigrations occurring in developing countries throughout the world.

III.2.3. Africa

The process of decolonization, of political turmoil, and of armed conflicts has resulted in considerable shifts of populations through the 1960s and onwards. Some minorities have been summarily expelled and the creation of new borders has sometimes split people off from their tribal kinsfolk. Droughts have also resulted in displacements. Finally there have also been considerable rural-urban shifts.

In North Africa, *Algeria,* which originally provided workers for France has now itself become a country of immigration due to its oil and industrial developments and has not only received many returnees from France but, in 1974 alone, absorbed 150000 workers from Tunisia and Morocco. In the same year, Libya took in 250000 immigrants, many from Egypt. Other migrant workers have been leaving North African countries for southern European locations, especially Spain, Italy and Greece.

In western Africa, movement has taken place southwards from the Sahara region to the Ivory Coast and Ghana, westwards from Mali and Guinea to Gambia and Senegal, and northwards from Dahomey and Senegal to France.

The main receiving countries in Central Africa have been Zaire and Gabon. In eastern Africa, the high immigration countries have been Kenya, Malawi, Tanzania and Uganda.

After 1945, there was a steady immigration of whites into Rhodesia (Zimbabwe) and the Republic of South Africa, mainly from UK. The current troubles in Zimbabwe led to thousands of refugees moving into neighbouring countries: Zambia, Mozambique and Botswana especially. In South Africa, whites comprised around 19% of the total population and, prior to the present difficulties, one third of its annual increase in poulations resulted from immigration. There has latterly been a net loss of migrants of around 1000 per month, with heaviest losses among those with high qualifications.

The story of *South Africa* with regard to the migration of black people bears recounting. Manpower for mining, industrial, agricultural and domestic purposes has been drawn from Botswana, South West Africa, Malawi, Swaziland, Mozambique, Lesotho and Angola. The compulsory return of the annual intake each year to their respective homelands has resulted in enormous social problems. In 1971 – 1972, it was estimated that 500000 men and women were living in single accommodation. In most urban areas, migrant labour formed 50% of workers, and this proportion was increasing. In 1969, 2.5 million black Africans (including 0.5 million domestics were working legally in white areas.

As mentioned earlier, the establishment of new States has resulted in some cases in discrimination against minority alien populations. In 1967, for instance, Senegal expelled Guineans and Cameroun asked Nigerians to leave; in 1968, the Ugandans expelled unemployed Kenyans and Tanzanians and, subsequently, Israelis and stateless Asians in 1972; in 1971, Zaire expelled non-Zairian Africans.

Mention may be made of the large number of refugees resulting from the continuing conflict between Ethiopia and Somalia. Also in the early 60's, over a quarter of a million Angolans moved into Zaire; and subsequently, with the granting of independence to Angola thousands of refugees and expatriates were forced to relocate in Portugal.

III.2.4. Asia

III.2.4.1. South-East Asia

In earlier centuries, the major emigrants were Chinese and Indians, the former extending southwards and forming minority enclaves of traders within plural societies such as Vietnam, Burma, Thailand, Indonesia and Malaysia; whilst the latter extended their influence through Burma, Malaysia, Indonesia and as far east as Fiji.

Since 1945, there has been an explosion of migration activity. In the decade 1960 – 1970 alone, the net emigration from south-east Asia was over 1 million and, as already stated, at least 25 million people have been displaced in the region.

Within the four years following the partition of India in 1947, 8.5 million Hindus moved from Pakistan to India and some 6.5 million Muslims moved in the reverse direction. Karachi alone tripled in size in that period. The flood of refugees was subsequently added to by the entry of Indian troops into Kashmir and the brief Indian – Pakistan war of 1965. The disturbances in Afghanistan in 1979/1980 have resulted in half a million refugees flooding into North-West Pakistan. In 1971, the conflict between East and West Pakistan, the intervention of India, and the creation of Bangladesh resulted in 10 million refugees moving into India. An influx of Tibetans into India resulted from annexation of Tibet by China and, in 1970, it was estimated there were 40 000 Tibetans there.

There has been a steady stream of Chinese into Hong Kong. Between 1931 – 1952, the population rose from 850 000 to 2.25 million and, although restrictions have more latterly been placed on the intake of immigrants from China, the population has now risen to over 5 million, assisted by the continuing influx of illegal immigrants (80 000 in 1979) and, now the advent of the Vietnamese ‹boat people›.

There was a vast exodus of a million North Vietnamese into South Vietnam following the Geneva agreement of 1954 and the subsequent civil war and overseas intervention resulted in still further displacements. Many Vietnamese refugees have emigrated to France, USA, Thailand, Malaysia, Phillipines, Australia, South America and Europe. The recent exodus of the ‹boat people›, largely of Chinese origin, to neighbouring countries and then to countries of resettlement have numbered more than half a million. A larger number of Chinese ethnic origin have moved over into China itself. The tragic situation of Kampuchea is currently apparent, the population being forced to move through hunger and the Vietnamese invasion, the result being an estimated million refugees are now at the Thai border, 250000 are in Thai camps over the border, and there are a lesser number of «stateless» refugees who have been accepted by UNHCR.

Korea, over the years, has had to deal with 2 million returnees from Japan and over 3 million who have moved internally from North to South Korea.

III.2.4.2. Asia Minor

As already mentioned, many Turks emigrated as guestworkers to European countries, of whom 84% went to the Federal German Republic. Migrant workers have also moved in substantial numbers from Palestine, Lebanon and Jordan to Libya. Kuwait and Saudi Arabia have absorbed workers from Egypt and Sudan. As of 1974, the foreign labour force in Saudi Arabia was 400000 out of a total million workers (Yemen, 200 – 250000; Jordan, 50000; Syria, 40000; Lebanon, 50000); in Bahrein, 35% of the total labour force were immigrants; whilst over 50% of the total population (75% of the total work force) in Kuwait were foreigners. Israel has absorbed nearly two million immigrants, among them about 800000 from the Arab countries, while the UNRWA took care of the Arab refugees from Israel (cfr page 342).

III.2.5. Oceania

Australia, which traditionally accepted predominantly UK immigrants prior to World War II, has since moved towards a pluralistic intake, with equal representation from other European countries – especially Italians, Greeks, Yugoslavians and Western Europeans. Australia accepted refugees from eastern European and Baltic countries soon after World War II; subsequently from the Hungarian and Czechoslovakian uprisings; and more recently, from the disturbances in Chile, Lebanon and Indo-China. One in five of the Australian population consists of first generation immigrants. It is estimated that there are 70000 illegal immigrants in Australia.

New Zealand has followed the same pattern as Australia, except that relatively more immigrants are of UK origin and there is a greater intake from the Pacific islands. Foreigners comprised 14.3% of the total population in 1971.

IV. Conclusions

An estimated 5.4 million people are living currently in camps, having fled terrorism, natural turmoil, rebellions and armed conflict. There are many millions more who are in limbo or have been forced into exile in the past and are currently facing problems of adjustment in new environments. There are large numbers also who have transplanted themselves, with or without their families, in an endeavour to improve their economic lot, a process which will inevitably intensify as the world population increase gains momentum. These phenomena must inevitably have important consequences for the mental health of a not inconsiderable section of humanity.

Bibliography

TABOR, P.: The Anatomy of Exile. Harrap, London 1972.

Name index

Subject index

359

361

Tripple burden of sex 182
Tunisia 345, 348
Turkey 186, 194, 340, 344, 346
Turkish, 112, 113, 114, 116, 119, 194, 338
Turks 12, 168, 170, 190, 295, 299, 338, 340, 345, 351

Uganda 134, 297
Ugandans 222
UN. = United Nations 320
UNESCO 93
UNHCR = United Nations High Commissioner for Refugees 335ff.
Unilingual 150, 158
United Kingdom see Great Britain
United States of America see USA
UNKRA (United Nations Korean Reconstruction Agency) 342
UNRRA (United Nations Relief and Rehabilitation Agency) 339, 341, 342
UNRWA (United Nations Relief and Works Agency for Palestine Refugees in the Near East) 342, 351
Uprooting 28, 74, 204, 308
Uprootedness 265, 267, 268
Urban influxes 39
Urbanization 12, 29, 300, 338
USA 16, 18, 19, 22, 35, 43, 70, 97, 100, 101, 102, 136, 147, 149, 150, 204, 225, 234ff., 278, 279, 320, 323, 329, 338, 342, 343, 346ff.
USSR 203, 339

Vendetta 55
Venezuela 347
Vietnam 43, 128, 343, 350, 351
Vietnamese 222, 239, 297, 350, 351
Voluntary 21, 22, 23, 25, 27, 28, 86, 90

Wales 32
Wage ladder 179
Wartime experiences 212
West Germany see Germany (West)
West Indian 136, 137, 279, 280, 328
West Indies 161, 280
Western Europe(an) 147, 181, 186, 234
Western Hemisphere 234
WHO (World Health Organisation) 344
Witch doctor 271
World Congress 13
World Psychiatric Organization 13
World War I 12, 215, 338, 339, 340
World War II 12, 22, 24, 27, 43, 85, 92, 186, 205, 214, 289, 317, 318, 335, 339, 341, 342, 343

Yugoslavia(n) 37, 167, 168, 170, 174, 178, 182, 186, 191, 226, 295, 340, 344, 345, 346, 351

Zaire 348, 349
Zambia 277
Zimbabwe 348
Zion 72

A little vocabulary

abdominal = pertaining to the abdomen (belly), part of the body containing stomach, bowels and other digestive organs

agenesis = imperfect development, corrosion

amalgamation = mix, fusing (e.g. of diverse peoples by intermarriage)

anomie = lack or loss of usual social standards or value systems

apathetic = lack of or not feeling emotions, uninterested

arthritis = inflammation of joint(s)

ascetic = severely abstinent, given to strict selfdenial, sensuous pleasures are voluntarily denounced

asthenic = of or characterized by asthenia

asthenia = lack or loss of strength, weakness, debility

atypical = not conforming to type

bimodal = of two forms

cardiovascular = involving heart and blood vessels

cerebral vascular = involving blood vessels in the brain

cerebrum = (principal part of) the brain

congenital = existing from birth e.g. defect, disease

cognitive = referring to intellect, knowing, perceiving

curb(ing) = restraint

deleterious = harmful (to mind or body)

dementia = mental disease characterized by serious mental impairment, mainly due to loss of intellectual power, brain disease, old age or injury

dichotymi = distinct division into two parts

duodenal ulcer = sore on the upper part of the intestine directly connected with the stomach

dysfunction = impairment of function, abnormal or imperfect functioning dysmorphophobia = morbid dread to be deformed or of deformity

dysphagia = a difficulty in swallowing

emaciate = let (person) starve

emaciated = in extremely bad state of nutrition, starved, famine-stricken

emphysema = enlargement of air vescicles of the lungs

endogenous = originating from within

epigastric = pertaining to or of the epigastrium, i.e. part of the abdominal surface in front of the stomach

ethnocentric = regarding one's own race (people) as the most important

euphoria = strong feeling of well-being

exogenous = originating from outside

gastric-intestinal = of stomach and alimentary canal

geriatrics = branch of science dealing with health and welfare of old people

hedonistic = of a doctrine that pleasure is the chief good

hypochondria = unnecessary anxiety or complaints about one's health

iatrogenic = caused by process of diagnosis or treatment

infarction = from infarct, region of dead tissue caused by blocking of blood-circulation

intrapsychic = being within the psyche (of the individual)

logopathy = any disorder of speech

lues = syphilis

malaise = bodily discomfort, feeling of uneasiness

maniform (agitation) = excessive enthusiasm

neurosis = functional nervous disease, especially a minor psychiatric reaction characterized by disorder of the personality functions or of the functions of bodily organs and resulting in personality difficulties. Behaviour showing inability to take rationally objective view of life

optometrist = sight tester

paranoia = mental derangement with delusions of gran-
deur, persecution etc.: abnormal tendency to suspect
and mistrust others. Hence paranoid
pathogen = agent causing disease
pathography = description of a disease, especially in the
development of a person
post-menopausal = after final cessation of menses
premorbid = present before disease
pseudo- = similar, but not genuine: False, pretended,
spurious
psyche = the human soul, the mind, the mental life
psychiatry = the medical speciality dealing with the study
and treatment of mental diseases
psychosis = mental disease characterized by severe mental derangement involving the whole personality
Hence: psychotic
psychosomatic = pertaining to the functional interrela-
tionship between mind and body
psychosomatic disease = bodily disease caused or ag-
gravated by mental disease
pulmonial = pertaining to or of the lungs

raison d'être = purpose that accounts for or justifies or originally caused things' existence

senescence = procedure of growing old
septicaemia = blood-poisoning
somatic = of the body
symptom = evidence of disease, something that indicates
presence of disease or a pathological condition
symptomatology = the sum of signs and evidences of diseases or of a patient's state. Systematic discussion of
symptoms

trauma = injury or wound, any experience that inflicts
serious damage on the body or on the mind
traumatic = adjective to trauma

ubiquitous = present everywhere at the same time (omni-present)

vegetative = concerned with growth and development
vegetative functions = bodily functions not subject to voluntary control